THE

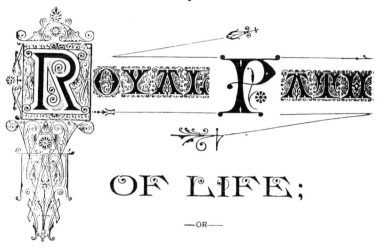

ROYAL PATH

OF LIFE;

—OR—

AIMS AND AIDS TO SUCCESS AND HAPPINESS.

BY

T.L. HAINES, A.M.
AND
L.W. YAGGY, M.S.
Author of "Our Home Counselor"

REVISED EDITION

KANSAS CITY, MO.:

WEVER & COMPANY.

WESTERN PUBLISHING HOUSE, CHICAGO, ILL.

1883

Engraved & Printed by Illman Brothers

THE PAST AND THE FUTURE.

FOR THE ROYAL PATH OF LIFE.

Preface.

THE subject matter of this book, success and happiness, has been the consideration of every eminent pen, from the days of Solomon to the present. To say any thing strictly new would be impossible. Nor would we presume that our knowledge and experience would be as valuable as the maxims of the wise and the sublime. Truths that have become a part of the standard literature. The best, therefore, that any one can expect to do is to recombine the experience of the past. Compile such thoughts and extracts as have chimed in with testimony of earnest and aspiring minds and offer them in a novel and fascinating form. In the words of the poet:

> "We have gathered posies from other men's flowers.
> Nothing but the thread that binds them is ours."

In life there is a Royal Path. Alas! That so many not being urged to seek life's prizes fail to find them. It is hoped that this book shall be a counselor to those who have become indifferent to life's purpose. A comfort to those who have long traveled on this Royal Path. We hope it shall serve to awaken the slumbering genius within the youth, stimulate and impel them to noble thoughts and actions, and lead them to honor, success, and happiness. Then the authors will consider themselves amply repaid for their labor.

OFTEN our wants and needs today center on some kind of self improvement or counseling. Who isn't trying to make a better life for themselves and those around them? It is the good news we want to see and hear in times of trouble. So we continually search for new ways to make our lives less complicated and more rewarding.

This is the main focus of our old book and why we want to share it with you. The valuable lessons on virtues were the same over one hundred years ago as they are today. They correct and encourage us from the inside out.

The original language, style, and manner serves to make the book more inspiring and endearing. The authors' chose to write it as a novel and the applications they used are sometimes contrary, but often humorous.

The principal thought is that God is our constant companion on the Royal Path through life. He will not fail to point us in the right direction and guide us over the rough and rocky ways of life.

Finally, we wish to dedicate this book to our own special young men and our families. God bless you, Andy, Scott, and Joe.

Bud and Debbie Neptune
Rural Route 1
Dawn, MO 64638

"Some books are to be tasted, others to be swallowed,
but a few are to be chewed and digested."

"Life is before you! From the fated road
You cannot turn; then take up the load,
Not yours to tread or leave the unknown way,
You must go o'er it, meet ye what ye may.
Gird up your souls within you to the deed,
Angels and fellow spirits bid you speed!"

–Butler

viii

CONTENTS.

x

Royal Path of Life.

Life

WE point to two ways in life. If the young man and maiden whose feet are lingering in the soft green meadows and flowery paths will only consider these ways. If they would choose soberly and earnestly before moving on, the one that leads to honor, success, and happiness. They have chosen wisely, "The Royal Path of Life." The other way is too well known to need description. It is a sad thing, after the lapse of twenty years, to find ourselves amid ruined hopes. To sit down with folded hands and say, "Thus far life has been a failure!" Yet, to how many is this the wretched summing up at the end of a single score of years from the time that reason takes the helm! Alas! That so few who start wrong, ever succeed in finding the "Royal Path." Life proving even to its last burdened years, a millstone about the neck.

Dear reader life is a "Royal Path" and to you it shall be a millstone about your neck or a diadem on your brow. Decide at once upon a noble purpose. Then take it up bravely, bear it off joyfully and lay it down triumphantly. Your greatest inheritance is a purpose in pursuit of which you will find employment and happiness for,

"The busy world shoves angrily aside the
man who stands with arms akimbo set Until
occasion tell him what to do; And he who
waits to have his task marked out Shall die
and leave his errand unfulfilled."

Life is not mean. It is grand. If it is mean to any he makes it so. God made it glorious. Its channels He paved with diamonds. Its banks He fringed with flowers. He overarched it with stars. Around it He spread the glory of the physical universe. The suns, moons, worlds, constellataions, and systems He revealed. All that is magnificent in motion, sublime in magnitude and grand in order and obedience. God would not have attended life with this broad march of grandeur if it did not mean something. He would not have descended to the blade of grass, the dew drop and the dust atom. Every moment of life letter to spell out some word that should bear the burden of a thought. How much life means words refuse to tell because they cannot. The very doorway of life is hung around with flowery emblems to indicate that it is for some purpose. The mystery of cause to effect, the dependence of one thing upon another, the mutual influence and affinity of all things. These assure us that life is for a purpose to which every outward thing doth point.

Trees bend under the wind make, music of it, then stand up again and grow more stalwartly straight up toward the heart of the heavens. A man is to learn of the oak and cling to his plans as the oak to its leaves, till pushed off by new ones. Be as tenacbous of life, when lopt, sending up branches straight as the old trunk. Then when cut off, sending up a brood of young oaks crowning the stump with vigorous defenders. He that floats lazily down the stream in pursuit of something borne along by the same current will find himself indeed moved forward. But unless he lays his hand to the oar and increases his speed by his own labor, will be always at the same distance from that which he was. In our voyage of life we must not DRIFT but STEER.

Every youth should form at the outset of his career the solemn purpose to make the most and the best of the powers which God has given him. Turn to the best possible account every outward advantage within his reach. This purpose must carry with it the assent of the reason, the approval of the conscience and the sober judgement of the intellect. It should then embody within itself whatever is vehement in desire, inspiring in hope, thrilling   in enthusiasm and intense in desperate resolve. Such a plan of life will save him from many a damaging contest with temptation. It will regulate his sports and recreations. It will go with him by day to trample under foot the allurements of pleasure. It will hold his eyes waking as he toils by the evening lamp. It will watch over his slumbers to jog him at the appointed hour and summon him to the cheerful duties of his chosen pursuit. Those who labor and study under the inspiration of such a purpose will soar out of sight of those who barely allow themselves to be carried along by the momentum of the machinery to which they are attached.

Many pass through life without even a consciousness of where they are and what they are doing. They gaze on whatever lies directly before them, "in fond amusement lost." Human life is a watchtower. It is the clear purpose of God that every one, the young especially, should take their stand on this tower. Look, listen, learn, wherever you go, whenever you tarry. Something is always transpiring to reward your attention. Let your eyes and ears be always open and you will often observe in the slightest incidents materials of advantage and means of personal improvement.

In nothing is childhood more strongly distinguished from manhood than in this, that the small child has no purpose. He has no plan of life. He has no will by which his energies are directed. He lives in a great measure to enjoy the passing scene. He finds his happiness in those agreeable consciousnesses which from hour to hour come to him by chance. If his life is governed by a plan, a purpose, it is the purpose of another. Not his own.

The man has his own purpose, his own plan, his own life and aim. The sorrowful experience of multitudes in this respect is that they are never men, but children all their days. Think out your work then work out your thought. No one can pursue a worthy object with all the powers of his mind and yet make his life a failure. A man may work in the dark but one day light shall arise upon his labor. And though he may never with his own lips declare the victory complete, some day others will behold in his life-work the traces of a great and thinking mind.

Take life as God intended. Take it just as though it was, as it is, an earnest, vital, essential affair. Take it just as though you personally were born to the task of performing a merry part in it. As though the world had waited for your coming. Take it as though it was a grand opportunity to do and to achieve, to carry forward great and good schemes to help and cheer a suffering, weary or heart-broken brother. The fact is life is undervalued by a great majority of mankind. It is not made half as much of as should be the case. Now and then a man stands aside from the crowd, labors earnestly, steadfastly, confidently, and straightway becomes famous for wisdom, intellect, skill, greatness of some sort. The world wonders, admires, idolizes. Yet it only illustrates what each may do if he takes hold of life with a purpose. One way is right to go. The hero sees it and moves on that aim and has the world under him for foot and sup-port. His approbation is honor, his dissent infamy. Man was sent into the world to be a growing and exhaustless force. The world was spread out around him to be seized and conquered. Realms of infinite truth burst open above him inviting him to tread those shining coasts along which Newton dropped his plummet and Herschel sailed. A Columbus of the skies. Some, because they have once or twice met with rebuffs sink in discouragement. Such should know, that our own errors may often teach us more than the grave precepts of others. We counsel the young man never to despair. If he can make nothing by any work that presents itself now, he can at least make himself. He can save himself from the sure death of a faint-hearted, halt-ing, irresolute spirit. He should never be cast down by mis-fortunes. If a spider breaks his web over and over he will mend it again. Do you not fall behind the very insect on your walls?. If the sun is going down look up to the stars. If earth is dark keep your eyes on heaven. With the presence and promise of God we can bare up under anything. We should press on and never falter or fear.

It is my firm conviction that man has only himself to blame if his life appears to him at any time void of interest and pleasure. Man may make life what he pleases and give it as much worth both for himself and others as he has energy for. Over his moral and intellectual being his sway is complete.

The first great mistake that men fall into is that they do not use integrity and truth and good sense in judging of what they are fit for. They take the things that they want and not the things that they deserve. They aspire after things that are pleasing to their ambition and not after things to which they are adapted by their capacity. When a man is brought into a sphere of his ambition for which he has not the requisite powers and where he is goaded on every side in the discharge of his duties, his temptation is at once to make up by fraud and appearance that which he lacks in reality. Men are seen going across lots to fortune. A poor business many of them make of it. Oftentimes, they lose their way. And when they do not, they find so many hills and valleys, so many swells and depressions, so many risings and fallings, so many ups and downs, that though by an airline the distance might be shorter in reality the distance is greater than by the lawful route. When they come back they are ragged and poor and mean. There is a great deal of going across-lots to make a beggar of a man's self in this world. Whereas the old-fashioned homely law that the man who is to establish himself in life, must take time to lay the foundations of reality and gradually and steadily build thereon. Though you slur it over and cover it up with fantasies and find it almost impossible to believe, it is so.

Rely not upon others. Let there be in your own bosom a calm, deep, decided and all-pervading principle. Look first, midst and last to God to aid you in the great task before you. Then plant your foot on the right. Let others live as they please tainted by low tastes, debasing passions, a moral putrefaction. Be ye the salt of the earth. Incorrupt in your deeds, in your inmost thoughts and feelings. Nay, more incorruptible like virtue herself. Your manners blameless. Your views of duty not narrow, false and destructive but a savor of life to all around you. Let your speech be always with grace seasoned with the salt of truth, honor, manliness, and benevolence. Wait not for the lash of guilt to scourge you to the path of God and heaven. Be of the prudent who foresee the evil and hide themselves from it. Not like the simple, who pass on and are punished. Life to youth is a fairy tale just opened. Old age, a tale read through ending in death. Be wise in time that you may be happy in eternity.

Man and Woman

MAN is bold. Woman is beautiful. Man is courageous. Woman is timid. Man labors in the field. Woman at home. Man talks to persuade. Woman to please. Man has a daring heart. Woman a tender, loving one. Man has power. Woman taste. Man has justice. Woman mercy.

Man has stength. Woman love. Man combats with the enemy, struggles with the world, woman is preparing his repast to sweeten his existence. He has crosses and the partner of his couch is there to soften them. His days may be sad and troubled, but in the chaste arms of his wife he finds comfort and repose. Without woman man would be rude, gross, and solitary. Woman spreads around him the flowers of existence as the creepers of the forests decorate the trunks of sturdy oaks with their perfumed garlands. Finally, the Christian pair live and die united. Together they rear the fruits of their union. In the dust, they lie side by side. They are reunited beyond the limits of the tomb.

Man has his strength and the exercise of his power. He is busy, goes about, thinks, looks forward to the future and finds consolation in it. Woman stays at home, remains face to face with her sorrow from which nothing distracts her. She descends to the very depths of the abyss it has opened, measures it and often fills it with her vows and tears. To feel, to love, to suffer, to devote herself will always be the text of the life of woman. Man has a precise and distinct language, the words being luminous speech. Woman possesses a peculiarly musical language interspersing the words with song. Woman is affectionate and suffers. She is constantly in need of something to rely upon like the honeysuckle upon the tree or fence. Man is attached to the fireside by his affection for woman and the happiness it gives him to protect and support her. Superior and inferior to man, humiliated by the hand of nature, but at the same time inspired by intuitions of a higher order than man can ever experience. She has fascinated him and innocently bewitched him forever. Man has remained enchanted by the spell. Women are generally better creatures than men. Perhaps they have taken less appetite, but they have much stronger affections. A man with a cruel heart has sometimes been saved by the strong head of a woman.

One has well said: "We will say nothing of the manner in which that sex usually conduct an argument; but the INTUITIVE JUDGEMENTS OF WOMEN are often more to be relied upon than the conclusions which men reach by an elaborate process of reasoning. No man that has an intelligent wife or who is accustomed to the society of educated women will dispute this. Times without number you must have known them to decide questions on the instant and with unerring accuracy, which you had been poring over for hours, perhaps with no other result than to find yourself getting deeper and deeper into the tangled maze of doubts and difficulties. It were hardly generous to allege that they achieve these feats less by reasoning than by a sort of sagacity which approximates to the sure instinct of the animal races. Yet, there seems to be some ground for the remark of a witty French writer, that when a man has toiled step by step up a flight of stairs, he will be sure to find a woman at the top; but she will not be able to TELL HOW SHE GOT THERE. How she got there however, is of little moment."

It is peculiar with what a degree of tact woman will determine whether a man is honest or not. She cannot give you reason for such an opinion, only that she does not like the looks of the man and feels that he is dishonest. A servant comes for employment, she looks him in the face and says he is dishonest. He gives good references and you employ him. He robs you. You may be quite sure he will do that. Years later another man comes. The same lady looks him in the face and says he, too, is not honest. She says so again fresh from her mere insight. But you also say he is not honest. You say, I remember I had a servant with just the same look about him three years ago, and he robbed me. This is one great distinction of the female intellect. It walks directly and unconsciously by more delicate insight and a more refined and trusted intuition, to an end to which men's minds grope carefully and ploddingly along. Women have exercised a most beneficial influence in softening the hard and untruthful outline which knowledge is apt to assume in the hands of direct scientific observers and experimenters. Women's intellect have prevented the casting aside of a mass of most valuable truth which is too fine to be caught in the material sieve. Intuition eludes the closest questioning of the microscope and the test-glass, which is allied with our passions and feelings. It especially holds the fine boundary-line where mind and matter, sense and spirit, wave their floating and indistinguishable boundaries and exercise their complex action and reaction.

When a woman is possessed of a high degree of tact she sees as by a kind of second sight when any little emergency is likely to occur. To use a more familiar expression, things do not seem to go right. She is thus aware of any sudden turn in conversation and prepared for what it may lead to. Above all, she can penetrate into the state of mind of those she is placed with to detect the gathering gloom upon another's brow before the mental storm has reached any for-midable height. She knows when the tone of voice has altered, if any unwelcome thought has presented itself, and when any pulse of feeling is beating higher or lower in con-sequence of some trifling circumstance. In such instances, woman with her tact will notice the fluctuations which constantly change the feeling of social life. She can change the current of feeling suddenly and in such a way that no one detects her. By the power which nature gives her, she saves society the pain and annoyance which arise very frequently from trifles, and the mismanagement of society of someone possessing less tact and social adaptation.

Man is the creature of interest and ambition. His nature leads him forth into the struggle and bustle of the world. Love is but the embellishment of his early life or a song piped in the intervals of the acts. He seeks for fame and fortune and space in the world's thought, for dominion over his fellow-man. A woman's life is the history of affections. The heart is her world. It is there her ambition strives for empire and her avarice seeks for hidden treasures. She sends forth her sympathies on adventure and embarks her whole soul in the traffic of affection. If ship-wrecked her case is hopeless, for it is the bankruptcy of the heart.

To a man the disappointment of love may occasion some bitter pangs. It wounds some feelings of tenderness. It blasts some prospects of felicity. He is an active being. He may dissipate his thoughts in the whirl of varied occupations or plunge into the tide of pleasure. If the scene of disappointment is too full of painful associations, he can shift his abode at will. Taking the wings of the morning, he can "fly to the uttermost parts of the earth and be at rest."

We find man the cap-stone of the climax of paradoxes. A complex budget of contradictions. A heterogeneous compound of good and evil. The most noble work of God bespattered by Lucifer. Immortal being cleaving to things not eternal. A rational being violating reason. An animal with discretion, glutting instead of prudently feeding appetite. Man is an original, harmonious, compact violating order and reveling in confusion. Man is immortal without realizing it. He is rational, but often deaf to reason. He is a combination of noble powers waging civil war, robbing instead of aiding each other. Yet, like the Siamese twins compelled to remain in the same compartment.

The following shows the love, tenderness, and fortitude of woman. The letter which was bedimmed with tears was written before the husband was aware that death was fixing its grasp upon the lovely companion. It was laid in a book which he was wont to pursue:

"When this shall reach your eyes dear G—, some day when you are turning over the relics of the past I shall have passed away. The cold white stone will be keeping its lonely watch over lips you have so often pressed and the sod will be growing green that shall hide from your sight, the dust of one who has so often nestled close to your warm heart. For many long and sleepless nights when all my thoughts were at rest, I have wrestled with the consciousness of approaching death. At last, it has forced itself on my mind. Many weary hours have I passed in the endeavor to reconcile myself to leaving you, whom I love so well and this bright world of sunshine and beauty. It is hard indeed to struggle on silently and alone with the sure conviction that I am about to leave forever and go alone into the dark valley. "But I know in whom I have trusted and leaning upon His arm, I fear no evil." Don't blame me for keeping all this from you. How could I subject you to such a sorrow as I feel at parting, when time will soon make it apparent. I could have wished to live if only to be at your side when your time shall come, and pillowing your head, commend your departing spirit to the Maker's presence. But it is not to be so and I submit. Yours is the privilege of watching for the spirit's final flight, and to transfer me to my Savior's bosom. And you shall share my last thought, the last faint pressure of my hand, the last kiss shall be yours. When flesh and heart have failed me my eyes shall rest on yours, and our spirits hold one communion. Fading from view, the last of earth and glories of that better world where partings are unknown. I know well the spot, dear G— where you will lay me. We have stood by the place and watched the mellow sunset as it flashes through the leaves and burnished the grassy mounds around us with stripes of gold. Each perhaps has thought that one of us would come alone; and whichever it might be, your name would be on the stone. We loved the spot and I know you'll love it none the less when you see the same quiet sunlight and gentle breezes play among the grass that grows over your Mary's grave. I know you'll go often alone and my spirit shall be with you and whisper among the waving branches, "I am not lost, but gone before."

A woman has no natural gift more bewitching than a sweet laugh. It is like the sound of flutes on the water. It leads from her in a clear sparkling rill and the heart that hears it feels as if bathed in the cool, exhilarating spring. Have you ever pursued an unseen figure through the trees led by a fairy laugh, now here, now there, now lost, now found? Men are pursuing that wandering voice to this day. Sometimes it comes to him in the midst of care and sorrow or irksome business and then he turns away to listen. Hearing it ring throughout the room like a silver bell, with power to scare away the evil spirits of the mind. How much we owe to that sweet laugh! It turns prose to poetry and flings showers of sunshine over the darkness of the woods in which we are traveling.

Quincy being asked why there were more women than men replied, "It is in conformity with the arrangements of nature. We always see more of heaven than of earth." He cannot be an unhappy man who has the love and smile of a woman to accompany him in every department of life. The world may look dark and cheerless outside. Enemies may gather in his path. But when he returns to his fireside and feels the tender love of woman, he forgets his cares and troubles and is comparatively a happy man. He is but half prepared for the journey of life who takes not with him that friend, who will forsake him in no emergency.

Woman will divide man's sorrows, increase his joys, lift the veil from his heart and throw sunshine amid the darkest scenes. No man can be miserable who has such a companion be he ever so poor, despised, and trodden on by the world.

No trait of character is more valuable in a female than the possession of a sweet temper. Home can never be made happy without it. It is like the flowers that spring up in our pathway reviving and cheering us. Let a man go home at night, wearied and worn by the toils of the day and how soothing is a word by a good disposition! It is sunshine falling on the heart. He is happy and the cares of life are for-gotten. Nothing can be more touching than to behold a woman who had been all tenderness and dependence and alive to every trivial roughness while treading the prosper-ous path of life, suddenly rising to be the comforter and sup-porter of her husband under misfortune. And she, standing firm while the most bitter winds of adversity arose. Like the vine being lifted by the sunshine, so it is beautifully ordained that woman should be man's stay and solace when smitten by sudden calamity.

A woman with true intelligence is a blessing at home, in her circle of friends and in society. Wherever she goes she carries with her a health giving influence. There is a beautiful harmony about her character that at once inspires a respect which soon warms into love. The influence of such a woman is of the most salutary kind. She strengthens right principles in the virtuous, incites the selfish and indifferent to good actions and gives to even the light and frivolous, a taste for food more substantial than the frothy gossip with which they seek to recreate their minds.

Thackeray says; "It is better for you to pass an evening once or twice a week in a lady's drawing room even though the conversation is slow and you know the girl's song by heart, than in a club, tavern, or pit of a theater. All amusements of youth to which virtuous women are not admitted are deleterious in their nature. All men who avoid female society have dull perceptions, gross tastes, and revolt against what is pure. The club swaggerers, who are sucking the butts of billiard cues all night, call female society insipid. Poetry is uninspiring to a jockey and beauty has no charms for a blind man. Music does not please a poor beast who does not know one tune from another. I can sit for a whole evening talking with a well regulated, kindly woman about her girl Fanny or her boy Frank and like the evening's entertainment. One of the great benefits a man may derive from a woman's society is that he is bound to be respectful to her. The habit is of great good to your moral men, depend on it. Our education makes us the most eminently selfish men in the world."

Tom Hood in writing to his wife says: "I never was anything till I knew you and I have been better, happier, and a more prosperous man ever since. Lay that truth by in lavender and remind me of it when I fail. I am writing fondly and warmly, but not without good cause. First, your own affectionate letter. Next, the remembrance of our dear children and pledges of our old familiar love. The impulse to pour out the overflowing of my heart to yours. And last, not least, the knowledge that your eyes will read what my hands are now writing. Perhaps there is an after-thought that whatever may befall me, my wife will have this acknowledgment of her tenderness, worth, and excellence from my pen."

Among all nations the women ornament themselves more than the men. Wherever found they are the same kind, obliging, humane and tender beings. They are ever inclined to be happy and cheerful or timorous and modest. They do not hesitate like a man to perform any hospitable or generous action. They are not haughty, arrogant, or supercilious but full of courtesy, fond of society, industrious, economical, ingenious. Some are more liable to err than man, but more virtuous and performing more good actions than man.

The gentle tendrils of a woman's heart sometimes twine around a proud and sinful spirit and like roses and jasmine around a lightening rod, clings for support to what brings down on her the blasting thunderbolt.

These are the natural traits of woman's character: The English woman is respectful and proud. The French is happy and agreeable. The Italian is ardent and passionate. The American is sincere and affectionate. With an English woman love is a principle, with French a caprice, with Italian a passion, with American a sentiment. A man is married to an English lady, united to a French, cohabits with an Italian, and is wedded to an American. An English woman is anxious to secure a lord, a French a companion, an Italian a lover, an American a husband. The Englishman respects his lady, the Frenchman esteems his companion, the Italian adores his mistress, the American loves his wife. At night the Englishman returns to his house, the Frenchman to his establishment, the Italian to his retreat, and the American to his home. When an Englishman is sick his lady visits him. When a Frenchman is sick his companion pities him. When an Italian is sick his mistress sighs over him. When an American is sick his wife nurses him. When an Englishman dies his lady is bereaved. When a Frenchman dies his companion grieves. When an Italian dies his mistress laments. When an American dies his wife mourns. An English woman instructs her offspring. A French woman teaches her progeny. An Italian rears her young. An American educates her child.

The true lady is known wherever you meet her. Ten women shall get into the omnibus though we never saw them, we shall point out the true lady. She does not constantly giggle at every little thing that transpires, or is not thrown into a state of confusion should someone appear in peculiar dress. She wears no flowered brocade to trodden underfoot, ballroom jewelry or rose-tinted gloves. She makes no parade of a watch nor does she draw off her dark glove to display ostentatious rings. The bonnet on her head is of plain straw, simply trimmed. She is quite as civil to the poorest as to the richest person who sits beside her and equally regardful of their rights. If she attracts attention, it is by the unconscious grace of her person and manner not by the ostentation of her dress. We are quite sorry when she disappears. A bachelor would go home to his solitary den with a resolution to become a better and a married man.

The strongest man feels the influence of woman's gentlest thoughts like the mightiest oak quivers in the softest breeze. We confess to a great distrust of that man who persistently underrates woman. Never did language better apply to an adjective than when it called the wife the "better half." We admire the ladies because of their beauty, respect them because of their virtues, adore them because of their intelligence and love them because WE CAN'T HELP IT.

Man was made to protect, love, and cherish, not to undervalue, neglect or abuse woman.

Treated well, educated and esteemed she rises in dignity. She becomes the refiner and imparts a milder, softer tone to man. No community has ever exhibited the refinements of civilization and social order where women were held in contempt and their rights not properly respected and preserved. Degrade woman and you degrade man more. She is the fluid of the thermometer of society placed there by the hand of the great Creator. Man may injure the instrument, but can neither destroy or provide a substitute for the mercury. Her rights are as sacred as those of the male. Her mental powers are underrated by those only who have either not seen or were so blinded by prejudice they would not see their development. Educate girls as you do boys, put women in the business arena designed for men and they will acquit themselves far better than boys would, if they were placed in the departments designed for females.

The perception of woman is more acute than that of man. A perception designed by an all-wise Creator for the preservation and perpetuity of our race. Her patience, fortitude, integrity, constancy, piety and devotion are naturally stronger than in the other sex. If she was first in transgression, she was first in prayer. Her seed has bruised the serpent's head. She stood by the expiring Jesus, when boasting Peter and the other disciples had forsaken their Lord. She was the last at his tomb to embalm his sacred body. The first to discover that he had burst the bars of death, risen from the cleft rock, and triumphed over death and the grave.

Under affliction the fortitude of woman is proverbial. As a nurse, one female will endure more than five men. That she is more honest than man, our prisons fully demonstrate. That she is more religiously inclined, the records of our churches will show. That she is more devotional, our prayer meetings will prove.

Woman has exercised a most remarkable judgement in regard to great issues. She has prevented the casting aside of plans which led to very remarkable discoveries and inventions. When Columbus laid a plan to discover the new world, he could not get a hearing till he applied to a woman for help. Woman equips man for the voyage of life. She generally does not lead but finds her peculiar and best attitude as helper. Though man executes a project, she fits him for it beginning in childhood. So everywhere man performs, woman trains the man. Every effectual person leaving his mark on the world is but another Columbus furnishing some Isabella in the form of his mother. She lays down her jewelry, her vanities and her comforts.

𝔐𝔬𝔱𝔥𝔢𝔯

I⊤ is true to nature, although it be expressed in a figurative form that a mother is both the morning and evening star of life. The light of her eye is always the first to rise and often the last to set on man's day of trial. She wields a power far more decisive than syllogisms in arguments or courts of last appeal in authority. Nay, where there has been no fear of God before the eyes of the young or his love has been unfelt and his law outraged, a mother's affection has held transgressors by the heart-strings. The means of leading them back to virtue and to God.

Woman's charms are certainly many and powerful. The rose just bursting into beauty has an irresistible bewitchingness. The blooming bride awakens admiration and interest, the blush of her cheek fills with delight. But the charm of maternity is more sublime than all these.

Heaven has imprinted in the mother's face something beyond this world. Something which claims kindred with the skies. The angelic smile, the tender look, the waking and watchful eye which keeps its fond vigil over her slumbering babe.

Mother! Ecstatic sound so twined round our hearts that they must cease to throb ere we forget it! "Tis our first love. "Tis part of religion. Nature has set the mother on such a pinnacle that our infant eyes and arms are first uplifted to her. We cling to it in manhood. We almost worship it in old age. Enter an apartment and behold the tender babe feeding on its mother's breast, the tide of life flowing through her generous veins as it nourishes.

"Can a mother's love be supplied? No! a thousand times no! By the deep, earnest yearning of our spirits for a mother's love. By the weary, aching void in our hearts. By the restless, unsatisfied wanderings of our affections ever seeking an object on which to rest. By our instinctive discernment of the true maternal love from the false, as we would discern between a lifeless statue and a breathing man. By the hallowed emotions with which we cherish in the depths of our hearts, the vision of a grass grown mound in a quiet graveyard among the mountains. By the reverent and holy love, the feeling akin to idolatry with which our thoughts hover about an angel form among the seraphs of Heaven, by all these we answer, no!"

"Often do I sigh in my struggles with the hard, uncaring world, for the sweet, deep, security I felt when of an evening nestled in her bosom, I listened to some quiet tale read in her tender and untiring voice. Never can I forget her sweet glance cast on me when I appeared asleep. Nor her kiss of peace at night. Years have passed since we laid her beside my father in the old church yard. Yet, still her voice whispers from the grave and her eye watches over me as I visit spots long since hallowed to the memory of my mother."

Oh! There is an enduring tenderness in the love of a mother that transcends all other affections of the heart. It is neither to be chilled by selfishness, daunted by danger, weakened by worthlessness, or stifled by ingratitude. She will sacrifice every comfort to his convenience, surrender every pleasure to his enjoyment, glory in his fame and exult in his prosperity. If misfortune overtake him, he will be the dearer to her from misfortune. If disgrace settle on his name, she will still love and cherish him in spite of his disgrace. If all the world cast him off, she will be all the world to him.

Alas! How little do we appreciate a mother's tenderness while she's living. How heedless are we in youth of all her anxieties and kindness? But when she is dead and gone and the cares and coldness of the world come withering to our hearts, we experience how hard it is to find true sympathy. How few there are who love us for ourselves or will befriend us in misfortune. Then it is, that we think of the mother we have lost.

Over the grave of a friend, brother, or sister we would plant the primrose. But over that of a mother we would let the grass shoot up, for there is something in the simple covering which nature spreads on the grave. A mother's grave. Earth has some sacred spots where we feel like losing shoes from our feet and treading with reverence. A place where friendship hands have lingered in each other and vows have been plighted, prayers offered, and tears of parting shed. Oh, how thoughts hover around such places and travel back through unmeasured space to visit them! But of all spots on this green earth, none is so sacred as that where rests waiting the resurrection, those we have loved and cherished.

There sleeps the nurse of infancy, the guide of our youth, the counselor of our riper years. Our friend when others deserted us. She whose heart was a stranger to every other feeling but love. There she sleeps and we love the very earth for her sake.

In what Christian country can we deny the influence which a mother exerts over the whole life of her children.

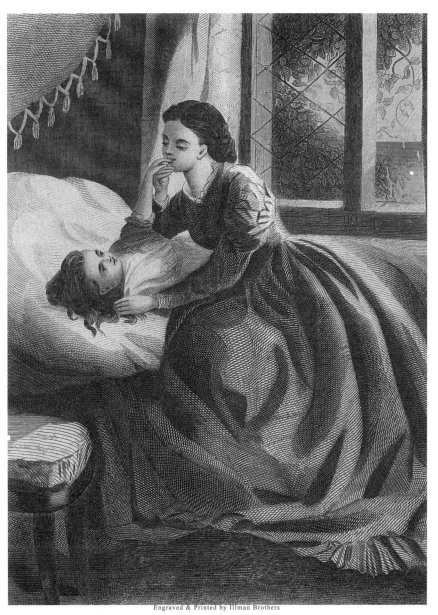

Engraved & Printed by Illman Brothers

THE MOTHER.

FOR THE ROYAL PATH OF LIFE.

The roughest and hardest wanderer while tossed on the ocean or scorching his feet on desert sands, revisits in his loneliness and suffering the smiles which maternal affection shed over his infancy. The reckless sinner even in his hardened career occasionally hears the whisperings of those holy precepts instilled by a virtuous mother. Although they may in the fullness of guilt be neglected, there are instances of having so stung the conscience as to have led to a deep and lasting repentance. The erring child will then, if a mother yet lives, turn to her for that consolation which the laws of society deny. In the lasting purity of a mother's love, they will find the way to heaven. How cheerfully does a virtuous son labor for a poverty stricken mother! How alive is he to her honor and high standing in the world! Should that mother be deserted and left in "worse than widowhood," how proudly he stands forth her comforter and protector. Indeed the more we reflect on the subject, the more we are convinced that no influence is so lasting. Such wide extent do we feel the necessity of guiding this sacred affection and perfecting that being from whom it emanates.

Science has sometimes tried to teach us that if a pebble be cast into the sea on any shore the effects are felt, though not perceived, over the whole area of the ocean. More wonderful still, science has tried to show the effects of all the sounds ever uttered by man or beast, or caused by inanimate things. These are still floating in the air. The present state is just the aggregate result of all these sounds. If these things be true, they furnish an emblem of the effects produced by a mother's power. Effects that stretch into eternity and operate there forever in sorrow or in joy. The mother can take man's whole nature under her control. She becomes what she has been called, "The divinity of infancy." Her smile is its sunshine, her word its mildest law until sin and the world have steeled the heart. She can shower around her the most genial of all influences. From the time when she first laps her little one in Elysium by clasping him to her bosom, "its first paradise," to the moment when that child is independent of her aid. Her smile, her word, and her wish is an inspiring force. A sentence of encouragement or praise is joy for a day. It spreads light on all faces and renders a mother's power more and more charm-like, as surely as ceaseless accusing, rebuking and correcting, chafes, sours and disgusts. So intense is her power that the mere remembrance of a praying mother's hand laid on the head in infancy has held back a son from ruin, when passion had waxed strong.

The mother is the angel-spirit of home. Her tender yearnings over the cradle of her infant babe, her guardian care of the child and youth, and her bosom companionship with the man of her love and choice make her the personal center of the interests, hopes, and happiness of the family. Her love glows in her sympathies and reigns in all her thoughts and deeds. It never cools, tires, dreads, or sleeps but ever glows and burns with increasing ardor. Her love is sweet and holy incense upon the altar of home devotion. Even when she is gone, the sainted mother in heaven sways a mightier influence over her child than when she was present. Her departed spirit still hovers over his affections, overshadows his path, and draws him by unseen cords to herself in heaven. But in glancing at a mother's position in our homes, we should not overlook the sorrows to which she is often exposed. A mother mourning by the grave of her first-born is a spectacle of woe. A mother watching the palpitating frame of her child as life ebbs away must evoke the sympathy of the most stern. A mother closing the dying eye, child after child, is one of the saddest sights of earth. When the cradle-song passes into a dirge, the heart is laden indeed.

Not long ago two friends were sitting together engaged in letter writing. One was a young man from India, the other a female friend, part of whose family resided in that far-off land. The former was writing to his mother in India. When the letter was finished his friend offered to enclose it in hers to save postage. This he politely declined, saying: If it be sent separately, it will reach her sooner and perhaps save her a tear." His friend was touched at his tender regard for his mother's feelings. Would that every boy and girl, every young man and woman as equally saving of a mother's tears. The Christian mother especially, can deeply plant and genially cherish the seeds of truth. Is her child sick? That is a text from which to speak to the Great Physician. Is it the sober calm of evening when even children grow sedate? She can tell of the Home where there is no night. Is it morning when all are buoyantly happy? The eternal day is suggested and its glories may be told. That is the wisdom which wins souls even more than the formal lesson, the lecture, or the task.

There is one suggestion more. Perhaps the saddest sentence that can fall on the ear regarding any child is, "He has no mother; she is dead!" It comes like a voice from the sepulchre and involves the consummation of all the sorrows that can befall the young. In that condition they are deprived of their most tender comforter and their wisest

counselor. They are left a prey to a thousand temptations or
ills. They are freed from the restraint of one who could curb
without irritating or guide without affecting superiority.
Now will mothers live with their children, as if they were to
leave them in a cold and inhospitable world? Will they
guide their little ones to Him who is pre-eminently the God
of the orphan and who inspired his servant to say; "Though
father and mother forsake me, the Lord will take me up."

Children

WOE to him who smiles not over a cradle and weeps not
over a tomb. He who has never tried the companionship of
a little child has carelessly passed by one of the greatest
pleasures of life, as one passes a rare flower without plucking it or knowing its value. The gleeful laugh of happy children is the best home music and the graceful figures of
childhood are the best statuary. We are all kings and queens
in the cradle. Each babe is a new marvel and miracle. The
perfection of the providence for childhood is willingly
acknowledged. The care which covers the seed of the tree
under tough husks. Stony cases provide for the human
plant, the mother's breast and the father's house. The size of
the nestler is comic. Its tiny beseeching weakness is com-
pensated perfectly by the happy look of the mother who is a
sort of high-reposing Providence to it. The parents welcome the puny struggler. Strong in his weakness, his little
arms more irresistible than the soldier's. His lips touched
with persuasion which Chatham and Pericles in manhood

could not. His unaffected lamentations when he lifts up his voice on high. The face all liquid grief as he tries to swallow his vexation. It softens all hearts to pity and to mirthful and clamorous compassion. The small despot asks so little that all reason and nature are on his side. His ignorance is more charming than all knowledge. His little sins more bewitching than any virtue.

His flesh is angel's flesh all alive. "Infancy, said Coleridge, "presents body and spirit in unity and the body is all animated." All day between his three and four sleeps, he coos like a pigeon-house, sputters, purrs, and puts on his faces of importance. When he fasts, the little Pharisee fails not to sound his trumpet before him. By lamplight he delights in shadows on the wall and by daylight, in yellow and scarlet. Carry him outdoors and he is overpowered by the light and the extent of natural objects, and is silent. Then begins the use of his fingers. He studies power, the lesson of his race.

Not without design has God implanted in the maternal breast that strong love of children which is felt everywhere. This lays deep and broad the foundation for the child's future education from parental hands. Nor without designs has Christ commanded, "Feed my lambs." Inculcate this on his church and the world at the earliest possible period. Nor can parents and all well-wishers to humanity, be too earnest and careful to fulfill the prompting of their nature and the command of Christ in this matter. Influence is as quiet and imperceptible on the child's mind as the falling of snowflakes on the meadow. One cannot tell the hour when the human mind is not in the condition of receiving impressions from exterior moral forces. In innumerable instances

the most secret and unnoticed influences have been in oper-
ation for months and even years, to break down the
strongest barriers of the human heart and work out its
morality. Yet, the fondness of parents and friends have been
unaware of the working of such unseen agents of evil. Not
all at once does any heart become utterly bad. The error is
in time and parents are not conscious how early the seeds of
vice are sown and take root. It is as the Gospel declares,
"While men slept, the enemy came and sowed tares and
went his way." If this then is the error, how shall it be cor-
rected and what is the antidote to be applied?

Never scold children, but soberly and quietly reprove.
Do not employ shame, except in extreme cases. The suffering is acute and it hurts self-respect in the child to reprove
him before the family. To ridicule, to tread down a child's
feelings ruthlessly is to wake in its bosom malignant feelings. A child is defenseless and is not allowed to argue. He
is often tried, condemned, and executed in a second. He
finds himself of little use. He is put at things he does not
care for and withheld from things which he does like. He is
made the convenience of grown-up people and is hardly
supposed to have any rights, except in a corner. He is sent
hither and thither and made to get up or sit down for everybody's convenience but his own. He is snubbed, catechised,
and learns to dodge government and elude authority. And
then be whipped for being "such a liar that no one can
believe him."

Children will not trouble you long. They grow up and
nothing on earth grows as fast as children. It was but yesterday that lad was playing with tops, a buoyant boy. He is
a man and gone now! There is no more childhood for him.

Life has claimed him. When a beginning is made, it is like a raveling stocking. Stitch by stitch it gives way till all are gone. The house has not a child in it and there is no more noise in the hall. No boys rush in pell-mell and it is very orderly now. There are no more skates, sleds, bats, balls, or strings left scattered about. Things are neat enough now. There is no delay for sleepy folks and there is no longer any task before you lie down. No looking after anybody or tucking up bed clothes. There are no disputes to settle, nobody to get off to school, no complaints, no opportunities for impossible things. No rips to mend, no fingers to tie up, no faces to wash, or collars to be arranged. There never was such peace in the house! It would sound like music to have some feet to clatter down the front stairs! Oh for some children's noise! What used to ail us that we were hushing their loud laughter, checking their noisy frolic, and reproving their slamming and banging the doors? We wish our neighbors would only lend us an urchin or two to make a little noise in these premises. A home without children. It is like a lantern and no candle, a garden and no flowers, a vine and no grapes, a brook and no water gurgling or gushing in its channel. We want to be tired, to be vexed, to be run over, to hear children at work with all its varieties.

Bishop Earle says: "A child is man in a small letter and yet the best copy of Adam, before he tasted of Eve or the apple. He is happy whose small practice in the world can only write his character. His soul is yet a white paper unscribbled with observations of the world, where it becomes a blurred notebook. He is purely happy because he knows no evil or has no means by sin to be acquainted with misery. He arrives not at the mischief of being wise, nor endures evils to come by foreseeing them. He kisses and loves all and when the smart of the rod is past, smiles on his beater. The older he grows, he is a stair lower from God. He is the Christian example and the old man's relapse. The one imitates his pureness and the other falls into his simplicity. Could he put off his body with his little coat, he could get eternity without a burden and exchange but one heaven for another."

Children are more easily led to be good by example of loving kindness and tales of well-doing in others, than threatened into obedience by records of sin, crime, and punishment. Then on the infant mind impress sincerity, truth, honesty, benevolence and their kindred virtues, and the welfare of your child will be insured. Not only during this life but the life to come.

Oh, what a responsibility to form a creature, frailest and feeblest that heaven has made, into the intelligent and fearless sovereign of the whole animated creation. The interpreter and adorer and almost the representative of Divinity!

Youth

MEN glory in raising great and magnificent structures and find a secret pleasure in seeing sets of their own planting grow up and flourish. But it is a greater and more glorious work to build up a man. See a youth of our own planting, from the small beginnings and advantages we have given him, grow up into a considerable fortune. See them take root in the world, shoot up to such a height, and spread their branches so wide. We who first planted him may ourselves find comfort and shelter under his shadow.

Much of our early gladness vanishes utterly from our memory. We can never recall the joy with which we laid our heads on our mother's bosom or rode our father's back in childhood. Doubtless, that joy is wrought up into our nature as the sunlight of long past mornings wrought up in the soft mellowness of the apricot. The time will soon come, if it has not already, when you must part from those who have surrounded the same paternal board. They mingled with you in the gay-hearted joys of childhood and the opening promise of youth. New cares will attend you in new situations. The relations you form or the business you pursue may call you far from the "playplace" of your "early days." In the unseen future, your brothers and sisters may be sundered from you. Your lives may be spent apart and in death you may be divided. Of you it may be said—

> "They grew in beauty, side by side,
>   They filled one home with glee;
> Their graves are severed far and wide,
>   By mount and stream and sea."

Let your own home be the center of your affections and the spot where your highest desires are concentrated. Do this and you will prove not only the hope but the stay of your kindred and home. Your personal character will elevate the whole family. Some may become degenerate sons and bring the gray hairs of their parents with sorrow, to the grave. You will be the pride and staff of a mother and an honor to your father. You will establish their house, give peace to their pillow, and be a memorial to their praise.

Spend your evening hours, boys and girls at home. You

may make them among the most agreeable and profitable of your lives. When vicious companions would tempt you away remember that God has said, "Cast not in thy lot with them; walk thou not in their way; refrain thy foot from their path. They lay in wait for their own blood; they lurk privily for their own lives. But walk thou in the way of good men and keep the paths of righteous."

Keep good company or none. Never be idle. If your hands cannot be usefully employed, attend to the cultivation of your mind. Always speak the truth. Make few promises. Live up to your engagements. Keep your own secrets if you have any. When you speak to a person, look him in the face. Good company and good conversation are the very sinews of virtue. Good character cannot be essentially injured except by your own acts. If one speak evil of you, let life be such that none will believe him. Drink no kind of intoxicating liquors. Always live, misfortune excepted, within your income. When you retire to bed, think over what you have been doing during the day. Make no haste to be rich if you would prosper. Small and steady gains give competency with tranquillity of mind. Never play at any kind of game of chance. Avoid temptation through fear, that you may not be able to withstand it. Never run into debt unless you see a way to get out again. Never borrow if you can possibly avoid it. Never speak evil of any one. Be just, before you are generous. Keep yourself innocent if you would be happy. Save when you are young to spend when you are old. Never think that which you do for religion is time or money misspent. Always go to meeting when you can. Read some portion of the Bible every day. Often think of death and your accountability to God.

An honest, industrious boy is always WANTED. He will be sought. His services will be in demand. He will be respected and loved. He will be spoken of in words of high commendation. He will always have a home. He will grow up to be a man of known worth and established character.

He will be WANTED. The merchant will want him for a salesman or clerk. The master mechanic will want him for an apprentice or a journeyman. Those with a job to let will want him for a contractor. Clients will want him for a lawyer. Patients will want him for a physician, congregations for a pastor, parents for a teacher of their children, and the people for an officer.

He will be WANTED. Townsmen will want him as a citizen, acquaintances as a neighbor, neighbors as a friend, families as a visitor, the world as an acquaintance and girls will want him for a beau and finally for a husband.

To both parents when faithful, a child is indebted beyond estimation. If one begins to enumerate their claims, to set in order their labors, and recount their sacrifices and privations, he is soon compelled to desist from his task. He is constrained to acknowledge that their love for him is surpassed only by that of the great Spring of all good. Who, to represent in the strongest language our measureless indebtedness to Him we call "Our Father in Heaven."

Parents do wrong in keeping their children hanging around home sheltered and enervated by parental indulgence. The eagle does better. It stirs up its nest when the young eagles are able to fly. They are compelled to shift for themselves for the old eagle literally turns them out and at the same time tears all down and feathers from the nest. It is this rude and rough experience that makes the king of birds so fearless in his flight and so expert in the pursuit of prey. It is a misfortune to be born with a silver spoon in your mouth, for you have it to carry and plague you all your days. Riches often hang like a dead weight or like a millstone about the necks of ambitious young men. Had Benjamin Franklin or George Law been brought up in the lap of affluence and ease, they would probably never have been heard of by the world at large. It was the making of the one that he ran away and the other that he was turned out of doors. Early thrown upon their own resources, they acquired the energy and skill to overcome resistance and to grapple with the difficulties that beset their pathway. Here I think they learned the most important lesson of their lives. A lesson that developed their manhood and forced on them necessity, the most useful and inexorable of masters. There is nothing like being bound out, turned out, or even kicked out to compel a man to do for himself. Rough handling of the last sort has often made drunken men sober. Poor boys at the foot of the hill should remember that every step toward the goal of wealth and honor gives them increased energy and power. They have a purchase and obtain a momentum the rich man's son never knows. The poor man's son has the heaviest weight to lift. Without knowing it, he is turning the longest lever and that with the utmost vim and vigor. Boys, do not sigh for the capital or indulgence of the rich, but use the capital you have. I mean those God-given powers which every healthy youth of good habits has in and of himself. All a man wants in this life is a skillful hand, a well informed mind, and a good heart. In our happy land and in these favored times of libraries, lyceums, liberty, religion, and education, the humblest and poorest can aim at the greatest usefulness and the highest excellence. A prospect of success calls forth all the endurance, perseverance, and industry that is in man.

We live in an age marked by its lack of respect. Old institutions however sacred are now fearlessly and often wantonly assailed. The aged are not treated with deference. Fathers and mothers are addressed with rudeness. The command now runs, one would think, not in the good old tenor of the Bible, "Children obey your parents in the Lord, for this is right," but thus: Parents obey your children. Some may go so far as to say this is right. "Why should I who am so much superior to my father and my mother bow down before them? Were they equal to me? Did they appear so well in society? And especially, were they not in destitute circumstances I could respect? My young friend, God, nature, and humanity forbid you to pursue this strain. Because our parents are poor are we absolved from all obligations to love and respect them? Nay, if our father was in narrow circumstances and still did all that he could for us we owe him instead of less regard, a hundred fold the more. If our mother with scanty means could promote our comfort and train us up as she did, then for the sake of reason, right, and common compassion let us not despise her in her need.

Let every child having pretence to heart or manliness or piety, and who is so fortunate as to have a father or mother living, consider it a sacred duty. Consult at any reasonable personal sacrifice the known wishes of a parent, until that parent is no more. The recollection of the same through the after pilgrimage of life will sweeten every sorrow, brighten every gladness, sparkle every teardrop with a joy ineffable. But be selfish still, have your own way, consult your own inclinations, yield to the bent of your own desires regardless of a parent's commands and counsels and beseeching tears, and as the Lord liveth, your life will be a failure. "The eye that mocketh at his father and dispiseth to obey his mother, the ravens of the valley shall pick it out and the young eagle shall eat it."

Consider finally that if you live on, the polluted joys of youth cannot be the joys of old age, though its guilt and the sting left behind will endure. We know well that the path of strict virtue is steep and rugged. But for the stern discipline of temperance, the hardship of self-denial, the crushing of appetite and passion, there will be the blessed recompense of cheerful, healthful manhood and an honorable old age. Yes higher and better than all temporal returns, live for purity of speech and thought. Live for an incorruptible character. Have the courage to begin the great race and the energy to pursue the glorious prize. Foresee your danger, arm against it, trust in God and you will have nothing to fear.

Home

WHAT, a hallowed name! How full of enchantment and how dear to the heart! Home is the magic circle within which the weary spirit finds refuge. It is the sacred asylum to which the care-worn heart retreats to find rest from the toils and inquietude of life.

Ask the lone wanderer as he plods his tedious way, bent with the weight of age and hair white with the frost of years. Ask him what is home. He will tell you "it is a green spot in memory. An oasis in the desert. A center about which the most fond recollections of his grief-oppressed heart cling with the tenacity of youth's first love. It was once a glorious, happy, reality but now it rests only as an image of the mind." Home! That name touches every fiber of the soul and strikes every cord of the human heart with its angelic fingers. Nothing but death can break its spell. What tender associations are linked with home! What pleasing images and deep emotions it awakens! It calls up the most fond memories of life and opens in our nature the purest, deepest, and richest gush of consecrated thought and feeling.

Some years ago, twenty thousand people gathered in the old Castle Garden, New York, to hear Jennie Lind sing as no other songstress ever had sung sublime compositions of Beethoven, Handle, etc. At length the Swedish Nightingale thought of her home, paused and seemed to fold her wings for a higher flight. She began with deep emotion to pour forth "Home, Sweet Home." The audience could not stand it. An uproar of applause stopped the music. Tears gushed from those thousands like rain. Beethoven and Handle were forgotten. After a moment the song came again, seemingly as from heaven, almost angelic. Home, that was the word bound as with a spell twenty thousand souls and Howard Payne triumphed over, the great masters of song. When we look at the brevity and simplicity of this home song we are ready to ask, what is the charm that lies concealed in it? Why does the dramatist and poet find his reputation resting on so apparently narrow a basis? The answer is easy. Next to religion, the deepest and most ineradicable sentiment in the human soul is that of the home affections. Every heart vibrates to this theme.

Home has an influence which is stronger than death. It

is law to our hearts and binds us with a spell which neither time nor change can break. The darkest villainies which have disgraced humanity cannot neutralize it. Gray-haired and demon guilt will make his dismal cell the sacred urn of tears, wept over the memories of home. These will soften and melt into tears of penitence even the heart of the unyielding. Ask the little child what is home? You will find that to him it is the world. He knows no other. The father's love, the mother's smile, the sister's embrace, the brother's welcome, throw about his home a heavenly halo and make it as attractive to him as the home of the angels. Home is the spot where the child pours out all its complaints. It is the grave of all its sorrows. Childhood has its sorrows and its grievances, but home is the place where these are soothed and banished by the sweet lullaby of a fond mother's voice.

Was paradise an abode of purity and peace or will the New Eden above be one of unmingled beatitude? Then "the Paradise of Childhood," "the Eden of Home," are names applied to the family abode. In that paradise, all may appear as smiling and serene to childhood as the untainted garden did to fallen man. Even the remembrance of it amid distant scenes of woe has soothed some of the saddest hours of life and crowds of mourners have spoken of

"A home, that paradise below
Of sunshine and of flowers
Where hallowed joys perennial flow
By calm sequestered bowers."

At home, childhood nestles like a bird which has built its abode among roses. There the cares and the coldness of earth are, as long as possible, averted. Flowers bloom there or fruits invite on every side, and there paradise is restored, could mortal power ward off the consequences of sin. This new garden of the Lord would then abound in beauty unsullied and trees of the Lord's planting, bearing fruit to his glory, would be found in plenty there. It would be reality and not mere poetry, to speak of

> "My own dear quiet home,
> The Eden of my heart."

Home of our childhood! What words fall upon the ear with so much of music in their cadence as those which recall the scenes of innocent and happy childhood, now numbered with the memories of the past! How fond recollection delights to dwell upon the events which marked our early pathway, when the unbroken home-circle presented a scene of loveliness vainly sought but in the bosom of a happy family. Intervening years have not dimmed the vivid coloring which memory has adorned, those joyous hours of youthful innocence. We are again borne on the wings of imagination of a father's care, a mother's love, and the cherished associations of brothers and sisters.

Home! How often we hear persons speak of the home of their childhood. Their minds seem to delight in dwelling upon the recollections of joyous days spent beneath the parental roof when their young and happy hearts were as light and free as the birds, that made the woods resound with the melody of their cheerful voices. What a blessing it is, when weary with care and burdened with sorrow to have a home to which we can go, and there in the midst of friends we love, forget our troubles and dwell in peace and quietness.

There is no happiness in life, there is no misery like that growing out of the dispositions which consecrate or desecrate a home. Peace at home, that is the blessing. "He is happiest be he king or peasant who finds peace in his home." Home should be made so truly home that the weary tempted heart could turn toward it anywhere on the dusty highway of life and receive light and strength. It should be the sacred refuge of our lives whether rich or poor. The affections and loves of home are graceful things especially among the poor. The ties that bind the wealthy and the proud to home may be forged on earth, but those which link the poor man to his humble hearth are of the true metal and bear the stamp of heaven. These affections and loves constitute the poetry of human life and so far as our present existence is concerned with all the domestic relations, are worth more than all other social ties. They give the first throb to the heart and unseal the deep fountains of its love. Home is the chief school of human virtue. Its responsibilities, joys, sorrows, smiles, tears, hopes, and solicitudes form the chief interest of human life.

There is nothing in the world so reverent as the character of parents. Nothing so intimate and endearing as the relation of husband and wife. Nothing so tender as that of parents and children. Nothing so lovely as those brothers and sisters. The little circle is made one by a singular union of the affections. The only fountain in the wilderness of life where man drinks of water totally unmixed with bitter ingredients. It pours forth for him in the calm and shady recess of domestic life.

Pleasure may heat the heart with artificial excitement, ambition may delude it with golden dreams, war may eradicate its fine fibers and diminish its sensitiveness, but it is only domestic love that can render it truly happy.

Even as the sunbeam is composed of millions of minute rays, the home life must be constituted of little tendernesses, kind looks, sweet laughter, gentle words and loving counsels. It must not be like the torchblaze of natural excitement which is easily quenched, but like the serene, chastened light which burns as safely in the dry east wind as in the stillest atmosphere. Let each bear the other's burden the while. Let each cultivate the mutual confidence, a gift capable of increase and improvement. Soon it will be found that kindliness will spring up on every side displacing constitutional unsuitability, want of mutual knowledge, even as we have seen sweet violets and primroses dispelling the gloom of the gray sea-rocks.

There is nothing on earth so beautiful as the household on which Christian love forever smiles and where religion walks a counselor and a friend. No cloud can darken it, for its twin-stars are centered in the soul. No storms can make it tremble, for it has a heavenly support and a heavenly anchor.

Home is a place of refuge. Our spirits tossed day by day upon the rough and stormy ocean of life, harassed by worldly cares and perplexed by worldly inquietude. The weary spirit yearns after repose. It seeks and finds it in the refuge which home supplies. Here the mind is at rest, the heart's turmoil becomes quiet, and the spirit basks in the peaceful delights of domestic love.

Yes, home is a place of rest. We feel it so when we seek and enter it after the busy cares and trials of the day are over. We may find joy elsewhere, but it is not the joy and satisfaction of home. The heart may soon tire of the world but of the home, never. In the world there is much of cold formality, much heartlessness under the garb of friendship, but in the home it is all heart, all friendship of the purest, truest character.

The road along which the man of business is not one of broken stones. Nor does the road ordinarily lead through pleasant scenes and by well-springs of delight. On the contrary it is a rough and rugged path beset with "wait a bit" thorns and full of pit-falls, which can only be avoided by the watchful care of circumspection. After every day's journey over this worse than rough turnpike road, the wayfarer needs something more than rest. He requires solace and he deserves it. He is weary of the dull prose of life and athirst for the poetry. Happy is the business man who can find that solace and that poetry at home.

Warm greetings from loving hearts, fond glances from bright eyes, the welcome shouts of children. The many thousand little arrangements for our comfort and enjoyment that silently tell of thoughtful and expectant love. The gentle ministrations that disencumber us and force us into an old and easy seat before we are aware of it. These and like tokens of affection and sympathy constitute the poetry which reconciles us to the prose of life. Think of this, wives and daughters of business men! Think of the toils, the anxieties, the mortification and wear that husbands and fathers undergo to secure comfortable homes, and compensate them for their trials by making them happy by their own firesides.

Is it not true that much of a man's energy and success, as well as happiness depends on the character of his home? Secure there, he goes forth bravely to encounter the trials of life. It encourages him to think of his pleasant home. It is his point of rest. The thought of a dear wife shortens the distance of a journey and alleviates the harassings of business.

It is a reserved power to fall back on. Home and home friends! How dear they are to us all! Well might we love to linger on the picture of home friends! When all other friends prove false, home friends removed from every bias but love are the steadfast and sure stays of our peace of soul. Friends, the best and dearest when the hour is darkest and the danger of evil the greatest. If one have none to care for him at home, if there be neglect or absense of love or coldness in our home and on our hearth, then even if we prosper outside it is dark indeed, inside! It is not seldom that we can trace alienation and dissipation to this source. If no wife or sister care for him who returns from his toil, well may he despair of life's best blessings. Without home friends, Home is nothing but a name.

The sweetest type of heaven is home. Heaven itself is the home for whose acquisition we are to strive the most strongly. Home in one form and another is the great object of life. It stands at the end of every day's labor and beckons us to its bosom. Life would be cheerless and meaningless did we not discern across the river that divides it from life beyond, glimpses of the pleasant mansions prepared for us.

Heaven! That land of quiet rest toward which those worn down and tired with the toils of earth, direct their frail barks over the troubled waters of life. And after a long and dangerous passage, find life, safe in the haven of eternal bliss. Heaven is the HOME that awaits us beyond the grave. There the friendships formed on earth and which death has severed are never more to be broken. Parted friends shall meet again never more to be separated.

It is an inspiring hope when we separate here on earth at the summons of death's angel and when a few more years have rolled over the heads of those remaining, if "faithful unto death," we shall meet again in heaven our eternal home. To dwell there in the presence of our Heavenly Father, and go no more out forever. At the best estate, we are only pilgrims and strangers. Heaven is to be our eternal home. Death will never knock at the door of that mansion and in all that land there will not be a single grave. Aged parents rejoice very much when on Christmas Day or Thanksgiving Day they have their children at home. But there is almost always a son or daughter absent from the country, perhaps absent from the world. But oh, how our Heavenly Father will rejoice in the long thanksgiving day of Heaven when He has all His children with Him in glory! How glad brothers and sisters will be to meet after so long a separation! Perhaps a score of years ago they parted at the door of the tomb. Now they meet again at the door of immortality. Once they looked through a glass darkly. Now, face to face, corruption, incorruption, mortality, immortality. Where are now all their sorrows and temptations and trials? Overwhelmed in the Red Sea of death while they, dry-shod, marched to glory. Gates of jasper, cap-stone of amethyst! Thrones of dominion do not so much affect my soul as the thought of home. Once there, let earthly sorrows howl like the storms and roll like the seas. Home! Let thrones rot and empires wither. Home! Let the world die in the earthquake struggles and be buried amid procession of planets and dirge of spheres. Home! Let everlasting ages roll in irresistible sweep. Home! No sorrow, no crying, no tears, no death, but home, sweet home, beautiful home! Glorious home! Everlasting home! Home with each other! Home with angels! Home with God! Home, Home! Through the rich grace of Christ Jesus, may we all reach it.

Family Worship

A PRAYERLESS family cannot be otherwise than irreligious. They who daily pray in their homes, do well. They that not only pray but read the Bible, do better. But they do best of all who not only pray and read the Bible, but sing the praises of God.

What scene can be more lovely on earth, more like the heavenly home and more pleasing to God than that of a pious family kneeling with one accord around the home-alter, uniting their supplications to their Father in heaven! How sublime the act of those parents who thus pray for the blessing of God upon their household! How lovely the scene of a pious mother gathering her little ones around her at the bedside and teaching them the privilege of prayer! And what a safeguard is this devotion against all the machinations of Satan! It is this which makes home a type of heaven, the dwelling place of God. The family altar is heaven's threshold. Happy are those at that altar who have been consecrated by a father's blessing, baptized by a mother's tears, and borne up to heaven on their joint petitions as a voluntary thank-offering to God. The home that has honored God with an altar of devotion may well be called blessed.

The influence of family worship is great, silent, irresistible, and permanent. Like the calm, deep stream it moves on in silent but overwhelming power. It strikes its roots deep into the human heart and spreads its branches wide over the whole being. Like the lily that braves the tempest, and the Alpine flower that leans its cheek upon the bosom of eternal snows. It is exerted amid the wildest storms of life and breathes a softening spell in our bosom, even when a heart-less world is drying up the fountains of sympathy and love.

It affords home security and happiness, removes family friction and causes all the complicated wheels of the home-machinery to move on noiselessly and smoothly. It pro-motes union and harmony, expunges all selfishness, allays petulant feelings and turbulent passions, destroys peevish-ness of temper and makes home holy and delightful. It caus-es the members to reciprocate each other's affections, hush-es the voice of recrimination and exerts a softening and har-monizing influence over every heart. The dew of Heaven falls upon the home where prayer is wont to be made. Its members enjoy the good and the pleasantness of dwelling together in unity. It gives tone and intensity to their affec-tions and sympathies. It throws sunshine around their hopes and interests. It increases their happiness and takes away the poignancy of their grief and sorrow. It availeth much there-fore, both for time and eternity. Its voice has sent many a poor prodigal home to his father's house. Its answer has often been, "This man was born there!" The child kneeling beside the pious mother and pouring forth its infant prayer to God must attract the notice of the heavenly host and receive into its soul, the power of a new life.

In order to do this the worship must be regular and devout and the whole family engage in it. Some families are not careful to have their children present when they wor-ship. This is very wrong. The children above all others are benefited and should always be present. Some do not teach the children to kneel during prayer and hence, they awk-wardly sit in their seats while the parents kneel. This is a sad mistake. If they do not kneel they naturally suppose they have no part or lot in the devotions, and soon feel that it is wrong for them to bow before the Lord. We have seen many cases where grown up sons and daughters have never bent the knee before the Lord and thought it wrong to kneel till they were Christians. In this way they were made more shy and stubborn and felt that there was an impassable barrier between them and Christ. This feeling is wrong and unnecessary. If family worship had been rightly observed, they would have felt that they were very near the Savior and would easily be inclined to give their hearts to Him. Indeed children thus trained, seldom grow to maturity without becoming practical Christians.

Family worship in itself embodies a hallowing influence that pleads for its observance. It must be that trials will enter a household. The conflict of wishes, the clashing of views, and a thousand other causes will ruffle the temper and produce jar and friction in the machinery of the family. There is needed then some daily agency that shall softly enfold the homestead with its hallowed and soothing power and restore the fine, harmonious play of its various parts. The father needs that which shall gently lift away from his thoughts the disquieting burden of his daily business. The mother that which shall smooth down the fretting irritation of her toil and trial. The child and domestic that which shall neutralize the countless agencies of evil that ever beset them. What so well adapted to do this as for all to gather when the day is done, around the holy page, and pour a united supplication and acknowledgment to that sleepless Power whose protection and scrutiny are ever around their path. When darker and sadder days begin to shadow the home, what can cheer and brighten the sinking heart so

much as resort to that fatherly One who can make the tears
of the loneliest sorrow to be the seedpearls of the brightest
crown? See what home becomes with religion as its life and
rule! Human nature is there checked and molded by the
amiable spirit and lovely character of Jesus. The mind is
expanded, the heart softened, sentiments refined, passions
subdued, hopes elevated, pursuits ennobled, the world cast
into the shade and heaven realized as the first prize. The
great want of our intellectual and moral nature is here met.
Home education becomes embodied with the spirit and elements of our preparation for eternity.

Compare an irreligious home with this and see the vast
importance of family worship. It is a moral waste. One
moves in the rotten atmosphere of injured feelings and misdirected power. Brutal passions become dominate. We hear
the stern voice of parental despotism. We behold a scene of
due strife and insubordination. There is throughout a heart-
blank. Domestic life becomes clouded by a thousand crosses
and disappointments. The solemn realities of the eternal
world are cast into the shade. The home-conscience and feeling becomes stiffly dignified. The sense of moral duty is distorted and all the true interests of home appear in a haze.
Natural affection is debased and love is prostituted to the base
designs of SELF. The entire family with all its tender chords,
ardent hopes and promised interests become engulfed in the
vortex of criminal worldliness! Family worship is included
in the necessities of our children and in the covenant promises of God. The penalties of its neglect and the rewards of our
faithfulness to it should prompt us to its establishment in our
homes. Its absence is a curse. Its presence a blessing. It is a
foretaste of heaven. Like manna it will feed our souls,

quench our thirst, sweeten the cup of life and shed a halo of glory and of gladness around our firesides. Let yours therefore, be the religious home. Be sure that God will delight to dwell therein, and His blessing will descend upon it. Your children shall "not be found begging bread," but shall be like "olive plants around your table," the "heritage of the Lord." Yours will be the home of love and harmony. It shall have the charter of family rights and privileges, the ward of family interests, the palladium of family hopes and happiness. Your household piety will be the crowning attribute of your peaceful home. The living stars that shall adorn the night of its tribulation and the pillar of cloud and of fire in its pilgrimage to a "better country." It shall strew the family threshold with the flowers of promise and enshrine the memory of loved ones gone before, in all the fragrance of that "blessed hope" of reunion in heaven which looms up from a dying hour. It shall give to the infant soul its "perfect flowering," and expand it in all the fullness of a generous love and conscience blessedness, making it "lustrous in the livery of divine knowledge." And then in the dark hour of home separation and bereavement, when the question is put to you mourning parents, "Is it well with the child? It is well with thee?" you can answer with joy, "It is well!"

Home Influence

OUR nature demands a home. It is the first essential element of our social being. This cannot be complete without the home relations. There would be no proper equilibrium of life and character without the home influence. The heart when bereaved and disappointed naturally turns for refuge to home-life and sympathy. No spot is so attractive to the weary one. It is the heart's moral oasis. There is a mother's watchful love and a father's sustaining influence. There is a husband's protection and a wife's tender sympathy. There is the circle of loving brothers and sisters happy in each other's love. Oh, what is life without these! A desolation, a painful, gloomy pilgrimage through "desert heats and barren sands."

Home influence may be estimated from the immense force of its impressions. It is the prerogative of home to make the first impression upon our nature and give that nature its first direction onward and upward. It uncovers the moral fountain, chooses its channel, and gives the stream its first impulse. It makes the "first stamp and sets the first seal" upon the molded nature of the child. It gives the first tone to our desires and furnishes ingredients that will either sweeten or embitter the whole cup of life. These impressions are indelible and durable as life. Compared with them, other impressions are like those made upon sand or wax. These are like "the deep borings into the flinty rock." To erase impressions, we must remove every stratum of our being. Even the infidel lives under the holy influence of a pious mother's impressions. John Randolph could never shake off the restraining influence of a little prayer his mother taught him when a child. It preserved him from the clutches of infidelity.

The home influence is either a blessing or a curse, either for good or for evil. It cannot be neutral. In either case it is mighty commencing with our birth, going with us through life, clinging to us in death and reaching into the eternal

world. It is that uniting power which arises out of the man-
ifold relations and associations of domestic life. The specif-
ic influences of husband and wife, of parent and child, of
brother and sister, of teacher and pupil united and harmo-
niously blended, that constitute the home influence.

Our habits too, are formed under the molding power of
home. The "tender twig" is there bent, the spirit shaped, the
principles implanted and the whole character is formed until
it becomes a habit. Goodness or evil are there "resolved into
necessity." Who does not feel this influence of home upon
all habits of life? The gray-haired father who wails in his
second infancy feels the traces of his childhood home in his
spirit, desires, and habits. Ask the strong man in the prime
of life whether the most firm and reliable principles of his
character, were not the inheritance of a parental home.

The most illustrious statesman, the most distinguished
warriors, the eloquent ministers, and the greatest benefactors of human kind owe their greatness to the fostering influence of home. Napoleon knew and felt this when he said,
"What France wants is good mothers, and you may be sure
then that France will have good sons." The homes of the
American revolution made the men of the revolution. Their
influence reaches yet, far into the inmost frame and constitution of our glorious republic. It controls the fountains of
her power, forms the character of her citizens and statesmen,
and shapes our destiny as a people. Did not the Spartan
mother and her home give character to the Spartan nation?
Her lessons to the child infused the iron nerve into the heart
of that nation and caused the sons in the wild tumult of battle, "either to live behind their shields or to die upon them!"
Her influence fired them with a patriotism which was

stronger than death. Had it been hallowed by the pure spirit and principles of Christianity, what a power of good it
would have been!

But alas! The home of an unbeliever had not the heart
and ornaments of the Christian family. Though "the monuments of Cornelia's virtues were the character of her children," yet these were not "the ornaments of a quiet spirit."
Had the central heart of the Spartan home been that of the
Christian mother, the Spartan nation would now perhaps
adorn the brightest page of history.

Home, in all well constituted minds is always associated
with moral and social excellence. The higher men rise in the
scale of being, the more important and interesting is home.
The Arab or forest man may care little for his home, but the
Christian man of cultured heart and developed mind will
love his home and generally love it in proportion to his moral
worth. He knows it is the planting ground of every seed of
morality, the garden of virtue, and the nursery of religion.

Our life abroad is but a reflex of what it is at home. We
make ourselves in a great measure, at home. This is especially true of woman. The woman who is rude, coarse, and
vulgar at home cannot be expected to be amiable, chaste and
refined in the world. Her home habits will stick to her. She
cannot shake them off. They are woven into the web of her
life. Her home language will be first on her tongue. Her
home by-words will come out to mortify her just when she
wants most to hide them in her heart. Her home vulgarities
will show their hideous forms to shock her most when she
wants to appear her best. Her home coarseness will appear
when she is in the most refined circles, and appearing there
will abash her more than elsewhere. All her home habits

will follow her. They have become a sort of second nature to her. It is much the same with men. It is indeed there, that every man must be known by those who would make a just estimate either of his virtue or felicity. Smiles and embroidery are alike and the mind is often dressed for show in painted honor and fictitious benevolence. Every young woman should feel, that just what she is at home she will appear abroad. If she attempts to appear otherwise, everybody will soon see through the attempt. We cannot cheat the world long about our real characters. The thickest and most opaque mask we can put on will soon become transparent. This fact we should believe without a doubt. Deception most often deceives itself. The deceiver is the most deceived. The liar is often the only one cheated. The young woman who pretends to what she is not, believes her pretense is not understood. People laugh in their sleeves at her foolish pretensions. Every young woman should form in her mind an ideal of a TRUE HOME. It should not be the ideal of a PLACE, but of the CHARACTER OF HOME. Place does not constitute home. Many a gilded palace and scene of luxury is not a home. Many a flower-girt dwelling and splendid mansion lacks all the essentials of home. A hovel is often more a home than a palace.

If the spirit of the congenial friendship link not the hearts of the family of a dwelling, it is not a home. If love reign not there, if charity spread not her downy mantle over all, if peace prevail not, if contentment be not a meek and merry dweller therein, if virtue rear not her beautiful children, and religion come not in her white robe of gentleness to lay her hand in benediction on every head, the home is not complete. We are all in the habit of building for ourselves ideal homes. But they are generally made up of outward things. A house, a garden, a carriage, and the ornaments and appendages of luxury. And if in our lives we do not realize our ideas, we make ourselves miserable and our friends miserable. Half the women in our country are unhappy because their homes are not so luxurious as they wish.

The grand idea of home is a quiet, secluded spot where loving hearts dwell, set apart and dedicated to improvement, intellectual and moral improvement. It is not a formal school of sober solemnity and rigid discipline where virtue is made a task and progress a sharp necessity, but a free and easy exercise of all our spiritual limbs. Obedience is a pleasure, discipline a joy, improvement a self-wrought delight. All the duties and labors of home when rightly understood are so many means of improvement. Even the trials of home are so many rounds in the ladder of spiritual progress, if we but make them so. It is not merely by speaking to children about spiritual things that we win them over. If that be all we do it will accomplish nothing, less than nothing. It is the sentiments which they hear at home. It is the maxims which rule our daily conduct. The likings and dislikings which we express. The whole regulation of the household in dress, food, and furniture. The recreations we indulge, the company we keep, the style of our reading, the whole complexion of daily life that creates the element in which our children are either growing in grace and preparing for an eternity of glory, or they are learning to live without God and to die without hope.

Home Amusements

"I HAVE been told by men who had passed unharmed through the temptations of youth, that they owed their escape from many dangers to the intimate companionship of affectionate and pure minded sisters. They have been saved from a hazardous meeting with idle company by some home engagement, of which their sisters were the charm. They have refrained from mixing with the impure because they would not bring home thoughts and feelings which they could not share with those trusting and loving friends. They have put aside the wine-cup and abstained from stronger potations, because they would not profane with their fumes the holy kiss with which they were accustomed to bid their sisters good-night."

A proper amount of labor well spiced with sunny sports is almost absolutely necessary to the formation of a firm, hardy, physical constitution and a cheerful and happy mind. Let all youth not only learn to choose and enjoy proper amusements, but let them learn to invent them at home and use them there. Let them form ideas of such homes as they shall wish to have their own children enjoy. Not half the people know how to make a home. One of the greatest and most useful studies of life is to learn how to make a home. A home as men, women, and children should dwell in. It is a study that should be early introduced to the attention of youth. It would be well if books were written upon this most interesting subject, giving practical rules and hints with a long chapter on AMUSEMENTS.

That was a good remark of Seneca when he said, "Great

is he who enjoys his earthen-ware as if it were plate, and not less great is the man to whom all his plate is no more than earthen-ware." Every home should be cheerful. Innocent joy should reign in every heart. There should be domestic amusements, fireside pleasures, quiet and simple they may be, but such as shall make home happy and not leave it that irksome place which will oblige the youthful spirit to look elsewhere for joy. There are a thousand and unobtrusive ways in which we may add to the cheerfulness of home. The very modulations of the voice will often make a great difference. How many shades of feeling are expressed by the voice! What a change comes over us at the change of its tones! No delicately tuned harpstring can awaken more pleasure or grating discord pierce with more pain.

Let parents talk much and talk well at home. A father who is habitually silent in his own house may be in many respects a wise man, but he is not wise in his silence. We sometimes see parents who are the life of every company which they enter and yet dull, silent, and uninteresting at home among the children. If they have not mental activity and mental stories sufficient for both, let them first provide for their own household. Ireland exports beef and wheat and lives on potatoes. They fare as poorly, who reserve their social charms for companions abroad and keep their dullness for home consumption. It is better to instruct children and make them happy at home than it is to charm strangers or amuse friends. A silent house is a dull place for young people, a place from which they will escape if they can. They will talk of being "shut up" there. The youth who does not love home is in danger.

The true mother loves to see her son come home to her.

He may be almost as big as her house; a whiskerando with as much hair on his face as would stuff her arm chair, and she be a mere shred of a woman. But he's "her boy" still. Even if he take unto himself a wife, he's her boy still for all that. She does not believe a word of the old rhyme—

> "Your son is your son till he gets him a wife;
> But your daughter's your daughter all the days of her life."

And what will bring our boys back to our homesteads but our making those homesteads pleasant to them in their youth. Let us train a few roses on the humble wall and their scent and beauty will be long remembered. Many a lad instead of going to a spree will turn to his old bed and return to his work again, strengthened, invigorated, and refreshed instead of battered, weakened, and perhaps disgraced.

Fathers and mothers remember this: if you would not have your children lost to you in after-life, if you would have your married daughters not forget their old home in the new one, if you would have your sons lend a hand to keep you in the old rose-covered cottage instead of letting you go to the naked walls of a workhouse, make home happy to them when they are young. Send them out into the world in the full belief that there is "no place like home," yes, "be it ever so humble." And even if the old home should in the course of time be pulled down or lost to your children, it will still live in their memories. The kind looks and kind words and thoughtful love of those who once inhabited it will not pass away. Your home will be like the poet's vase—

> "You may break, you may ruin, the vase if you will,
> but the scent of the roses will cling to it still."

Music is an accomplishment usually valuable as a home enjoyment, as rallying round the piano the various members of a family and harmonizing their hearts as well as their voices, particularly in devotional songs. We know no more agreeable and interesting spectacle than that of brothers and sisters playing and singing together those elevated compositions in music and poetry which gratify the taste and purify the heart. Their parents sit delighted. We have seen and heard an elder sister thus leading the family choir, who was the soul of harmony to the whole household and whose life was a perfect example. Parents should not fail to consider the great value of home music. Buy a good instrument and teach your family to sing and play. Then they can produce sufficient amusement at home themselves and the sons will not think of looking elsewhere for it. The reason that so many become dissipated and run to every place of amusement no matter what its character making every effort to get away from home at night, is the lack of entertainment at home.

To Young Men

YOUNG MEN! You are wanted. From the street corners, from the saloons and playhouses, from the loafers' rendezvous, from the idlers' promenade turn yours steps into the highway of noble aim and earnest work. There are prizes enough for every successful worker, crowns enough for every honorable head that goes through the smoke of conflict to victory.

There is within the young man an upspringing of lofty

sentiment which contributes to his elevation. There are obstacles to be surmounted and difficulties to be vanquished. Yet with truth for his watch word and leaning on his own noble purposes and indefatigable exertions, he may crown his brow with imperishable honors. He may never wear the warrior's crimson wreath, the poet's chaplet of bays, or the statesman laurels. No grand universal truth may ,at his bidding, stand confessed to the world. It may never be his to bring to a successful issue, a great political revolution. To be the founder of a republic, whose name shall be a "distinguished star in the constellation of nations," yea more, though his name may never be heard beyond the narrow limits of his own neighborhood, yet is his mission none the less a high and holy one.

Not only in the field of battle, but also the consecrated cause of truth and virtue in the moral and physical world calls for champions. The field for doing good is "white unto the harvest." If he enlists in the ranks and his spirit faints not, he may write his name among the stars of heaven. Beautiful lives have blossomed in the darkest places, just as pure white lilies full of fragrance on the slimy, stagnant waters. No possession is so productive of real influence as a highly cultivated intellect. Wealth, birth, and official station may and do secure to their possessors an external, superficial courtesy. But they never did and they never can command the reverence of the heart. It is only to the man of large and noble soul. Those who blend a cultivated mind with an upright heart yields the tribute of deep and genuine respect.

But why do so few young men of early promise whose hopes, purposes, and resolves were as radiant as the colors of the rainbow fail to distinguish themselves? The answer is, they are not willing to devote themselves to that toilsome culture which is the price of great success. Whatever aptitude for particular pursuits nature may donate to her favorite children, she conducts none but the laborious and the studious to distinction.

God puts the oak in the forest and the pine on its sand and rocks and says to men, "There are your houses; go hew, saw, frame, build, and make." God makes the trees, man must build the house. God supplies the timber, men must construct the ship. God buries iron in the heart of the earth, men must dig it, smelt it, and fashion it. What is useful for the body and still more what is useful for the mind is to be had only by exertion. Exertion that will work men more than iron is wrought. That will shape men more than timber is shaped.

Great men have ever been men of thought as well as men of action. As the magnificent river rolling in the pride of its mighty waters owes its greatness to the hidden springs of the mountain nook, so does the wide-sweeping influence of distinguished men date its origin from hours of privacy. Men resolutely employed in efforts after self-development. The invisible spring of self-culture is the source of every great achievement.

Away then young man with all dreams of superiority unless you are determined to dig after knowledge, like men search for concealed gold! Remember that every man has in himself the seminal principle of great excellence, and he may develop it by cultivation if he will TRY. Perhaps you are what the world calls poor. What of that? Most of the men whose names are as household words were also the children of poverty. Captain Cook the circumnavigator of the globe was born in a mud hut and started in life as a cabin boy. Lord Eldon who sat on the woolsack in the British parliament for nearly half a century was the son of a coal merchant. Franklin the philosopher, diplomatist, and statesman was but a poor printer's boy whose highest luxury at one time was only a penny roll, eaten in the streets of Philadelphia. Ferguson the profound philosopher was the son of a half-starved weaver. Johnson, Goldsmith, Coleridge, and multitudes of others of high distinction knew the pressure of limited circumstances and have demonstrated that even poverty is no insuperable obstacle to success.

Up then young man and gird yourself for the work of self-cultivation! Set a high price on your leisure moments. They are sands of precious gold. Properly expended they will procure for you a stock of great thoughts. Thoughts that will fill, stir, invigorate, and expand the soul. You must seize on the unparalleled aids furnished by stream and type in this unequaled age.

The great thoughts of great men are now to be procured at prices almost nominal. You can therefore, easily collect a library of choice standard works. But above all learn to reflect, even more than you read. Without thought, books are the sepulchre of the soul. They only confine it. Let thought and reading go hand in hand and the intellect will rapidly increase in strength and gifts. Its possessor will rise in character, in power, and in positive influence. A great deal of talent is lost in the world for the want of a little courage. Every day sends to the grave a number of obscure men who have only remained because their timidity has prevented them from making a first effort. And who if they could have been induced to begin, would in all probability have gone great lengths in the career of fame. The fact is, that to do anything in this world worth doing we must not stand back shivering and thinking of the cold and the danger, but jump in and scramble through as well as we can. It will not do to be perpetually calculating tasks and adjusting nice chances. It did very well before the flood where a man could consult his friends upon an intended publication for a hundred and fifty years, and then live to see its success afterward. But at present a man waits and doubts and hesitates, consults his brother, his uncle, particular friends till one fine day he finds that he is sixty years of age. He has lost so much time in consulting his first cousin and particular friends that he has no more time to follow their advice.

Man is born to dominion, but he must enter it by conquest and continue to do battle for every inch of ground added to his sway. His first exertions are put forth for the acquisition of the control and the establishment of the authority of his own will. With his first efforts to reduce his own physical powers to subjection, he must simultaneously begin to subject his mental faculties to control. Through the combined exertion of his mental and physical powers, he labors to spread his dominion over the widest possible extent of the world.

Thus self-control and control over outward circumstances are alike, the duty and the birthright of man. But self-control is the highest and most noble form of dominion. "He that ruleth his own spirit is greater than he that taketh a city,"

If you intend to marry, if you think your happiness will be increased and your interests advanced by matrimony, be sure and "look where you're going." Join yourself in union with no woman who is selfish for she will sacrifice you, or one who is fickle for she will become estranged. Have naught to do with a proud one for she will ruin you. Leave a coquette to fools who flutter around her. Let her own fireside accommodate a scold. Flee from a woman who loves scandal as you would flee from the evil one. "Look where you're going" will sum it all up.

Gaze not on beauty too much lest it blast thee, nor too long, lest it blind thee, nor too near, lest it burn thee. If thou like it, it deceives thee. If thou love it, it disturbs thee. If thou lust after it, it destroys thee. If virtue accompany it, it is the heart's paradise. If vice associate it, it is the soul's purgatory. Beauty is the wise man's bonfire and the fool's furnace. The Godless youth is infatuated by a fair face and is lured to his fate by a charming smile. He takes no counsel of the Lord and is left to follow his own shallow fancies or the instigations of his passions. The time will surely come in his life when he will not so much want a pet as a heroine. One who will be there when the waves of misfortune are breaking over him and one home comfort, and another, and another is swept away. The piano and grand instrument gone to the creditors. The family turned out on the sidewalk by the heartless landlord, then what is the wife good for if her lips that accompanied the piano in song cannot lift alone the notes, "Jesus, lover of my soul?" The strongest arm in this world is not the arm of a blacksmith, nor the arm of a giant. It is the ARM OF A WOMAN when God has put into it through faith and submission to His will, His own moral omnipotence. If there is one beautiful spot on earth it is the home of the young family, consecrated by piety. The abode of the Holy Spirit above which the hovering angels touch their wings forming a canopy of protection and sanctity.

There is no moral object so beautiful as a conscientious young man. We watch him as we do a star in the heaven. Clouds may be before him, but we know that his light is behind them and will beam again. The blaze of other's popularity may outshine him, but we know that though unseen he illuminates his own true sphere. He resists temptation, not without a struggle for that is not virtue, but he does resist and conquer. He bears the sarcasm of the wicked and it stings him for that is a trait of virtue. He heals the wound with his own pure touch. He heeds not the watchword of fashion if it leads to sin. The Atheist who says not only in his heart but with his lips, "There is no God!" controls him not. He sees the hand of a creating God and rejoices in it. Woman is sheltered by fond arms and loving counsel. Old age is protected by its experience. Manhood by its strength. But the conscientious young man stands amid the temptations of the world like a self-balanced tower. Happy is he who seeks and gains the prop and shelter of morality. Onward then, conscientious youth. Raise thy standard and nerve thyself for goodness. If God has given thee intellectual power, awaken in that cause. Never let it be said of thee, he helped to swell the tide of sin by pouring his influence into its channels. If thou art weak in mental strength, throw not that drop into a polluted current. Awake, arise, young man! Assume that beautiful garb of virtue! It is difficult to be pure and holy. Put on thy strength. Let truth be the lady of thy love. Defend her.

A young man came to an aged professor of a distinguished continental university with a smiling face and informed him that the long and fondly cherished desire of his heart was at length, fulfilled. His parents had given their consent to his studying of the law.

For some time he continued explaining how he would spare no labor or expense in perfecting his education. When he paused, the old man who had been listening to him with great patience and kindness gently said, "Well! and when you have finished your studies, what do you mean to do then?" "Then I shall take my degree," answered the young man. "And then?" asked the revered friend. "And then," continued the youth, "I shall have a number of difficult cases and shall attract notice and win a great reputation." "And then?" repeated the holy man. "Why then" replied the youth, "I shall doubtless be promoted to some high office in the State." "And then?" "And then," pursued the young lawyer, "I shall live in honor and wealth and look forward to a happy old age." "And then?" repeated the old man. "And then," said the youth, "and then—and then—I shall die." Here the venerable listener lifted up his voice and again asked with solemnity and emphasis, "And then?" Whereupon the aspiring student made no answer, cast down his head, and in silence and thoughtfulness retired. The last "And then?" had pierced his heart like a sword and made an impression which he could not dislodge.

To Young Women

WHAT is womanhood? Is there any more important question for young women to consider than this? It should be the highest ambition of every young woman to possess a true womanhood. Earth presents no higher object of attainment. To be a woman in the truest and highest sense of the word, is to be the best thing beneath. To be a woman, is something more than to live eighteen or twenty years. Something more than to grow to the physical stature of women. Something more than to wear flounces, exhibit drygoods, sport jewelry, or catch the gaze of lewd-eyed men. Something more than to be a belle, a wife, or a mother. Put all these qualifications together and they do but little toward making a true woman.

Beauty and style are not the surest passports to womanhood. Some of the most noble specimens of womanhood that the world has ever seen have presented the most plain and unprepossessing appearance. A woman's worth is to be estimated by the real goodness of her heart, the greatness of her soul, and the purity of and sweetness of her character. A woman with a kindly disposition and well-balanced temper is both lovely and attractive be her face ever so plain, and her figure ever so homely. She makes the best of wives and the truest of mothers. She has a higher purpose in living than the beautiful, yet vain and supercilious woman, who has no higher ambition than to flaunt her finery on the street or to gratify her inordinate vanity by extracting flattery and praise from society, whose compliments are as hollow as they are insincere.

Beauty is a dangerous gift. It is even so. Like wealth it has ruined thousands. Many of the most beautiful women are destitute of common sense and common humanity. No gift from heaven is so general and so widely abused by woman as the gift of beauty. In about nine cases in ten it makes her silly, senseless, thoughtless, giddy, vain, proud, frivolous, selfish, low and mean. "She is beautiful and she knows it," is as much as to say she is spoiled. A beautiful girl is very likely to believe she was made to be looked at. She sets herself up for a show at every window, in every door, on every corner of the street, in every company at which opportunity offers an exhibition of herself. And believing and acting thus, she soon becomes good for nothing else. When she comes to be a middle-aged woman she is that weakest most sickening of all human things, a faded beauty.

These facts have long since taught sensible men to beware of beautiful women. Sound them carefully before they give them their confidence. Beauty is shallow, only skin deep. It is fleeting, only for a few years' reign. It is dangerous, tempting to vanity and lightness of mind. It is deceitful, dazzling, often to bewilder. It is weak, reigning only to ruin. Beauty is gross leading often to sensual pleasure. And yet we say, it need not be so. Beauty is lovely and ought to be innocently possessed. It has charms which ought to be used for good purposes. It is a delightful gift which ought to be received with gratitude and worn with grace and meekness. It should always minister to inward beauty. Every woman of beautiful form and features should cultivate a beautiful mind and heart.

Young women ought to hold a steady moral sway over their male associates so strong as to prevent them from becoming such lawless rowdies. Why do they not? Because they do not possess sufficient FORCE of character. They have not sufficient resolution and energy of purpose. Their virtue is not vigorous. Their moral wills are not resolute. Their influence is not armed with executive power. Their goodness is not felt as an earnest force of

benevolent purpose. Their moral convictions are not regarded as solemn resolves to be true to God and duty, come what
may. This is the virtue of too many women. They would not
have a drunkard for a husband, but they would drink with a
fast young man. They would not use profane language, but
they are not shocked by its incipient language and love the
society of men whom they know are as profane as Lucifer
out of their presence. They would not be dishonest, but they
will use a thousand deceitful words and ways and countenance the society of men known as hawkers, sharpers, and
deceivers. They would not be irreligious, but they smile
upon the most irreligious men, even show that they love to
be wooed by them. They would not be licentious, but they
have no stunning rebuke for licentious men and will even
admit them on parole into their society.

This is the virtue of too many women. A virtue scarcely worthy the name. Really no virtue at all, a milk and water
substitute, a hypocritical hollow pretension to virtue as
unwomanly as it is disgraceful. We believe that a young
lady by her constant, consistent, Christian example may
exert an untold power. You do not know the respect and
almost worship which young men no matter how wicked
they may be themselves, pay to a consistent Christian lady
be she young or old. If a young man sees that the religion
which in youth he was taught to revere, is lightly thought of
or perhaps sneered at by the young ladies with whom he
associates, we can hardly expect him to think that it is the
thing for him. Men love to trust their fortunes in the hands
of the Christian character. The good, love to gather around
the Christian lady for the blessing of their smiles. They
strew their pathway with moral light. They bless with

effort. They teach sentiments of duty and honesty in every act of their lives.

Such is the rectitude of character which every young woman should cultivate. Nothing will more surely secure confidence and esteem. There is special need of such cultivation, for young women are doubted in many respects more generally than any other class of people. Many people seldom think of believing many things they hear from the lips of young women, so little is genuine integrity cultivated among them. We are sorry to make such a remark. We wish truth did not compel it. We would that young women would cultivate the strictest regard for truth in all things. In small as well as in important matters. Exaggeration or false coloring is as much a violation of integrity as a direct falsehood. Equivocation is often falsehood. Deception in all forms is opposed to integrity. Mock manners, pretended emotions, affectation, policy plans to secure attention and respect are all sheer falsehoods and in the end injure those who are guilty of them. Respect and affection are the outgrowth of confidence. She who secures the most firm confidence will secure the most respect and love. Confidence can only be secured by integrity. The young woman with a high sense of duty will always secure confidence and having this she will secure respect, affection, and influence.

You have great influence. You cannot live without having some sort of influence any more than you can without breathing. One thing is just as unavoidable as the other. Beware then what kind of influence it is that you are constantly exerting. An invitation to take a glass of wine or to play a game of cards may kindle the fires of intemperance or gambling, which will burn forever. A jest given at the expense of religion, any of the numerous ways in which you may show your disregard for the souls of others may be the means of ruining many for time and eternity.

We want the girls to rival the boys in all that is good and refined and ennobling. We want them to rival the boys as they well can in learning, in understanding, in virtues. In all noble qualities of mind and heart, but not in any of those things that have caused them justly or unjustly to be described as savages. We want girls to be gentle, not weak, but gentle and kind and affectionate. We want to be sure that wherever a girl is there should be a sweet, subduing, and harmonizing influence of purity, truth, and love, pervading and hallowing from center to circumference, the entire circle in which she moves. If the boys are savages, we want her to be their civilizer. We want her to tame them, to subdue their ferocity, to soften their manners and to teach them all needful lessons of order, sobriety, meekness, patience, and goodness. The little world of self is not destined to waste its fires in the narrow chamber of a single human heart. No, a broader sphere of action is hers, a more expansive benevolence. The light and heat of her love are to be seen and felt far and wide. Who would not rather thus live a true life than sit shivering over the smoldering embers of self-love? Happy is that maiden who seeks to live this true life! As time passes on her own character will be elevated and purified. Gradually will she return toward that order of her being, which was lost in the decline of mankind from that original state of excellence in which they were created. She will become more and more a true woman. She will grow wiser, better, and happier. Her path through the world will be as a shining light and all who know her will call her blessed.

A right view of life then which all should take at the out-set, is the one we have presented. Let every young lady seriously reflect upon this subject. Let her remember that she is not designed by her Creator to live for herself alone. She has a higher and more noble destiny, that of doing good to others and making others happy. As the quiet streamlet which runs along the valley nourishes a luxuriant vegeta-tion, causing flowers to bloom and birds to sing along its banks so do a kind look and happy countenance spread peace and joy around.

Kindness is the ornament of man. It is the chief glory of woman. It is indeed woman's true prerogative, her scepter and her crown. It is the sword with which she conquers and the charm with which she captivates. Young lady would you be admired and beloved? Would you be an ornament to your sex? A blessing to your race? Cultivate this heavenly virtue. Wealth may surround you with its blandishments. Beauty, learning, or talents may give you admirers. But love and kindness alone can captivate the heart. Whether you live in a cottage or a palace, there graces can surround you with perpetual sunshine. Making you and all around you happy.

Seek ye then fair daughters the possession of that inward grace. The essence shall permeate and vitalize the affections, adorn the countenance, make sweetly flowing the voice and impart a hallowed beauty even to your motions! Not merely that you may be loved would we urge this, but that you may in truth be lovely. That loveliness which fades not with time nor is marred or alienated by disease. But which neither chance nor change can in any way despoil. We urge you gen-tle maiden, to beware of the silken enticements of the stranger until your love is confirmed by protracted acquaintance. Shun the idler though his coffers overflow with pelf. Avoid the irreverent, the scoffer of hallowed things. Avoid him, "who looks upon the wine while it is red." Avoid him too, "who hath a high look and a proud heart," and who "privily slandereth his neighbor." Do not heed the specious prattle about "first love," and so place irrevocably the seal upon your future destiny before you have sounded, in silence and secrecy, the deep fountains of your own heart. Wait rather, until your own character and that of him who would woo you is more fully developed. Surely, if this "first love" cannot endure a short probation fortified by "the pleasures of hope," how can it be expected to survive years of intimacy, scenes of trial, distracting cares, wasting sickness and all the homely routine of practical life. Yet it is these that constitute life and the love that cannot abide them is false and will die.

Daughter And Sister

THERE are few things which men are more proud of than their daughters. The young father follows the sportive girl with his eye, as he cherishes an emotion of complacency, not so tender but quite as active as the mother's. The aged father leans on his daughter as the crutch of his declining years. An old proverb says that a son is son till he is married, but the daughter is daughter forever. This is something like the truth. Though the daughter leaves the parental roof, she is still followed by kindly regards. The gray-haired father drops in every day to greet the beloved face. When he pats the cheeks of the little grandchildren, it is chiefly because the bond which unites him to them passes through the heart of his darling Mary. She is his daughter still. There are other ministries of love more conspicuous than hers but none in which a gentler, lovelier spirit dwells, and none to which the heart's warm requitals more joyfully respond. There is no such thing as a comparative estimate of a parent's affection for one child or another. There is little which he needs to covet, to whom the treasure of a good child has been given. A good daughter is the steady light of her parent's house. The father's idea is indissolubly connected with that of his happy fireside. She is the morning sunlight and his evening star. The grace and vivacity and tenderness of her sex have their place in the mighty sway which she holds over his spirit. The lessons of recorded wisdom which he reads with her eyes come to his mind with a new charm, as they blend with the beloved melody of her voice. He scarcely knows weariness which her song does not make him forget, or gloom which is proof against the brightness of her young smile. She is the pride and ornament of his hospitality. The gentle nurse of his sickness and the constant agent in those nameless, numberless acts of kindness which one chiefly cares to have rendered, because they are unpretending but all-expressive proofs of love.

But now turning to the daughters themselves, one of their first duties at home is to make their mother happy. Shun all that would pain or even perplex her. "Always seeking the pleasure of others, always careless of her own," is one of the finest enconiums ever pronounced upon a daughter, True: at that period of life when dreams are realities, and realities seem dreams, this may be forgotten. Mothers may find only labor and sorrow where they had a right to expect repose. But the daughter who would make her home and her mother happy, should learn that next to duty to God our Savior, comes duty to her who is always the first to rejoice in our joy, and to weep when we weep. Of all the proofs of heartlessness which youth can give, the strongest is indifference to a mother's happiness or sorrow.

How large and cherished a place does a good sister's love always hold in the grateful memory of one who has been blessed with the benefits of this relation, as he looks back to the home of his childhood! How many are there who in the changes of more mature years, have found a sister's love for themselves their ready and adequate resource. With what a sense of security is confidence reposed in a good sister, and with what assurance that it will be uprightly and considerately given is her counsel sought! How intimate is the friendship of such sisters not widely separated in age from one another! What a reliance for warning, excitement, and sympathy has each secured in each! How many are the brothers to whom when thrown into circumstances of temptation, the thought of a sister's love has been a constant holy presence rebuking every wayward thought!

The relationship of brothers and sisters forms another important element in the happy influences of home. A boisterous or a selfish boy may try to domineer over the weaker or dependent girl, but generally the latter exerts a softening, sweetening charm. The brother animates and heartens and the sister mollifies, tames, and refines. The vine and its sustaining elm are the emblems of such a relation. By such agencies our "sons may become like plants grown up in their youth, and our daughters like corner-stones polished after the similitude of a temple."

Sisters scarcely know the influence they have over their brothers. A young man testifies that the greatest proof of the truth of the Christian religion was his sister's life. Often the simple request of a lady will keep a young man from doing wrong. We have known this to be the case very frequently. Young men have been kept from breaking the Sabbath, from drinking, from chewing, just because a lady whom they respected and for whom they had an affection requested it. A tract given, an invitation to go to church, a request that your friend read the Bible daily will often be regarded when a more powerful appeal from other sources would fall unheeded upon the heart. Many of the gentlemen whom you meet in society are away from the influence of parents and sisters. They will respond to any interest taken in their welfare. We all speak of a young man's danger from evil associates and the bad influence which his dissipated gentlemen associates have upon him. We believe it is all true that a gentleman's character is formed to a greater extent by the ladies that he associates with, before he becomes a complete man of the world. We think in other words, that a young man is pretty much what his sister and young lady friends choose to make him. We knew a family where the sisters encouraged their young brothers smoke thinking it was manly, and to mingle with merry, dissipated fellows because they thought it "smart." They did mingle with them, body and soul and abused the same sisters shamefully. The influence began further back than with their gentleman companions. It began with their sisters and was carried on through the forming years of their character. On the other hand, if sisters are watchful and affectionate they may in various ways, by entering into any little plan with interest or by introducing their younger brothers into good ladies' society, lead them along till their character is formed. Then a high respect for ladies and a manly self-respect will keep them from mingling in low society.

Associates

Thou art noble; yet, I see,
Thy honorable Metal may be wrought
From that it is disposed. Therefore 'Tis meet
That noble Minds keep ever with their Likes:
For who so firm, that cannot be seduced?

–Shakespeare

AN author is known by his writings, a mother by her daughter, a fool by his words, and all men by their companions.

Relationships with persons of decided virtue and excellence is of great importance in the formation of a good character. The force of example is powerful. We are creatures of imitation and by a necessary influence our tempers and habits are formed on the model of those with whom we familiarly associate. Better to be alone than in bad company. Evil communications corrupt good manners. Ill qualities are catching as well as disease. The mind is at least as much if not a great deal more liable to infection than the body. Go with mean people and you think life is mean.

The human race requires to be educated. It is doubtless true that the greater part of that education is obtained through example rather than precept. This is especially true respecting character and habits. How natural is it for a child to look up to those around him for an example of imitation?

How readily does he copy all that he sees good or bad? The importance of a good example on which the young may exercise this powerful and active element of their nature is a matter of the utmost moment. To the phrenologist, every faculty assumes an importance almost infinite, perhaps none more than that of imitation. It is a trite but true maxim that "a man is known by the company he keeps." He naturally assimilates by the force of imitation to the habits and manners of those by whom he is surrounded. We know persons who walk much with the lame who have learned to walk with a hitch or limp. Vice stalks in the streets unabashed and children copy it. Witness the urchin seven years old trying to ape his seniors in folly by smoking the cigarstumps which they have cast aside. In time when his funds improve, he will wield the long nine and be a full-fledged "loafer." This faculty is usually more active in the young than in adult life. It serves to lead them to imitate that which their seniors do before their reasoning powers are sufficiently developed and instructed to enable them to reason out a proper course of action. Thus by copying others they do that which is appropriate, right or wrong, without knowing why or the principles and consequences involved in their actions.

The awfully sad consequences of evil associations is exhibited in the history of almost all criminals. The case of a man named Brown recently executed in Toronto, Canada is an example. He was born in Cambridgeshire, England of parents who were members of the Church of England. In a sketch of his life written at his dictation, he attributes his downfall to early disobedience and to bad companions which led to dissipation and finally plunged him into associations with the most dissolute and lawless characters. They led him on in transgressions and sin which ended in his being brought to the scaffold. On the gallows, he made the following speech: "This is a solemn day for me, boys! I hope this will be a warning to you against bad company. I hope it will be a lesson to all young people and old, rich or poor. It was what brought me here today to my last end, though I am innocent of the murder I am about to suffer for. Before my God I am innocent of the murder! I never committed this or any other murder. I know nothing of it. I am going to meet my Maker in a few minutes. May the Lord have mercy on my soul! Amen, amen." What a terrible warning his melancholy example affords to young men never to deviate from the straight line of duty. Live with the culpable and you will be very likely to die with the criminal. Bad company is like a nail driven into a post which after the first or second blow may be drawn out with little difficulty. But being once driven in up to the head the pinchers cannot take hold to draw it out, and can only be done by the destruction of the wood. You may be ever so pure, but you cannot associate with bad companions without falling into bad odor. Evil company is like tobacco smoke—you cannot be long in its presence without carrying away taint of it. "Let no man deceive himself," says Petrarch, "by thinking that the contagions of the soul are less than those of the body. They are yet greater; they sink deeper and come on more unsuspected." With impure air, we take diseases. With bad company, vice and imperfection. Avoid as much as you can the company of all vicious persons whatever for no vice is alone and all are infectious.

Men carry unconscious signs of their life about them.

Those that come from the forge and those from the lime and mortar. Those from dusty travel bear signs of being workmen and of their work. One need not ask a merry face or a sad one whether it has come from joy or from grief. Tears and laughter tell their own story. Should one come home with fruit, we say "You have come from the orchard." If with hands full of wild flowers, "You have come from the field." If one's garments smell of mingled odors we say, "You have walked in a garden." So with associations. Those that walk with the just, the upright, have the sweetest incense that has ever anointed man. Let no man deceive himself.

Do you love the society of the vulgar? Then you are already debased in your sentiments. Do you seek to be with the profane? In your heart you are like them. Are jesters and buffoons your choice friends? Do you love and seek the society of the wise and good? Is this your habit? Had you rather take the lowest seat among these than the highest seat among others? Then you have already learned to be good. You may not make very much progress, but even a good beginning is not to be despised. Hold on to your way, and seek to be the companion of those that fear God. You shall be wise for yourself and wise for eternity.

No man of position can allow himself to associate without prejudice with the profane, the Sabbath-breakers, the drunken and the licentious for he lowers himself without elevating them. The chimney sweep is not made the less black by rubbing against the well-dressed and the clean for they are inevitably defiled. Nothing elevates us so much as the presence of a spirit similar to our own. What is companionship, where nothing that improves the intellect is communicated and where the larger heart contracts itself to the model and dimension of the smaller?

Washington was wont to say, "Be courteous to all, but intimate with few and let those few be well tried before you give them your confidence." It should be the aim of young men to go into good society. We do not mean the rich, the proud and fashionable, but the society of the wise, the intelligent, and good. Where you find men that know more than you do and from whose conversation one can gain information, it is always safe to be found. It has broken down many a man by associating with the low and vulgar where the ribald song and the indecent story were introduced to excite laughter. If you wish to be respected and desire happiness and not misery, we advise you to associate with the intelligent and good. Strive for moral excellence and strict integrity and you will never be in the sinks of pollution or on the benches of retailers and gamblers. Once habituate yourself to a virtuous course. Once secure a love of good society. No punishment would be greater than by accident to be obliged for half a day to associate with the low and vulgar. Try to frequent the company of the wise. In book and life it is the most wholesome society. Learn to admire rightly, that is the great pleasure of life. Note what the great men admire. They admire great things. Narrow spirits admire basely and worship meanly. Some persons choose their associates as they do other useful animals, preferring those from whom they expect the most service. Procure no friends in haste, nor if once secured, in haste abandon them. Be slow in choosing an associate and slower to change him. Slight no man for poverty nor esteem any one for his wealth. Good friends should not be easily forgotten nor used as suits of apparel which, when we have worn them threadbare cast off and call for new. When once you profess yourself a friend, endeavor to be always such. He can never have any true friends that will be often changing them. Whoever moves you to part with a true and tried friend has certainly a design to make way for a treacherous enemy. To part with a tried friend without very great provocation is unreasonable levity. Nothing but plain malevolence can justify disunion. The loss of a friend is like that of a limb. Time may heal the anguish of the wound but the loss cannot be repaired.

When you have once found your proper associate, then stick to him. Make him your friend, a close friend. Do all you can to improve him and learn all you can of him. Let his good qualities become yours. One is not bound to bear a part in the follies of a friend, but rather to dissuade him from them. Even though he cannot consent to tell him plainly, as Phocion did Antipater who said to him, "I cannot be both your friend and flatterer." It is a good rule always to back your friends and face your enemies. Whoever would reclaim his friend and bring him to a true and perfect understanding of himself may privately admonish, but never publicly reprehend him. An open admonition is an open disgrace.

Have the courage to cut the most agreeable acquaintance you have when you are convinced he lacks principle. A friend should bear with a friend's infirmities, but not with his vices. He that does a base thing in zeal for a friend burns the golden thread that ties their hearts together.

If you have once chosen the proper person as an associate and a friend, then you have a friend for lifetime. You will always cherish and honor him. But the neglected child, the reckless youth, the wrecked and wretched man will haunt you with memories of melancholy with grief and despair. How we will curse those associates that dragged us down to ruin and destruction and how we love to repeat the names of old friends.

"Old friends!" What a multitude of deep and varied emotions are called forth from the soul by the utterance of these two words. What thronging memories of other days crowd the brain when they are spoken. Ah, there is magic in the sound and the spell which it creates as both sad and pleasing. As we sit by our fireside while the winds arc making wild melody throughout the walls of our cottage, and review the scenes of by-gone years which flit before us in swift succession. Dim and shadowy as the recollections of a dream. How those "old familiar faces" will rise up and haunt our vision with their well remembered features. But ah, where are they? Those friends of our youth. Those kindred spirits who shared our joy and sorrows when first we started in the pilgrimage of life. Companions of our early days.

They are endeared to us by many a tie and we now look back through the vista of years upon the hours of our communion, as upon green oasis in a sandy waste. Years have passed over us with their buds and flowers, their fruits and snows; and where now are those "old familiar faces?" They are scattered and over many of their last narrow homes the thistle waves its lonely head, "after life's fitful fever they sleep well." Some are buffeting the billows of time's stormy sea in distant lands. Though they are absent, our thoughts are often with them.

Influence

AWAY up among the Alleghanies, there is a spring so small that a single ox on a summer's day could drain it dry. It steals its unobtrusive way among the hills till it spreads out into the beautiful Ohio. Then it stretches away a thousand miles leaving on its banks more than a hundred villages and cities and many a cultivated farm. Then joining the Mississippi it stretches away some twelve hundred miles more till it falls into the emblem of eternity. It is one of the greatest tributaries to the ocean. Obedient only to God, it shall roar till the angel with one foot on the sea and the other on the land shall assert that time shall be no more. So with moral influence! It is a rill, a rivulet, an ocean, and as boundless and fathomless as eternity.

"The stone flung from my careless hand into the lake splashed down into the depths of the flowing water and that was all." No, it was not all. Look at those concentric rings rolling their tiny ripples among the sedgy reeds, dippling the overhanging boughs of yonder willow. It produced an influence slight but conscious to the very shores of the lake itself. That stray word, that word of pride or scorn flung from my lips in casual company produces a momentary depression and that is all. No, it is not all. It deepened that man's disgust at godliness and it sharpened the edge of that man's sarcasm. It shamed that half-converted one out of his penitent misgivings and produced an influence, slight but eternal, on the destiny of a human life. Oh, it is a terrible power that I have. This power of influence and it clings to me. I cannot shake it off. It is born with me. It has grown with my growth and is strengthened with my strength. It speaks, it walks, it moves. It is powerful in every look of my eye, in every word of my lips, in every act of my life. I cannot live to myself. I must either be a light to illumine or a tempest to destroy. I must either be an Abel who by his immortal righteousness being dead yet speaking, or a Cain, the sad continuance of whose otherwise forgotten name is the proof that man perishes not alone in his iniquity. Dear reader, this necessary element of power belongs to you. The sphere may be contracted, your influence may be small, but a sphere and influence you surely have. Every human being is a center of influence for good or for ill. No man can live unto himself. The meshes of a net are not more surely knit together than man to man. We may forget this secret, silent influence. But we are exerting it by our deeds. We are exerting it by our words. We are exerting it by our very thoughts. He is wise with a wisdom more than that of earth who seeks to put forth the highest power for good, be his home a hut or a hall, a cabin or a palace.

Habit

Habit in a child is at first like a spider's web, if neglected it becomes a thread of twine, next a cord of rope and finally a cable. Then who can break it? There are habits contracted by bad example or bad management before we have judgement to discern their approaches or because the eye of reason is laid asleep or has not compass of view sufficient to look around on every quarter.

Oh, the tyranny and despotism of a bad habit! Coleridge one of the subtler intellects and finest poets of his time, battled for twenty years before he could emancipate himself from his tyrant opium. He went into voluntary imprisonment. He hired a man to watch him day and night and keep him from tasting the pernicious drug. He formed resolution after resolution. Yet during all the best years of his life, he wasted his substance and his health, neglected his family and lived degraded and accursed because he had not resolution to abstain. He would lay plans to cheat the very man whom he paid to keep the drug from him and bribe the jailer to whom he had voluntarily surrendered himself.

Terrible, TERRIBLE is the despotism of a bad habit. The case of Coleridge is an extreme one, of course, but there are many whose eyes these lines will meet. They are as truly the slaves of a perverted appetite as he. Their despot may be opium, tobacco, drink, or worse. They are so completely under the DOMINION of their master that nothing short of a moral war of independence, which should task all their own strength and all they could borrow from others would suffice to deliver them.

John B. Gough uses the following as a powerful illustration: I remember once riding from Buffalo to Niagara Falls. I said to a gentleman, "What river is that, sir?"

"That," he said, "is Niagara river."

"Well, it is a beautiful stream," said I; "bright and fair and glassy. How far off are the rapids?"

"Only a mile or two," was the reply.

"Is it possible that only a mile from us we shall find the water in the turbulence which it must show near to the falls?"

"You will find it so, sir." And so I found it; and the first
sight of Niagara I shall never forget. Now launch your bark on
that Niagara river; it is bright, smooth, beautiful and glassy.

There is a ripple at the bow; the silver wave you leave
behind adds to the enjoyment. Down the stream you glide,
oars, sails, and helm in proper trim and you set out on your
pleasure excursion. Suddenly some one cries out from the
bank," "Young men, ahoy!"

"What is it?"

"The rapids are below you!"

"Ha, ha! we have heard of the rapids but we are not such
fools as to get there. If we go too fast then we shall up with
the helm and steer to the shore; we will set the mast in the
socket, hoist the sail, and speed to the land. Then on boys;
don't be alarmed. There is no danger."

"Young men, ahoy there!"

"What is it?"

"The rapids are below you!"

"Ha, ha! we will laugh and quaff, all things delight us.
What care we for the future! No man ever saw it. Sufficient
for the day is the evil thereof. We will enjoy life while we
may; will catch pleasure as it flies. This is enjoyment; time
enough to steer out of danger when we are sailing swiftly
with the current."

"Young men, ahoy!"

"What is it?"

"Beware! Beware! The rapids are below you!"

Now you see the water foaming all around. See how fast
you pass that point! Up with the helm! Now turn! Pull
hard! Quick! Quick! pull for your lives! Pull till the blood
starts from the nostrils, and the veins stand like whip-cords

upon the brow! Set the mast in the socket! hoist the sail ah! ah! it is too late! Shrieking, cursing, howling, blaspheming, over they go.

Thousands go over the rapids every year through the power of habit, crying all the while, "When I find out that it is injuring me I will give it up!"

Few people form habits of wrong-doing deliberately or willfully. They glide into them by degrees and almost unconsciously and before they are aware of danger, the habits are confirmed and require resolute and persistent effort to effect a change. "Resist beginning," was the maxim of the ancients and should be preserved as a landmark in our day. Those who are prodigal or passionate, or indolent, or visionary soon make shipwreck of themselves and drift about the sea of life, the prey of every wind and current vainly shrieking for help till at last they drift away into darkness and death.

Take care that you are not drifting. See that you have fast hold of the helm. The breakers of life under the lee and adverse gales continually blow on the shore. Are you watching how she heads? Do you keep a firm grip of the wheel? If you give way but for one moment, you may drift hopelessly into the boiling vortex. Young men, take care! It rests with ourselves alone under God whether you reach port triumphantly or drift to ruin.

Be not slow in the breaking of a sinful custom. A quick, courageous resolution is better than a gradual deliberation. In such a combat, he is the bravest soldier who lays about him without fear or wit. Wit pleads, fear disheartens. He that would kill hydra, had better strike off one neck than five heads. Fell the tree, and the branches are soon cut off.

Whatever be the cause says Lord Kames, it is an established fact that we are much influenced by custom. It hath an effect upon our pleasures, upon our actions and even upon our thoughts and sentiments. Habit makes no figure during the vivacity of youth. In middle age it gains ground. In old age, it governs without control. In that period of life generally speaking, we eat at a certain hour, take exercise at a certain hour, go to rest at a certain hour all by the direction of habit. Then a particular seat, table, bed comes to be essential. A habit in any of these cannot be contradicted without uneasiness.

Man, it has been said is a bundle of habits and habit is second nature. Metastasio entertained so strong an opinion as to the power of repetition in act and thought that he said, "All is habit in mankind, even virtue itself."

Evil habits must be conquered or they will conquer us and destroy our peace and happiness. Vicious habits are so great a stain upon human nature, said Cicero, and so odious in themselves that every person actuated by right reason would avoid them if he was sure they would always be concealed both from God and man, and if no future punishment entailed upon them. Vicious habits when opposed, offer the most vigorous resistance on the first attack. At each successive encounter this resistance grows fainter and fainter, until finally it ceases altogether and the victory is achieved.

Habit is man's best friend or worst enemy. It can exalt him to the highest pinnacle of virtue, honor, and happiness, or sink him to the lowest depths of vice, shame, and misery.

We may form habits of honesty or knavery, truth or falsehood, of industry or idleness, frugality or extravagance. Habits of patience or impatience, self-denial or self-indulgence, of kindness, cruelty, politeness, rudeness, prudence, perseverance, circumspection. In short there is not a virtue nor a vice, not an act of body nor of mind, to which we may not be chained down by this despotic power.

It is a great point for young men to begin well. It is in the beginning of life that the system of conduct is adopted which soon assumes the force of habit. Begin well and the habit of doing well will become quite as easy as the habit of doing badly. Pitch upon that course of life which is the most excellent and habit will render it the most delightful. Well begun is half ended says the proverb; and a good beginning is half the battle. Many promising young men have irretrievably injured themselves by a first false step at the commencement of life. While others of much less promising talents, have succeeded simply by beginning well and going onward. The good practical beginning is to a certain extent, a pledge, a promise, and an assurance of the ultimate prosperous issue. There is many a poor creature now crawling through life, miserable himself and the cause of sorrow to others who might have lifted up his head and prospered. If instead of merely satisfying himself with resolutions of well-doing, he had actually gone to work and made a good practical beginning.

Company

Congenial passions souls together bind,
And every calling mingles with its kind;
Soldier unites with soldier, swain with swain,
The mariner with him that roves the main.

-F. Lewis

THAT we may be known by the company we frequent has become proverbial. For when unrestrained, we are prone to choose and associate with those whose manners and dispositions are agreeable and congenial to ours. Hence, when we find persons frequenting any company whatsoever, we are disposed to believe such company is congenial with their feelings. Not only in regard to their intellectual capacities and accomplishments, but also their moral disposition and their particular manner in life.

Good company not only improves our manners, but also our minds. Intelligent associates will become a source of enjoyment as well as our edification. If pious, they will improve our morals. If polite, they will tend to improve our manners. If educated, they will add to our knowledge and correct our errors. On the other hand if immoral, ignorant, vulgar, their impress will most surely be left upon us. It therefore becomes a matter of no trivial concern to select and associate with proper company, while avoiding that which is certainly prejudicial. We should always seek the company of those who are known to possess good merit and natural endowments. For then by being assimilated in manners and disposition, we rise.

Whereas by associating with those who are untaught in every respect, we become assimilated with them and by that assimilation become offensive. On the whole, much care and judgement are necessary in selecting properly that company we have chosen. Yet this is not a point of so great interest among women, as men. They are not thrown into associations of such diversity of character as the latter. Nevertheless, the greater care and prudence are requisite to women should they happen in such circles, to avoid the pernicious influence of such associations.

Good company is that which is composed of intelligent and worthy persons. Whose language is wise and good. Whose sentiments are pure and edifying. Whose deportment is such as pure and well-educated and correct morals dictate. Whose conduct is directed and restrained by the precepts of religion.

When we have the advantage of such company, it should be the object of our zeal "to imitate their real perfections, copy their politeness, their carriage, their address, and their easy turn of conversation. But we should remember let them shine ever so bright, their vices, (if they have any) are so many blemishes which we should no more endeavor to imitate than we should make artificial warts on our faces because some very handsome lady happened to have one by nature. We should on the contrary, think how much more handsome she would have been without it.

What can be more pleasing and more angelic than a young lady, virtous and adorned with the graces and elegances of finished politeness, based upon a sound intellect and well improved mind!

"For her inconstant man might cease to range,
And gratitude forbid desire to change."

The reflection is pleasing. It is the power of all to acquire an elegance of manner, although they may be deprived of the advantages to be derived from a liberal education. At least they may attain to that degree of elegance and manners, by judicious selection of company that will render them pleasing in any social circle whether at home or abroad. This will excite interest and grow into respect from which springs that pure, ardent, and affectionate attachment. It alone forms the only generous and indissoluble connection between the sexes, and which the lapse of time serves only to confirm and nought but death can destroy.

If so much importance is attached to the prudent selection of company and associates, if this be of such vital interest to every young female, how careful should she be not to take to her bosom for life a companion of dissolute habits and morals? Such an act might destroy all the domestic felicity she might have hoped to enjoy and be a source of constant sorrow to her through life.

> "Oh shun my friend, avoid that dangerous coast
> Where peace expires, and fair affection's lost."

For no connection or friendship can be fond and lasting, where a conformity of inclination and disposition does not exist. But where this exists, all passions and finer feelings of the soul gently harmonize and form one common and lasting interest.

Force of Character

WHAT you can effect depends on what you are. You put your whole self into all that you do. If that self be small, lean, and mean your entire life-work is paltry. Your words have no force. Your influence has no weight. If that self be true, high, pure, kind, vigorous, and forceful your strokes are blows, your notes staccatos, your work massive and your influence cogent. You can do what you will. Whatever your position, you are a power. You are felt as a kingly spirit and you are as one having authority. Too many think of character, chiefly in its relation to the life beyond the grave. We certainly would not have less thought of it with reference to that unknown future. The margin of which some of us undoubtedly are at this moment standing. But we do wish that more consideration were bestowed upon its earthly uses. We would have young men as they start in life, regard character as a capital. Its much surer to yield full returns than any other capital, unaffected by panics and failures, fruitful when all other investments lie dormant. As certain a promise in the present life, as in that which is to come.

Franklin also attributed his success as a public man not to his talents of his powers of speaking for these were but moderate, but to his known integrity of character. "Hence it was," he says, "that I had so much weight with my fellow citizens. I was but a bad speaker, never eloquent, subject to much hesitation in my choice of words, hardly correct in language, and yet I generally carried my point." Character creates confidence in men in every station of life. It was said of the first Emperor Alexander of Russia that his personal character was equivalent to a constitution. During the wars of the Fronde, Montaigne was the only man among the French who kept his castle gates unbarred. It was said of him that his personal character was worth more to him than a regiment of horse.

There are trying and perilous circumstances in life which show how valuable and important a good character is. It is a sure and strong staff of support when everything else fails. It is the Acropolis which remains impregnable, imparting security and peace when all the other defenses have been surrendered to the enemy. The higher walks of life are treacherous and dangerous. The lower full of obstacles and impediments. We can only be secure in either by maintaining those principles which are just, praiseworthy, and pure and which inspire bravery in ourselves and confidence in others.

Truthfulness, integrity, and goodness, qualities that hang not on any man's breath form the essence of manly character. As one of our old writers has it, "that inbred loyalty unto virtue which can serve her without a livery." He who possesses these qualities united with strength of purpose carries with him a power which is irresistible. He is strong to do good, he is strong to resist evil and strong to bear up under difficulty and misfortune. When Stephen of Coloma fell into the hands of his base assailants and they asked him in derision, "Where is now your fortress?" "Here," was his bold reply, placing his hand upon his heart. It is in misfortune that the character of the upright man shines forth with the greatest luster. When all else fails, he takes stand upon his integrity and his courage. In the famous pass of Thermopyle. The three hundred Spartans withstood the enemy with such vigor that they were obliged to retire wearied and conquered during three successive days, till suddenly coming up from the rear they crushed the brave defenders to pieces.

Strength of character consists of two things, power of will and power of self-restraint. It requires two things, therefore, for its existence. Strong feelings and strong command over them. Now it is here we make a great mistake. We mistake strong feelings for strong character. A man bears all before him, before whose frown domestics tremble and whose bursts of fury make the children of the household quake. He has his will obeyed and his own way in all things and we call him a strong man. The truth is, that is the weak man. It is his passions that are strong. He, mastered by them, is weak. You must measure the strength of a man by the power of the feelings he subdues, not by the power of those which subdue him. Hence, composure is very often the highest result of strength.

Did we never see a man receive a flagrant insult and only grow a little pale and then reply quietly? This is a man spiritually strong. Did we never see a man in anguish stand as if carved out of solid rock being master of himself? One bearing a hopeless daily trial remain silent and never tell the world what cankered his home peace. That is strength. He who with strong passions remains decent. He who is keenly sensitive with manly powers of indignation in him can be provoked, and yet restrain himself and forgive. These are the strong men, the spiritual heroes.

The truest criterion of a man's character and conduct is invariably to be found in the opinion of his nearest relations, having daily and hourly opportunities of forming a judgement of him, will not fail in doing so. It is a far higher testimony in his favor for him to secure the esteem and love of a few individuals within the privacy of his own home. Better than the good opinion of hundreds in his immediate neighborhood or that of ten times the number residing at a distance. The most trifling actions that affect a man's credit are to be regarded. The sound of your hammer at five in the morning or nine at night heard by a creditor, makes him easy six months longer. But if he sees you at a billiard table or hears your voice at a tavern when you should be at work, he sends for his money the next day.

Deportment, honesty, caution, and a desire to do right carried out in practice are to human character what truth, reverence, and love are to religion. They are the unvaried elements of a good reputation. Such virtues can never be reproached although the cruel and despicable may scoff at them. It is not so much in their affected revulsion at them as it is in the wish to reduce them to the standard of their own degraded natures and vitiated passions. Let them scoff and sneer. Let them laugh and ridicule as much as they may. A strict, upright, onward course will convince the world and them that there is more manly independence in one forgiving smile than in all the pretended exceptions to worthiness in the society of the mean and cruel. Virtue must have its admirers and firmness of principle, both moral and religious, and will ever command the proudest encomium of the intelligent world to the exclusion of every other thing connected with human existence.

That character is power is true in a much higher sense than that knowledge is power. Mind without heart, intelligence without conduct, cleverness without goodness are powers in their way. But they may be powers only for mischief. We may be instructed or amused by them. But it is sometimes as difficult to admire them as it would be to admire the dexterity of a pickpocket or the horsemanship of a highwayman.

Integrity

YOUNG men look about them and see a great measure of worldly success awarded to men without principle. They see the trickster crowned with public honors. They see the swindler rolling in wealth. They see the sharp man, the over-reaching man, the unprincipled man, the liar, the dema-gogue, the time-server, the trimmer, the scoundrel who cun-ningly manages. Though constantly disobeying moral law and trampling upon social courtesy, keeps himself out of the clutches of the legal police. All the while carrying off the prizes of wealth and place. This is a demoralizing puzzle and a fearful temptation. Multitudes of young men are not strong enough to stand before it. They ought to understand that in this wicked world there is a great deal of room where there is integrity. Great trusts may be sought by scoundrels, but great trusts never seek them. Perfect integrity is at a pre-mium even among scoundrels. There are some trusts that they will never confer on each other. There are occasions where they need the services of true men. They do not find them in shoals and in the mud, but alone and in pure water.

Integrity is the foundation of all that is high in character among mankind. Other qualities may add to its splendor, but if this essential requisite be wanting all their luster fades. Our integrity is never worth so much to us as when we have lost everything to keep it. Integrity without knowledge is weak. Knowledge without integrity is dangerous and dread-ful. Integrity however rough, is better than smooth dissimu-lation. Let a man have the reputation of being fair and upright in his dealings, and he will possess the confidence of all who know him. Without these qualities every merit will prove unavailing. Ask concerning a man, "Is he active and capable?" Yes. "Industrious, temperate, and regular in his habits?" O, yes, "Is he honest? is he trustworthy?" Why I am sorry to say, he is not to be trusted. He needs watching. He is a little tricky and will take an undue advantage, if he can. "Then I will have nothing to do with him," will be the invariable reply. Why then is honesty the best policy? Because without it, you will get a bad name and everybody will shun you.

The world is always asking for men who are not for sale. Men who are honest, sound, true to the heart's core. Men who will condemn wrong in friend or foe, in themselves as well as others. Men whose consciences are as steady as the needle to the pole. Men who will stand for the right if the heavens totter and the earth reels. Men who can tell the truth and look the world and the devil right in the eye. Men who neither brag nor run. Men who neither flag nor flinch. Men who do not cry, nor cause their voices to be heard on the streets, who will not fail nor be discouraged till judgement be set in the earth. Men who know their message and tell it. Men who know their places and fill them. Men who know their own business. Men who will not lie. Men who are not too lazy to work, not too proud to be poor. Men who are willing to eat what they have earned and wear what they have paid for. It is always safe to trust those who can trust themselves, but when a man suspects his own integrity it is time he was suspected by others. Moral degradation always begins at home. Honesty is never gained or lost suddenly or by accident.

Avoid and young men especially, all base, servile,

underhanded, sneaking ways. Part with anything rather than your integrity and conscious rectitude. Flee from injustice as you would from a viper's fangs. Avoid a lie as you would the gates of hell. Some there are who are callous as to this. Some there are who in stooping to mercantile dishonor and business in driving the immoral bargain, think they have done a clever action. Things are often called by their wrong names. Duplicity is called shrewdness and wrong-heartedness is called long-headedness. Evil is called good and good evil. Darkness is put for light and light for darkness. Well! be it so. You may be prosperous in your own eyes. You may have realized an envied fortune. You may have your carriage, and plate, and servants, and pageantry. But better the shielding and the crust of bread with a good conscience, than the stately dwelling or palace without it. Better than the marble mausoleum which gilds and smothers tales of heartless villainy and fraud. And would you not far rather have that heap of grass we were wont often to gaze upon in an old village churchyard, with the simple record of a cotter's virtues: "Here lies an honest man!" There is nothing more sad than to be carried like a vessel away from the straight course of principle. To be left a stranded outcast thing, on the sands of dishonor. A man bolstering himself up in a position he is not entitled to. "That is a man of capital," says the world pointing to an unscrupulous and successful swindler. Capital! What is capital? Is it what a man has? Is it counted by pounds and pence, stocks and shares, by houses and lands? No! capital is not what a man has, but what a man is. Character is capital. Honor is capital. That is the most fearful of ruin when character is gone, when integrity is sold, when honor is bartered for a miserable mess of earthly pottage. God save us from ruin like this! Perish what may, gold, silver, houses, lands. Let the winds of misfortune dash our vessel on the sunken rock, but let integrity be like the valued keepsake which the sailor boy lashed with the rope round his body. The only thing we care to save. Let one die, but let angels read if friends cannot afford to erect the grave stone: "Here lies an honest man."

Poor Boys and Eminence

MANY men have been obscure in their origin and birth, but great and glorious in life and death. They have been born and nurtured in villages, but have reigned and triumphed in cities. They were first laid in the mangers of poverty and obscurity, but have afterwards become possessors of thrones and palaces. Their fame is like the pinnacle which ascends higher and higher until at last, it becomes a most conspicuous and towering object of attraction.

Columbus was the son of a weaver and a weaver himself. Cervantes was a common soldier. Homer was the son of a small farmer. Moliere was the son of a tapestry maker. Demosthenes was the son of a cutler. Terrence was a slave. Oliver Cromwell was the son of a London brewer. Howard was an apprentice to a grocer. Franklin was the son of a tallow-chandler and soap boiler. Dr. Thomas, Bishop of Worcester was the son of a linen-draper. Daniel Defoe was a hostler and son of a butcher. Whitfield was the son of an inn-keeper. Virgil was the son of a porter. Horace was the son of a shop keeper. Shakespeare was the son of a wood stapler. Milton was the son of a money scrivener. Robert Burns was a plowman in Ayrshire. Mohammed, called the prophet was a driver of asses. Madame Bernadotte was a washerwoman of Paris. Napoleon was of an obscure family of Corsica. John Jacob Astor once sold apples on the streets of New York. Catherine, Empress of Russia was a camp-follower. Cincinnatus was plowing in his vineyard when the dictatorship of Rome was offered him. Elihu Burritt was a blacksmith. Daniel Webster while young, worked on a farm. Henry Clay was "the mill-boy of the slashes."

The young man who thinks of taking a short cut to fortune should deliberately write down the names of a dozen of our richest men. He will find that the largest part of the wealth of the Astors and Browns and Stewarts and Vanderbilts was accumulated after they had passed their fiftieth year.

"Without fame or fortune at forty, without fame or fortune always," is the sentiment of many. More often expressed by the saying, that if a man is not rich at forty he never will be. It is after forty that Sir Walter Scott became the great unknown. It was after forty that Palmerston was found to be England's greatest prime minister of the century. At that age, many who now appear prominently in our political history were obscure citizens. Howe of the sewing machine was utterly destitute at thirty-five, a millionaire six years later.

A long time ago, a little boy twelve years old on his road to Vermont stopped at a country tavern and paid for his lodging and breakfast by sawing wood instead of asking for food as a gift. Fifty years later, the same boy passed that same little inn as George Peabody, the banker whose name is the synonym of magnificent charities, the honored of two hemispheres. He was born poor in Danvers, Mass., and by beginning right and pursuing a course of strict honesty, integrity, activity, and Christian benevolence he has been able to amass great wealth. Some years since, he made a generous gift to his native town. He also remembered the city of Baltimore, Maryland where he long resided by a liberal donation. For nearly twenty-five years, having done business in London and being past sixty years old he had given nearly $750,000 to be devoted to the benefit of the poor of that city.

When Cornelius Vanderbilt was a young man his mother gave him fifty dollars of her savings to buy a small sailboat. He engaged in the business of transporting market-gardening from Staten Island to New York city. When the wind was not favorable, he would work his way over the shoals by pushing the boat along by poles sure to get his freight to market in season. This energy gave him a command of full freights and he accumulated money. After awhile, he began to build and run steamboats. He died worth more than eighty-five millions of dollars.

Mr. Tobin, formerly President of the Hudson River Railroad Company is a millionaire. He is not yet forty years of age. He began life as a steamboat clerk with Commodore Vanderbilt. When he took his position, the Commodore gave him two orders: first, to collect fare of everybody and have no deadheads on the boat; second, to start the boat on time and wait for nobody. The Commodore then lived at Staten Island. Tobin obeyed his orders so literally that he collected fare of the Commodore the first evening and left him on the wharf the next morning as the boat could not wait. The Commodore was coming down the wharf leisurely and supposed of course, the boat would wait for him. He proved a man after Vanderbilt's own heart. He became his confidential clerk and broker.

Stephen Girard left his native country at the age of ten or twelve years as a cabin boy on a vessel. He came to New York in that capacity. His deportment was distinguished by such fidelity, industry, and temperance that he won the attachment and confidence of his master who generally bestowed upon him the appellation of "my Stephen." When his master gave up business, he promoted Girard to the command of a small vessel. Girard was a self-taught man and the world was his school. It was a favorite theme with him when he afterwards grew rich, to relate that he commenced life with a sixpence and to insist that a man's best capital was his industry. All professions and all occupations which afford a just reward for labor were alike honorable in his estimation. He was never too proud to work.

In the time of the yellow fever in 1793, when consternation had seized the whole population of the city of Philadelphia, Stephen Girard then a rich merchant, offered his services as a nurse in the hospital. His offers were accepted and in the performance of the most loathsome duties he walked unharmed in the midst of the pestilence. He used to say to his friends, "When you are sick, if anything ails you do not go to a doctor, but come to me. I will cure you."

Far back in the teens of the present century, a young man asked for employment in the Springfield armory. He was poor and modest and had no friends so he went away without work. Feeling the man within him, he sought work until he found it. An age later he visited that armory a second time, not as a common day-laborer but as the ablest speaker of the House of Representatives and for many years

Governor of Massachusetts.

Of P. R. Spencer the author of the Spencerian system of penmanship, it is said "the smooth sand beach of Lake Erie constituted the foolscap in and on which, for want of other material, he perfected the system which meets such general favor in our common and commercial schools and in our business and literary circles." We reflect upon the immense popularity of his system passing beyond the limits of our own country, has been re-engraved in England and is used in the model counting rooms of London, Liverpool and Manchester. It is also the adopted system of the English Department of the University of Zurich in Switzerland. We must accord to its honored author, chaste and elevated powers of conception with bold and tireless grasp and just apprehension. We agree that the barefooted boy of fifty years ago must have been thinking and thinking right and thinking with no ordinary mind. He gave to his comings in the sands that vitality of science the world has adopted and embalmed as the most beautiful imagery of "the art."

Masons and bricklayers can boast of Ben Jonson who worked at the building of Lincoln's Inn with a trowel in his hand and a book in his pocket. Edwards and Telford the engineers, Hugh Miller the geologist, and Allen Cunningham the writer and sculptor. John Hunter the physiologist, Ronevey and Opie the painters, Professor Lee the orientalist, and John Gibbons the sculptor were carpenters. Wilson the ornithologist, Dr. Livingstone the missionary traveler, and Tannahill the poet were weavers. Samuel Drew the essayist and Gifford the editor of the "Quarterly Review," were shoemakers. Admiral Hobson, one of the gallanted of British seaman was originally a tailor.

Engraved & Printed by Illman Brothers

YOUTH.

FOR THE ROYAL PATH OF LIFE.

It is not good for human nature to have the road of life made too easy. Better to be under the necessity of working hard and faring badly, than to have everything given to our hand, a pillow of down to repose upon. Indeed to start in life with comparatively small means seems so necessary as a stimulus to work, that it may almost be set down as one of the essential conditions to success in life. Hence an eminent judge when asked what contributed most to success at the bar replied, "Some succeed by great talent, some by high connections, some by miracle, but the majority by commencing without a shilling."

So it is a common saying that the men who are most successful in business who begin with fortunes, generally lose them. Necessity is always the first stimulus to industry and those who conduct it with prudence, perseverance, and energy will rarely fail. Viewed in this light, the necessity of labor is not a chastisement but a blessing. The very root and string of all that we call progress in individuals and civilization in nations. It may indeed be questioned whether a heavier curse could be imposed on man, than the complete gratification of all his wishes without effort on his part leaving nothing for his hopes, desires, or struggles. That life is destitute of any motive or necessity for action must be of all others, the most distressing and the most insupportable to a rational being.

Occupation

THE man who has no occupation is in a bad plight. If he is poor, want is ever and always pinching him. If he is rich, weariness is a more relentless tormentor than want. An unoccupied man cannot be happy, nor can one who is improperly occupied. We have swarms of idlers among us the worst of whom are gentleman idlers. That is, men who pursue no useful occupation and sponge their way often enjoying the luxuries of life. Living upon the hard earnings of others, they are the cancers of community, false patterns of men, and leeches on the body politic.

In this widespread and expanding country no one need be without some useful occupation. All trades and professions are open from the honest hod-carrier to the highest place in the agricultural, commercial, and mechanical departments. Occupations from the humblest, but no less useful teacher of A, B, C, up to the pinnacle of professional fame. The occupations that require manual labor are the surest, most healthy and most independent.

Man or woman with no business and nothing to do are an absolute pest to society. They are thieves stealing what is not theirs. Beggars eating what they have not earned. Drones wasting the fruits of others' industry. Leeches sucking the blood of others. Evil-doers setting an example of idleness and dishonest living. Hypocrites shining in stolen and false colors. Vampires eating out the life of the community. Frown upon them, O youth. Learn in your heart to despise their course of life.

Many of our most interesting youth waste a great portion of their early life in fruitless endeavors at nothing. They have no trade, no profession, no object before them. They have nothing to do and yet have a great desire to do something. Something worthy of themselves. They try this and that and the other. They offer themselves to do anything and everything and yet know how to do nothing. Educate themselves they cannot, for they know not what they should do it for. They waste their time, energies, and little earnings in endless changes and wanderings. They have not the stimulus of a fixed object to fasten their attention and awaken their energies, not a known prize to win. They wish for good things but have no way to attain them. They desire to be useful but little means for being so. They lay plans, invent schemes, form theories, build castles but never stop to execute and realize them. Poor creatures! All that ails them is the want of object, a single object. They look at a hundred things and see nothing. If they would look steadily at one, they would see it distinctly. They grasp at random at a hundred things and catch nothing. It is like shooting among a scattered flock of pigeons, the chances of hitting one is doubtful. This will never do, no never. Success, respectability, and happiness are found in a permanent business. An early choice of some business, devotion to it, and preparation for it should be made by every youth.

When the two objects business and character like the great end of life are before a youth, what then? Why, he must attain those objects. Will wishes and prayers bring them into his hands? By no means. He must work as well as wish, labor as well as pray. His hand must be as stout as his heart, his arm as strong as his head. Purpose must be followed by action. The choosing of an occupation however, is not a small thing. Great mistakes are made and often the most worthy pursuits are left. The young man who leaves the farm-field for the merchant's desk or the lawyer's or doctor's office thinking to dignify or ennoble his toil, makes a sad mistake. He passes by that step from independence to dependence. He barters a natural for an artificial pursuit. He must be the whim of customers and the trickster of trade, either to support himself or to acquire a fortune. The more artificial a man's pursuit the more debasing it is, morally and physically. To test it, contrast the merchant's clerk with the plow-boy. The former may have the most exterior polish, but the latter under his rough outside, possesses true stamina. We wish that young men might judge of the dignity of labor by its usefulness rather than by the superficial glosses it wears. Therefore we never see a man's nobility in his kid gloves and toilet adornments, but in that sinewy arm whose outlines browned by the sun betoken a hardy, honest toil under whose farmer's or mechanic's vest the kingly heart may beat.

Above all, the notion that the "three black graces," Law, Medicine, and Ministry must be worshiped by the candidate for respectability and honor, has done incalculable damage to society. It has spoiled many a good carpenter, done injustice to the sledge and the anvil, cheated the goose and the shears out of their rights, and committed fraud on the corn and the potato field. Thousands have died of broken hearts in these professions. Thousands who might have been happy at the plow or opulent behind the counter. Thousands dispirited and hopeless look upon the healthful and independent calling of the farmer with envy and chagrin. Thousands more by the worse fate still are reduced to necessities which degrade them in their own estimation, rendering the most brilliant success but a wretched compensation for the humiliation. Their often compelled to grind out of the misery of their fellow men, the livelihood which is denied to their legitimate exertions. The result of all this, is the world is full of men who disgusted with their vocations and getting their living by their weakness instead of by their strength are doomed to hopeless inferiority. "If you choose to represent the various part in life," says Sydney Smith, "by holes in a table of different shapes, some circular, some square, some oblong, some triangular with persons acting these parts, we shall generally find that the triangular person has gotten into the square hole, the oblong into the triangular, while the square person has squeezed himself into the round hole." A French writer on agriculture serves that it is impossible profitably to improve land by trying forcibly to change its natural character, like bringing sand to clay or clay to sand. The only true method is to adapt the cultivation to the nature of the soil. The same is true with moral and intellectual qualities. Exhortation, self-determination may do much to stimulate and stir a man on in a wrong career against his better judgement. But when the crisis comes, this artificial character thus laboriously induced will break down, failing at the very time when it is most needed.

No need of spurs to the little Handel or the boy Bach to study music, when Bach steals midnight interviews with a smuggled clavichord in a secret attic or Handel copies whole books of studies by moonlight for want of a candle, rudely denied. No need of whips to the boy-painter West, when he begins in a garret and plunders the family cat for bristles to make his brushes. On the other hand to spend years at college, at the workbench or in a store and then find that the calling is a wrong one is disheartening to all but men of the toughest fiber. The discovery shipwrecks the feeble and plunges ordinary minds into despair. Doubly trying is this discovery when one feels that the mistake was made in defiance of friendly advice to gratify a freak of fancy or an idle whim. The sorrows that come upon us by the will of God or through the mistakes of our parents, we can submit to with comparative resignation. But the sorrows which we have wrought by our own hand, the pitfalls into which we have fallen by obstinately going our own way, these are the sore places of memory which no time and no patience can salve over. Be what nature intended for you and you will succeed. Be anything else and you will be ten thousand times worse than nothing.

It is an uncontroverted truth that no man ever made an ill figure who understood his own talents, nor a good one who mistook them. Let no young man of industry and perfect honesty despair because his profession and calling is crowded. Let him always remember that there is room enough at the top, or rise above the crowd at the base of the pyramid. This will be decided by the way in which he improves the first ten years of his active life, and secures to himself a thorough knowledge of his profession and a sound moral and intellectual culture.

Employment

I TAKE it that men and women were made for business, for activity, for employment. Activity is the life of us all. To do and to bear is the duty of life. We know that employment makes the man in a very great measure. A man with no employment, nothing to do, is scarcely a man. The secret of making men is to put them to work and keep them at it. It is not study, not instruction, not careful moral training, not good parents, not good society that makes men. These are means. But back of these, lies the grand molding influence of men's life. It is employment. A man's business does more to make him than every thing else. It hardens his muscles, strengthens his body, quickens his blood, sharpens his mind, corrects his judgement, wakes up his inventive genius, puts his wits to work, starts him on the race of life, arouses ambition, makes him feel that he is a man and must fill a man's shoes, do a man's work, bear a man's part in life and shows himself a man in that part. No man feels himself a man who is not doing a man's business. A man without employment is not a man. He does not prove by his works that he is a man. He cannot act a man's part. A hundred and fifty pounds of bone and muscle is not a man. A good cranium full of brains is not a man. The bone and muscle and brain must know how to act a man's part, do a man's work, think a man's thoughts, mark out a man's path, and bear a man's weight of character and duty before they constitute a man.

A man is body and soul in action. A statue if well dressed, may appear to be a man. So may a human being. But to be a man and appear to be are two different things. Human beings grow, men are made. The being that grows to the stature of a man is not a man till he is made one. The grand instrumentality of man-making is employment. The world has long since learned that men cannot be made without employment. Hence, it sets its boys to work. The world gives them trades, callings, and professions. It puts the instruments of man-making into their hands and tells them to work out their manhood. And most of them do it somehow, not always very well. The men who fail to make themselves a respectable manhood are the boys who are put to no business. The young men who have nothing to do. The male beings that have no employment. We have them about us, walking nuisances, pestilential gasbags, fetid air-bubbles. They burst and are gone. Our men of wealth and character, of worth and power have been early bound to some useful employment. Many of them were unfortunate orphan boys who were compelled to work for bread. The children of penury and lowly birth. In their early boyhood they buckled on the armor of labor, took upon their little shoulders heavy burdens, assumed responsibilities, met fierce circumstances, contended with sharp opposition, chose the most rugged path of employment because they yielded the best remuneration and braved the storms of toil till they won great victories for themselves. They stood before the world in the beauty and majesty of noble manhood. This is the way men are made. There is no other way. Their powers are developed in the field of employment.

Men are not born. They are made. Genius, worth, power of mind are more made than born. Genius born may grovel in the dust. Genius made will mount to the skies. Our great and good men who stand along the paths of history bright and shining lights are witnesses of these truths. They stand as everlasting pleaders for employment.

True Greatness

THE forbearing use of power is a sure attribute of true greatness. Indeed we may say, power whether physical, moral, purely social or political is one of the touchstones of genuine greatness.

The power the husband has over his wife, in which we must include the impunity with which he may be unkind to her. The father over his children. The old over the young. The young over the aged. The strong over the weak. The officer over his men. The master over his hands. The magistrate over the citizens. The employer over the employed. The rich over the poor. The educated over the unlettered. The experienced over the confiding. The forbearing and inoffensive use of all power or authority or a total abstinence from it where the case admits, will show the true greatness in a plain light.

"You are a plebeian," said a patrician to Cicero. "I am a plebeian," said the eloquent Roman. "The nobility of my family begins with me. That of yours will end with you. I hold no man deserves to be crowned with honor whose life is a failure. And he who lives only to eat and drink and accumulate money, is a failure. The world is no better for his living in it. He never wiped a tear from a sad face. Never kindled a fire upon a frozen hearth. I repeat with emphasis, he is a failure. There is no flesh in his heart. He worships no God but gold." These were the words of a heathen.

Man is to be rated not by his hoards of gold, not by the simple or temporary influence he may for a time, exert. But by his unexceptionable principles, relative both to character and religion. Strike out these and what is he? A brute without a virtue! A savage without a sympathy! Take them away and his manship is gone. He no longer lives in the image of his maker! A cloud of sin hangs darkly on his brow. There is ever a tempest on his countenance, the lightning in his glance, the thunder in words and the rain and whirlwind in the breathing of his angry soul. No smile gladdens his lip to tell that love is playing there. No sympathizing glow illuminates his cheek. Every word burns with malice and that voice, the mystic gift of heaven, grates harshly on the timid ear as rushing thunders beating amid falling cliffs and tumbling cataracts.

That which especially distinguishes a high order of man from a low order of man. That which constitutes human goodness, human greatness, human nobleness is surely not the degree of enlightenment with which men pursue their own advantage. But it is self-forgetfulness. It is self-sacrifice. It is the disregard of personal pleasure, personal indulgence, personal advantage, remote and present because some other line of conduct is more right.

The truest greatness is that which is unseen, unknown. Public martyrdom of every shade has a certain eclat and popularity connected with it that will often bear men up to endure with courage, its trials. There are those who suffer alone without sympathy for truth or principle, unnoticed by men, maintaining their post in obscurity and amid discouragement. There are those who patiently fulfill their trust. These are the real heros of the age and the suffering they bear is true greatness.

Let man go abroad with just principles and what is he? He is an exhaustless fountain in a vast desert. A glorious sun shining ever, dispelling every vestige of darkness. There is love animating his heart, sympathy breathing in every tone. Tears of pity. Dew drops of the soul gather in his eye and gush impetuously down his cheek. A good man is abroad and the world knows and feels it. Beneath his smiles, lurks no degrading passions. Within his heart, there slumbers no guile. He is not exalted in moral pride, not elevated in his own views, but honest, moral and virtuous before the world. He stands throned on truth. His fortress is wisdom and his dominion is the vast and limitless world, always upright, kind and sympathizing. He is always attached to just principles and actuated by the same governed by the highest motives in doing good.

Idleness

MANY moralists have remarked that pride has of all human vices, the widest dominion and lies hidden under the greatest variety of disguises. Disguises like the moon's veils of brightness both its luster and its shade. They betray it to others though they hide it from themselves.

It is not our intention to degrade pride from its preeminence, yet we know not whether idleness may not maintain a very doubtful and obstinate position. Idleness predominates in many lives where it is not suspected. Being a vice which terminates in itself, it may be enjoyed without injury to others. Therefore is it not watched like fraud, which endangers property or like pride which naturally seeks its gratification in other's inferiority.

Idleness is a silent and peaceful quality that neither raises envy by ostentation nor hatred by opposition. There are some who profess idleness in its full dignity. They boast because they do nothing and thank their stars that they have nothing to do. They sleep every night until they cannot sleep any longer, and then rise only that exercise may enable them to sleep again. They prolong the reign of darkness by double curtains and never see the sun, but to tell him how they hate his beams. Their whole labor is to vary the posture of indulgence, and their day differs from their night, like a couch or chair differs from a bed. These are the true and open votaries of idleness who exist in a state of unruffled stupefied laziness. Forgetting and forgotten they have long ceased to live and at their death the survivors can only say that they have ceased to breath. Such a person is an annoyance. He is of no use to anybody. He is an intruder in the busy thoroughfare of every-day life. He is of no advantage. He annoys busy men. He makes them unhappy. He may have an income to support his idleness or he may sponge on his good-natured friends. But in either case, he is despised. He is a criminal prodigal and a prolific author of want and shame. He is a confused work-shop for the devil to tinker in and no good can ever be expected from him. In short, he is a nuisance in the world and needs abatement for the public good. Idleness is the bane of body and mind, the nurse of haughtiness, the chief author of all mischief, one of seven deadly sins. The cushion upon which the devil reposes and a great cause not only of depression, but of many other diseases. The mind is naturally active and if it be not occupied about some honest business, it rushes into mischief or sinks into melancholy. Of all contemptible things, there is nothing half so wretched as a lazy man. The Turks say the devil tempts everybody, but the idle man tempts the devil. When we notice that a man can be a professional loafer, a successful idler, with less capital, less brains than are required to succeed in any other profession, we cannot blame him so much after all. Those are things that the idler is generally destitute of. We can notice it as an actual fact that they succeed in their business. It costs them no energy, no brains, no character, "no nothing." They are dead beats. They are a sort of dead men that cannot be buried.

Idleness is an ingredient in the upper current, which was scarcely known and never countenanced in the good old linsey-woolsey, tow and linen, mush and milk, pork and potato times of the pilgrim fathers and revolutionary patriots. We now have those among us who would rather go hungry and be clad in rags than to work. We also have a numerous train of gentleman idlers who pass down the stream of life at the expense of their fellow passengers. They live well and dress well as long as possible by borrowing and sponging. Then they take to gambling, swindling, stealing and robbing. They often pass on for years before justice overtakes them. So long as these persons can keep up fashionable appearances and elude the police, they are received into the company of the upper ten thousand. Many an idle knave by means of a fine coat, a lily hand and a graceful bow has been received into the polite circles of society with eclat. They have walked rough-shod over a worthy young mechanic or farmer who had too much good sense to make a dash or imitate the shines of an itinerant dandy. A fine dress in the eyes of some covers more sins than charity.

If thus the young man wishes to be nobody, his way is easy. He need only go to the drinking saloon to spend his leisure time. He need not drink much at first, only a little beer or some other drink. In the meantime, play dominoes, checkers or something else to kill time so that he is sure not to read any useful books. If he reads at all, let it be of the dime novels of the day. Thus go on, keep his stomach full and his head empty and he will soon graduate a nobody. Unless he should turn out a drunkard or a professional gambler which is worse than a nobody. Young man, if you do not wish to be a nobody or somebody much worse than nobody then guard your youth. A lazy youth will be a lazy man just as sure as a crooked sapling makes a crooked tree. Whoever saw a youth grow up in idleness who did not make a lazy, shiftless vagabond when he was old enough to be a man, though he was not a man by character. The great mass of thieves, paupers,and criminals have come to what they are by being brought up to do nothing useful. Laziness grows on people. It begins in cob-web and ends in iron chains. If you will be nothing just wait to be somebody. That man waits for an opportunity to do much at once, may breathe out his life in idle barren zeal. The young man idle is an old man needy. Idleness travels very leisurely along and poverty soon overtakes her. To be idle is to be poor. It is said that pride and poverty are inconsistent companions, but when idleness unites them the depth of wretchedness is complete. Leisure is sweet to those who have earned it, but burdensome to those who get it for nothing.

Arouse yourself young man! Shake off the wretched and disgraceful habits of the do-nothing if you have been so unfortunate as to incur them. Go to work at once! "But what shall I do?" you ask. ANYTHING, rather than continue in dependent, enfeebling, and demoralizing idleness. If you can get nothing else to do, sweep the streets. But you are "ashamed" to do that. If so your shame has been very slow in manifesting itself, seeing how long you have been acting on life's great stage, the despicable parts of drone and loafer WITHOUT shame!

Idler! Take the foregoing home to yourself. Don't try to persuade yourself that the cap doesn't fit you. Honestly acknowledge its fitness. It will be a great point gained to become honest with yourself. It will be a step forward. A step toward that justice to others which your present conduct absolutely ignores!

Education

MANUFACTURERS find intelligent, educated mechanics more profitable to employ even at higher wages than those who are uneducated. We have never met any one who had much experience in employing large numbers of men who did not hold this opinion. As a general rule, those manufacturers are most successful who are most careful to secure intelligent and skillful workmen.

It requires extensive observation to enable one even partially, to appreciate the wonderful extent to which all the faculties are developed by mental cultivation. The nervous system grows more vigorous and active. The touch is more sensitive. There is greater mobility in the hand.

We once knew of a weaving room filled with girls, above average in character and intelligence. There was one girl who had been highly educated. Though length of arms and strength of muscle are advantages in weaving and though this girl was short and small, she always weaved the greatest number of pieces in the room. She also drew the largest pay at the end of every month. We might fill many pages with similar cases which have come under our own observation, but there is no occasion. It has long since been settled by the general observation of manufacturers that intelligent workmen will do more and better work than uneducated ones.

The excess in the amount of work performed is not the most important respect in which an intelligent workman is superior. He is far more likely to be faithful to the interests of his employer. He saves from waste and turns to profit every thing that comes to his hand. There is also the exalted satisfaction of being surrounded by thinking, active, and inquiring minds.

Such are some of the advantages to the "Captains of Industry," which result from the employment of intelligent workmen. Not in one article nor any number of articles, could these advantages be fully set forth. If it is impossible to state the advantages to the employer, how vain must be the effort to describe those which result to the workman himself!

The increase of wages is the least and lowest of the rich rewards of mental culture. The whole being is enlarged and exalted. The scope of view is widened. The objects of interest are increased. The subjects of thought are multiplied. Life is filled with emotion. The man is raised in the scale of creation.

To English travelers, nothing in the United States has excited so much wonder and admiration as Lowell, Nashua, Manchester, Lawrence, and the other manufacturing towns of New England. That here factory girls play on the piano and sustain a creditable magazine by their own contributions. Their residences are clean, commodious, and elegant. Here factory men are intelligent gentlemen well-read in literature and totally unacquainted with beer and its inspirations. For many years this has been the crowning marvels of America, to all travelers of right feeling and good judgement.

Daniel Webster says: "Knowledge, does not comprise all which is contained in the large term of education. The feelings are to be disciplined, the passions are to be restrained. True and worthy motives are to be inspired. A profound religious feeling is to be instilled and pure morality inculcated under all circumstances. All this is comprised in education." Too many have imbibed the idea that to obtain sufficient education to enable a man to appear advantageous upon the theater of public life, his boyhood and youth must be spent within the walls of some classical seminary of learning. Then he could commence his career under the high floating banner of a collegiate diploma, to them the first round in the ladder of fame.

That a refined, classical education is desirable and one of the ACCOMPLISHMENTS of a man, we admit. That it is indisputably necessary and always makes a man more useful, we deny. He who has been in a school of learning since his childhood and within the limited circumference of his school and boarding room may have mastered all the classics. But he is destitute of that knowledge of men and things indisputably necessary to prepare him for action, either in private or public life. Classic lore and polite literature are very different from that vast amount of common intelligence fit for every day use. He must have to render his relationships with society pleasing to himself and agreeable to others. He may have a large fund of FINE SENSE, but if he lacks COMMON SENSE he is like a ship without a rudder. Let boys and girls be taught first and last all that is necessary to prepare them for the common duties of life. If the classics and polite literature can be worked between the coarser branches, they will be safe as silk goods enclosed in canvas or a bale. We wish not to undervalue high seminaries of learning, but rather to stimulate those to persevere in the acquirement of science and those who are deprived of the advantage of their dazzling lights. Franklin Sherman and others emerged from the work shop and illuminated the world as brightly as the most profound scholar from a college. In this enlightened age and in our free country, all who will may drink deeply at the pure fountain of science. Ignorance is a voluntary misfortune. By a proper improvement of time, the apprentice or the mechanic may lay in a stock of useful knowledge. This will enable him, when he arrives at manhood, to take a respectable stand by the side of those who have grown up in the full blaze of a collegiate education. With a better prospect of success at the start, he is much better stocked with common information. Without it, man is a poor, helpless creature.

Education of every kind has two values. Value as knowledge and value as discipline. Besides its use for guidance in conduct, the acquisition of each order of facts has also its use as mental exercise. Its effects as preparative for complete living have to be considered under both of these heads.

Education cannot be acquired without pains and application. It is troublesome and deep digging for pure water. But once you come to the springs, they rise up and meet you. Every grain helps fill the bushel. So does the improvement of every moment increase knowledge.

Says Swedenborg: "It is of no advantage to man to know much unless he lives according to what he knows. Knowledge has no other end than goodness. He who is made good is in possession of a far richer treasure than he whose knowledge is the most extensive, yet destitute of goodness. What the latter is seeking by his great acquirement the former already possesses."

One of the most agreeable consequences of knowledge is the respect and importance which it communicates to old age. Men rise in character often as they increase in years. They are venerable from what they have acquired and pleasing from what they can impart. Knowledge is the treasure, but judgement the treasurer of a wise man. Superficial knowledge, pleasure dearly purchased, and subsistence at the will of another are the disgrace of mankind.

The chief properties of wisdom are to be mindful of things past, careful for things present and provident of things to come.

He that thinks himself the happiest man is really so, but he that thinks himself the wisest is generally the greatest fool.

A wise man, says Seneca, is provided for occurrences of any kind. The good he manages, the bad he vanquishes. In prosperity he betrays no presumption and in adversity he feels no despondency.

By gaining a good education you shall have your reward in the rich stores of knowledge you have thus collected, and which shall ever be at your command. It is more valuable than earthly treasure. While fleets may sink and storehouses consume, and banks may totter and riches flee, the intellectual investments you make will be permanent and enduring. Unfailing as the constant flow of Niagara or Amazon, a bank whose dividends are perpetual, whose wealth is undiminished however frequent the drafts upon it. Which though moth may impair, yet thieves cannot break through nor steal.

Nor will you be able to fill these storehouses till they are full. Pour into a glass a stream of water and at last it fills to the brim and will not hold another drop. But you may pour into your mind through a whole lifetime, streams of knowledge from every conceivable quarter and no only shall it never be full, but it will constantly thirst for more and welcome each fresh supply with a greater joy. Even more to all around, you may impart of these gladdening streams which have so fertilized your own mind. Yet, like the candle from which a thousand other candles may be lit without diminishing its flame, your supply shall not be impaired. On the contrary, your knowledge as you add to it will itself attract still more as it widens your realm of thought. Thus will you realize in your own life the parable of the ten talents for "to him that hath, shall more be given."

The beginning of wisdom is to fear God, but the end of it is to love him. The highest learning is to be wise. The greatest wisdom is to be and do good. The wise man looks forward into the future and considers what will be his condition millions of ages hence, as well as what it is at present.

Opportunity

MANY do with opportunity as children do at the seashore. They fill their little hands with sand then let the grains fall through one by one, till they are all gone.

Four things do not come back. The spoken word, the sped arrow, the past life, and the neglected opportunity. Opportunity has hair in front, behind it is bald. If you seize it by the forelock you may hold it, but if allowed to escape not Jupiter himself can catch it again.

Opportunities are the offers of God. Heaven gives us enough when it gives us opportunity. Great opportunities are generally the result of the wise improvement of small ones. Wise men make more opportunities than they find. If you think your opportunities are not good enough, you had better improve them. Remember you are responsible for talents, for time, and for opportunities. Improve them as one that must give an account. Make hay while the sun shines. Gather roses while they bloom.

As a general rule, those who have no opportunities despise small ones. Those who despise small opportunities, never get large ones. Opportunity does not only do great work, but if not heeded is often most disastrous.

A shipmaster once said, "It was my lot to fall in with the ill-dated steamer, the Central America. The night was closing in, the sea rolling high. But I hailed the crippled steamer, and asked if they needed help. "I am in a sinking condition," cried Captain Herndon. "Had you not better send your passengers on board directly?" I said. "Will you not lay by me till morning?" answered Captain Herndon. "I will try," I replied. "But had you not better send your passengers on board now?" "Lay by me till morning, again said Captain Herndon. I tried to lay by him, but at night such was the heavy roll of the sea I could not keep my position and I never saw the steamer again. In an hour and a half after the captain said "Lay by me till morning," the vessel with its living freight went down. The captain and crew and a great majority of passengers found a grave in the deep." There is so little time for over-squeamishness at present that the opportunity slips away. The very period of life at which a man chooses to venture is so confined that it is no bad rule to preach up the necessity, in such instances, of a little violence done to the feelings. Efforts can be made in defiance of strict and sober calculation in order to not pass one opportunity after another.

What may be done at any time will be done at no time. Take time while time is for time will away, say the English. When the fool has made up his mind the market has gone by, say the Spanish. A little too late, much too late, say the Dutch. Some refuse roast meat, and afterwards long for the smoke of it, say the Italian.

There is sometimes wanting only a stroke of fortune to discover numberless latent good and bad qualities, which would otherwise have been eternally concealed. As words written with a certain liquor, appear only when brought near the fire.

Accident does very little toward the production of a great result in life. Though sometimes what is called a "happy hit" may be made by a bold venture, the old and common highway of steady industry and application is the only safe road to travel.

It is not accident that helps a man in the world, but purpose and persistent industry. These make a man sharp to discern opportunities and turn them to account. To the feeble, the sluggish, and purposeless the happiest opportunities avail nothing. They are passed by and no meaning is seen in them.

Spare Moments

IF we are prompt to seize and improve even the shortest intervals of possible action and effort, it is astonishing how much can be accomplished. Watt taught himself chemistry and mechanics while working at his trade as a mathematical instrument maker. He availed himself of every opportunity to extend his knowledge of language, literature and the principles of science. Stephenson taught himself arithmetic and mensuration while working as an engineer during the night shifts. He studied mechanics during his spare hours at home thus preparing himself for the great work of his life, the invention of the railway locomotive.

With perseverance, the very odds and ends of time may be worked up into results of the greatest value. An hour in every day withdrawn from frivolous pursuits would if profitably employed, enable any man of ordinary capacity to master a complete science. It would make an unlearned man a well-informed man in ten years. We must not allow the time to pass without yielding fruits in the form of something learned worthy of being known. A good principle cultivated or some good habit strengthened. Dr. Mason Good translated Lucretius while riding in his carriage in the streets of London, going his rounds among his patients. Dr. Darwin composed nearly all his works in the same way while riding about in his "sulky," from house to house in the country. He wrote down his thoughts on little scraps of paper which he carried about with him for the purpose. Hale wrote his "contemplations" while traveling on a circuit. Dr. Burney learned French and Italian while traveling on horseback

from one musical pupil to another in the course of his profession. Kirk White learned Greek while walking to and
from a lawyer's office. We personally know a man of eminent position in a northern manufacturing town who learned
Latin and French while going messages as an errand boy in
the streets of Manchester.

Elihu Burritt attributed his first success in self-improvement not to genius which he disclaimed, but simply to the
careful employment of those invaluable fragments of time
called "odd moments." While working and earning a living
as a blacksmith, he mastered some eighteen ancient and
modern languages and twenty two European dialects. With
which, he was exceedingly modest and thought his achievements nothing extraordinary. Like another learned and
wise man of whom it was said, he could be silent in ten languages, Elihu Burritt could do the same in forty. "Those
who have been acquainted with my character from my
youth up," said he, writing to a friend, "will give me credit
for sincerity when I say, that it never entered into my head
to blazon forth any acquisition of my own. All that I have
accomplished or expect or hope to accomplish has been and
will be by that prodding, patient, persevering process of
accretion which builds the ant-hill. Particle by particle,
thought by thought and fact by fact. If ever I was actuated
by ambition, its highest and warmest aspirations reached no
further than the hope to set before the young men of my
country an example in employing those invaluable fragments of time called "odd moments."

Daguesseau one of the great chancellors of France, by
carefully working up his odd bits of time wrote a bulky and
able volume in the successive intervals of waiting for dinner.

Madame de Gentis composed several of her charming volumes while waiting for the princess to whom she gave her daily lessons. Jeremy Bentham in like manner disposed of his hours of labor and repose so that not a moment should be lost, the arrangement being determined on the principle that it is a calamity to lose the smallest portion of time. He lived and worked habitually under the practical consciousness that man's days are numbered and that the night cometh when no man can work.

What a solemn and striking admonition to youth is that inscribed on the dial at All Souls, Oxford, England, "Periunt et imputantur," the hours perish and are laid to our charge. For time like life, can never be recalled. Melanchthon noted down the time lost by him that he might thereby reanimate his industry and not lose an hour. An Italian scholar put over his door an inscription intimating that whosoever remained there should join in his labors. "We are afraid," said some visitors to Baxter, "we break in upon your time." "To be sure you do," replied the disturbed and blunt divine. Time, was the estate out of which these great workers and all other workers carved a rich inheritance of thoughts and deeds for their successors.

Sir Walter Scott found spare moments for self-improvement in every pursuit and turned even accidents to account. Thus it was in the discharge of his functions as a writer's apprentice, that he first penetrated into the Highlands and formed those friendships among the surviving heroes of 1745, which served to lay the foundation for a large class of his works. Later in life when employed as quartermaster of the Edinburgh Light Cavalry, he was accidentally disabled by the kick of a horse. Confined for some time to his house,

Scott was a sworn enemy to idleness. He set his mind to work and in three days composed the first canto of "The Lay of the Last Minstrel," his first great original work.

Let not the young man sit with folded hands calling on Hercules. Thine own arm is the demi-god. It was given thee to help thyself. Go forth into the world trustful, but fearless. Exalt thine adopted calling or profession. Look on labor as honorable and dignify the task before thee whether it be in the study, office, counting room, workshop, or furrowed field. There is an equality in all and the resolute will and pure heart may ennoble either.

Books

No man has a right to bring up his children without surrounding them with books. It is a wrong to his family. He cheats them. Children learn to read by being in the presence of books. The love of knowledge comes with reading and grows upon it. The love of knowledge in a young mind is almost a warrant against the inferior excitement of passions and vices.

A little library growing larger every year is an honorable part of a young man's history. It is a man's duty to have books. A library is not a luxury, but one of the necessaries of life. It is not like a dead city of stones, yearly crumbling and needing repair, but like a spiritual tree. There it stands and yields its precious fruit from year to year and from age to age.

Carlyle saw the influence of books many years ago, "I say of all the priesthoods and aristocracies there is no class comparable for importance to the priesthood as the writers of books."

The art of writing and of printing as a sequence to it is really the most wonderful thing in the world. Books are the soul of actions. The only audible, articulate voice of the accomplished facts of the past. The men of antiquity are dead. Their fleets and armies have disappeared. Their cities are ruins. Their temples are dust. Yet all these exist in magic preservation, in the books they have bequeathed us. Their manners and their deeds are as familiar to us as the events of yesterday. These papers and books, the mass of printed matter which we call literature are really the teacher, guide, and law-giver of the world today.

The influence of books upon man is remarkable. They make the man. You may judge a man more truly by the books and papers which he reads than by the company which he keeps, for his associates are often in a manner imposed upon him. But his reading is the result of choice, and the man who chooses a certain class of books and papers unconsciously becomes more colored in his views, more rooted in his opinions, and the mind becomes fettered in his views.

All the life and feeling of a young girl fascinated by some glowing love romance is colored and shaped by the page she reads. If it be false, weak, and foolish she will be false, weak, and foolish too. But if it be true, tender, and inspiring then something of its truth, tenderness, and inspiration will grow into her soul and become a part of her very self. The boy who reads deeds of manliness, of bravery and noble daring feels the spirit of emulation grow within him. The seed is planted which will bring forth fruit of heroic endeavor and exalted life.

A good book is the most appropriate gift that friendship can make. It never changes. It never grows unfashionable or old. It is soured by no neglect, is jealous of no rival. But always its clean, clear pages are ready to amuse, interest, and instruct. The voice that speaks the thought may change or grow still forever. The heart that prompted the kindly and cheering word may grow cold and forgetful. But the page that mirrors it is changeless, faithful, and immortal. The Book that records the incarnation of divine love is God's best gift to man. The books which are filled with kindly thought and generous sympathy are the best gifts of friend to friend. Every family ought to be well supplied with a choice supply of books for reading. This may be seen from the consequences of its neglect and abuse on the one hand and from its value and importance on the other. Parents should furnish their children the necessary means, opportunities, and direction of a Christian education. Give them proper books. "Without books," says the quaint Bartholin, "God is silent, justice dormant, science at a stand, philosophy lame, letters dumb and all things involved in Cimmerian darkness." Bring them up to the habit of properly reading and studying these books. " A reading people will soon become a thinking people and a thinking people must soon become a great people." Every book you furnish your child and which reads with reflection, is "like a cast of the weaver's shuttle adding another thread to the indestructible web of existence." It will be worth more to him than all your hoarded gold and silver.

Dear Reader be independent and make up your mind what is best for you to read and read it. Master a few good books. Life is short and books are many. Instead of having your mind a garret crowded with rubbish make it a parlor of rich furniture, beautifully arranged, in which you would not be ashamed to have the whole world enter. "Readers," says Addison, "who are in the flower of their youth, should labor at those accomplishments which may set off their persons when their bloom is gone, and to lay in timely provisions for manhood and old age." Says Dr. Watts: "A line of the golden verses of the Pythagoreans recurring in the memory hath often tempted youth to frown on temptation to vice." No less worthy is the following: "There are many silver books, and a few golden books. But I have one book worth more than all called the Bible and that is a book of blank notes." The parent who lives for his children's souls, will often consider what other books are most likely to prepare his little ones for prizing aright that Book of Books, and make that object the pole star of his endeavors.

Every book has a moral expression, though as in the human face it may not be easy to say what it consists in. We may take up some exquisite poem or story with no distinctly religious bearing and feel that it is religious. It strikes a chord so deep in human nature that we feel it is only the divine nature. "God who encompasses," that can respond to what it calls forth. When we feel the inspiring influence of books, when we are lifted on the wings of ancient genius we should jealously avoid the perversion of the gift. The children of this world have their research and accomplishment and enough is done for pleasure and fame. The Christian scholar will rebuke himself unless he find it in his heart to be more alive in devotion to heavenly things. He will know at the very moment when he has breathed the aroma of poetry and eloquence. Some books are to be tasted, others to be swallowed, and some few to be chewed and digested. That is, some books are to be read only in parts. Others to be read, but not curiously. And some few to be read wholly and with diligence and attention. Some books also may be read by deputy and extracts made of them by others. That would be only in the less important arguments, and the meaner sort of books. Distilled books are like common distilled waters, flashy things.

"Not to know what was before you were," as has been truly said, "is to be always a child." And it is equally true that he never becomes a complete man who learns nothing of the former days from reading. "Books," says a good writer, "are the crystalline founts which hold in eternal ice the imperishable gems of the past."

Good books are invaluable as a moral guard to a young man. The culture of a taste for such reading keeps one quietly at home and prevents a thirst for exciting recreations and debasing pleasure. It makes him scorn whatever is low, coarse, and vulgar. It prevents that weary and restless temper which drives so many to the saloon if not the gambling table, to while away their leisure hours. Once form the habit of domestic reading, and you will at any time prefer an interesting book to frequenting the haunts of vice.

Chief among the educational influences of a household are its books. Therefore good sir or madam, wherever you economize do not cut off the supply of good literature. Have the best books, the best papers, and the best magazines even if you turn your old black silk once more and make the old coat do duty another season. Nothing will compensate to your boys and girls for the absence of those quiet, kindly teachers who keep such order in their schools and whose valuable friendship never cools or suffers change. You may go without pies and cake or without butter on your bread, but if you care for your family's best happiness and progress you will not go without the best of books, such as Shakespeare and the best authors of the day.

In books, we live continually in the decisive moments of history and in the deepest experience of individual lives. The flowers which we cull painfully and at long intervals in our personal history, blossom in profusion here. The air is full of a fragrance which touches our own life only in the infrequent springs. In our libraries we meet great men on a familiar footing, and are at ease with them. We come to know them better perhaps than those who bear their names and sit at their tables. The reserve that makes so many fine natures difficult of access is entirely lost. No crudeness of manner, no poverty of speech or unfortunate personal peculiarity mars the relationship of author and reader. It is a relation in which the interchange of thought is undisturbed by outward conditions. We lose our narrow selves in the broader life that is opened to us.

We forget the hindrances and limitations of our own work in the full comprehension of that stronger life that cannot be bound nor confined. It grows in all soils and climbs heavenward under every sky. It is the privilege of greatness to understand life in its height and depth. Hazlitt has told us of his first interview with Coleridge. The moonlight walk homeward when the eloquent lips of the great conversationalist awoke the slumbering genius within him, and made the old familiar world strange and wonderful under a sky that seemed full of new stars. Such relationships with gifted men is the privilege of few. But in the seclusion of the library, there often grows up an acquaintance more thorough and inspiring. Books are rich not only in thought and sentiment, but in character. Where shall we find in any capitals such majesty as "doth hedge about" the kings of Shakespeare, or such brave and accomplished gentlemen as adorn his courts and measure wit and courtesy with the fair and graceful women of his fancy.

The best society in the world is that which lives in books. No taint of vulgarity attaches to it, no petty strife for place and power disturbs its harmony, no falsehood stains its perfect truth. Those who move habitually in these associations find a strength which is the more controlling because it is molded by genius into forms of grace and refinement.

There is a certain monotony in daily life and those whose aims are high, but who lack the inherent strength to stand true to them amid adverse influences, gradually drop out of the ever-thinning ranks of the aspiring. They are conquered by the routine and disheartened by the discipline and labor that guard the prizes of life. Even to the strongest, there are hours of weakness and weariness. To the weak and to the strong in their times of weakness, books are inspiring friends and teachers. Against the feebleness of individual efforts, books proclaim the victory of faith and patience. Out of the uncertainty and discouragement of one day's work, they prophesy the fuller and richer life. Life grows strong and deep through conflict, sets itself more and more in harmony with the most noble aims and is at last crowned with honor and power.

Reading

THERE are four classes of readers. The first is like the hour-glass, with their reading being like the sand. It runs in and runs out and leaves no vestige behind. A second is like a sponge which imbibes everything and returns it in the same state, only a little dirtier. A third is like a jelly bag, allowing all that is pure to pass away, retaining only the refuse and dregs. The fourth are like workers in the diamond mines of Golconda who casting aside all that is worthless, obtain only pure gems. One's reading is usually a fair index of his character. Observe in almost any house you visit, the books which lie customarily on the center-table. Note what is taken by preference from the public or circulating library. You will judge in no small degree not only the intellectual tastes and the general knowledge of the family, but also what is of far deeper importance. You may pronounce on the moral attainments and the spiritual advancement of most of the household. "A man is known," it is said, "by the company he keeps." It is equally true that a man's character may be to a great extent ascertained, by knowing what books he reads.

The temptation to corrupt reading is usually strongest at the period when the education of the schoolroom is about closing. The test of the final utility however, is the time when our youth leave these schools. If the mind be now awakened to a manly independence and start on a course of vigorous self culture, all will be well. But if on the other hand, it sinks into a state of inaction, indifferent to its own needs and to all the highest ends and aims of life then woe to the man. For very few ever rouse themselves in mid-life to a new intellectual taste, or to an untried application of their time and powers to that culture for which the Creator formed and endowed them.

To read books which present false pictures of human life, is decidedly dangerous and we would say stand aloof! Life is neither a tragedy nor a farce. Men are not all either knaves or heroes. Women are neither angels nor furies. And yet if you depended upon much of the literature of the day, you would get the idea that life instead of being something earnest, something practical, is a fitful and fantastic and extravagant thing. How poorly prepared are that young man and that young woman for the duties of today, who spent last night wading through brilliant passages descriptive of mag-nificent knavery and wickedness! The man will be looking all day long for his heroine in the tin shop, by the forge, in the factory, in the counting-room and he will not find her. He will be dissatisfied. A man who gives himself up to the discriminate reading of novels will be nerveless, inane, and a nuisance. He will be fit neither for the store, nor for the shop, nor the field. A woman who gives herself up to the indiscriminate reading of novels will be unfitted for the duties of wife, mother, sister and daughter. There she is hair disheveled, countenance vacant, cheeks pale, hands trem-bling, bursting into tears at midnight over the fate of some unfortunate lover. In the daytime when she ought to be busy, staring by the half hour at nothing, biting her fingernails to the quick. The carpet that was plain before will be plainer after having wandered in tessellated halls of castles. Your industrious companion will be unattractive, now that you have walked in the romance through parks with plumed

princesses or lounged in the arbor with the polished desper-
ado. Abstain from all those books which, while they have
some good things about them have also an admixture of evil.
You have read books that had the two elements in them, the
good and the bad. Which stuck to you? The bad! The heart
of most is like a sieve, which lets the small particles of gold
fall through, but keeps the great cinders. Once in a while
there is a mind like a lodestone, when plunged amid steel
and brass fillings gathers up the steel and repels the brass. If
you attempt to plunge through a hedge of burrs to get one
blackberry, you will get more burrs than blackberries. You
cannot afford to read a bad book however good you are. You
say, "The influence is insignificant." I tell you that the
scratch of a pin has sometimes produced the lockjaw. Alas if
through curiosity as many do you pry into an evil book, your
curiosity is as dangerous as that of the man who should take
a torch into a gunpowder mill merely to see whether it would
blow up or not.

Inferior books are to be rejected in an age and time when
we are courted by whole libraries. And no man's life is long
enough to compass even those which are good and great and
famous. Why should we bow down at puddles? We can
approach freely to the crystal spring-heads of science and
letters. Half the reading of most people is snatched up at random. Many stupefy themselves over the dullness of authors
who ought to never to have escaped oblivion. The invention
of paper and printing may be said to have overdone the matter and made it too easy to be born into the world of author-
ship. The race would be benefited by some new invention for
strangling nine out of ten who sue for publicity. No man can
do his friend or child a more real service than to snatch from

his hand the book that relaxes and effeminates him, lest he destroy the solids and make his fiber flaccid by the slops and hashes of a catch-penny press. But especially is he a bene-factor who instills the principle, that no composition should be deliberately sought which is not good, beneficial, and above mediocrity.

To those who plead the want of time to read, be as frugal of your hours as you are of your dollars and you can create time in the busiest day. Horace Greeley the editor of an almost incredible circulation, tells us as a boy he would "go reading to the woodpile, to the garden, to the neighbors." His father was poor and needed his services through the day. It was a mighty struggle with him to get Horace to bed. "I would take a pine knot," he says, "put it on the backlog, pile my books around me and lie down and read all through the long winter evenings. Silent, motionless, and dead to the world around me. Alive only to the world to which I was transported by my book."

In this country, talent has a fair field to rise by culture from the humblest walks of life to attain the highest distinc-tion of which it is capable. "Why," inquired a bystander of a certain carpenter who was bestowing great labor in planing and smoothing a seat for the bench in a courtroom, "why do you spend so much time on that seat?" "I do it to make it easy for myself," was the reply. He kept his word. By indus-try, perseverance, and self-education, he rose step by step until he actually DID afterwards, sit as judge on that very bench he had planed as a carpenter.

Consider that what we carry to a book is always quite as important as what we receive from it. We may strike the keys of the best instrument from earliest morn till latest night, but unless there be music in our soul it can produce no harmony for us. While to an earnest, inquiring, self-poised mind, "a good book is the plectrum by which our silent lyres are struck." Master your reading and let it never master you. Then it will serve you with an ever-increasing fidelity. Only read books aright, and they will charge your mind with the true electric fire. Take them up as among your best friends. Every volume you read will join the great company of joyous servitors who will wait around your immortal intellect. Then too, your daily character will bear the signatures of the great minds you commune with in secret. And as the years pass on, you will walk in the light of an ever enlarging multitude of well chosen, silent, but never-erring guides.

To read with profit the books must be of a kind calculated to inform the mind, correct the head, and better the heart. These books should be read with attention, understood and remembered, and their precepts put in practice. It depends less on the number than quality. One good book well understood and remembered is of more use than to have a superficial knowledge of fifty, equally sound. Books of the right character produce reflection and induce investigation. They are a mirror of the mind for mind to look into. Of all the books ever written no one contains so instructive, so sublime, and so great a variety as the Bible. Resolve to read three chapters each day for one year, and you will find realities there. They are more wonderful than any pictures of fiction that have been drawn by the pencilling of the most practiced novel writer, in the dazzling galaxy of ancient or modern literature.

Our advice in regard to reading only the best selected works leads us to say, read slowly. We sometimes rush over pages of valuable matter because at a glance they seem to be dull. We leap along to see how the story, if it be a story is to end. We do everything in this age in a hurry. We demand not only fast horses, but fast writers, fast preachers, and fast lecturers. Said a noted seaman's preacher in one of our large cities, "I work in a hurry, I sleep in a hurry, and if I ever die, I expect to die in a hurry." This is the history of much of the present reading. No one can too highly appreciate the magic power of the press or too deeply deprecate its abuses. Newspapers have become the great highway of that intelligence which exerts a controlling power over our nation, catering the everyday food of the mind. Show us an educated family of boys and girls and we will show you a family where newspapers and periodicals are plenty. Nobody who has been without these   private tutors can know their educating power for good or evil. Have you ever thought of the innumerable topics of discussion which they suggest at the breakfast table? How early our children become acquainted with important public measures? How their attention is awakened by the great philanthropic questions of the day and the general spirit of education is evoked by these quiet visitors? Reading that makes home pleasant, cheerful and chatty thins the haunts of vice and the thousand and one avenues of temptation. Good reading should certainly be regarded, when we consider the influence on the minds of the young as a great social and moral light.

A child beginning to read becomes delighted with a newspaper because he reads of names and things which are familiar. He will progress accordingly. A newspaper in one year is worth a quarter's schooling to a child. Every father must consider that information is connected with advancement. The mother of a family being one of its heads and having a more immediate charge of children, should also consider the value. A mind occupied becomes fortified against the ills of life and is braced for emergency. Children amused by reading or study are of course more considerate and easily governed.

How many thoughtless young men have spent their earnings in a tavern or grog shop who ought to have been reading! How many parents who have not spent twenty dollars for books for their families would have given thousands to reclaim a son or daughter who had ignorantly or thoughtlessly fallen into temptation!

Take away the press and the vast educating power of the school and the college would soon come to an end. Look one moment at the immense influence a single writer has had on an age, or on the world. Shakespeare in creating the drama, or Bacon and Descartes in founding different systems of philosophy. Who may estimate the influence of Charles Dickens upon society when by the magic of his pen touched the underworld of poverty, of want, and sin? The rich and merry glided on not thinking what was beneath their feet. There marched all this ghastly array of ragged and hungry children, sorrowful women, and discouraged men, the famished forms from the poor-house, and the ugly visage of the criminal. They marched into the parlors of wealth and culture and there, had them tell the story of their woes and their suffering. Who can tell the influence of a MacDonald, or a Beecher, or an Egleston in entering the wide realm of romance and compelling it to serve truth, humanity and religion? Who knows the influence of Thomas Paine and Jefferson in strengthening the cause of liberty in our struggle for national independence? Take one single writer of our own land, Mrs. Harriet Beecher Stowe. The single tale of "Uncle Tom's Cabin," stirred the heart of this vast nation to its profoundest depths. At the simple moving of her pen, millions of swords and bayonets gleamed and flashed in the air. Vast armies met in deadly array and fought face to face till liberty, re-baptized in blood, was given to man as man. This vast world moves along lines of thought and sentiment and principle made eloquent by the clang of the printing press.

Perseverance

"CONTINUAL dropping wears a stone," as persevering labor gains our objects. Perseverance is the virtue wanted, a lion-hearted purpose of victory. It is this that builds, constructs, and accomplishes whatever is great, good, and valuable.

Perseverance built the pyramids of Egypt's plains, erected the gorgeous temple at Jerusalem, reared the seven-hilled city, inclosed in the adamant of Chinese empire. It scaled the stormy, cloud-capped Alps and opened a highway through the watery wilderness of the Atlantic. Perseverance leveled the forests of a new world and reared in its stead a community of states and nations. It has wrought from the marble block the exquisite creations of genius, painted on the canvas the gorgeous mimicry of nature, and engraved on the metallic surface the viewless substance of the shadow. Perseverance has put in motion millions of spindles, winged as many flying shuttles, harnessed a thousand iron steeds to as many freighted cars. It set them flying from town to town and nation to nation, tunneled mountains of granite, and annihilated distance with the lighting's speed. Perseverance has whitened the waters of the world with the sails of a hundred nations, navigated every sea and explored every land. It has reduced nature in her thousand forms to as many sciences, taught her laws, prophesied her future movements, measured her untrod spaces, counted her myriad hosts of worlds, and computed their distances, dimensions, and velocities.

But greater still are the works of perseverance in the world of mind. What are the productions of science and art compared with the splendid achievements won in the human soul? What is a monument of constructive genius compared with the living domes of thought, the sparkling temples of virtue, and the rich, glory-wreathed sanctuaries of religion which perseverance has wrought out and reared in the souls for good?

What are the toil-sweated productions of wealth piled in vast profusion around Girard or a Rothchild, when weighed against the stores of wisdom and the treasures of knowledge? There is strength, beauty, and glory with which this victorious virtue has enriched and adorned a great multitude of minds during the march of a hundred generations. How little can we tell or know the labors of brain and heart, the conscience struggles it cost to make a Newton, a Howard, or a Channing? How many days of toil, how many nights of weariness, how many months and years of vigilant, powerful effort was spent to perfect in them what the world has bowed to in reverence! Their words have a power, their names a charm, and their deeds a glory. How was this wealth of soul to be theirs? Why are their names watchwords of power set high on the temple of fame? Why does age feel a thrill of pleasure when they are mentioned?

They were the sons of perseverance of unremitting industry and toil. They were once as weak and helpless as any. Once as destitute of wisdom, virtue, and power as any infant. Once, the very alphabet of that language which they have wielded with such magic effect, was unknown to them. They toiled long to learn it, to get its sounds, understand its dependencies. Longer still, to obtain the secret of its highest charm and mightiest power. Yet even longer for those living, glorious, thoughts which they bid it be known to an astonished and admiring world. Their characters now given to the world and to millions yet unborn, as patterns of greatness and goodness were made by that untiring perseverance which marked their whole lives. From childhood to old age, they knew no such word as fail. Defeat only gave them power. Difficulty only taught them the necessity of redoubled exertions. Dangers gave them courage. The sight of great labors inspired in them corresponding exertions. So it has been with all men and all women who have been eminently successful in any profession or calling of life. Their success has been wrought out by persevering industry. Successful men owe more to their perseverance than to their natural powers, their friends, or the favorable circumstances around them. Genius will falter by the side of labor. Great powers will yield to great industry. Talent is desirable, but perseverance is more so. It will make mental powers, or at least will strengthen those already made. Yes, it will make mental power. The most available and successful kind of mental power is that made by the hand of determination.

It will also make friends. Who will not befriend the

persevering, energetic youth, the fearless man of industry? Who is not a friend to him, who is a friend to himself? He who perseveres in business, hardships, and discouragements will always find ready and generous friends in every time of need. He who perseveres in a course of wisdom, rectitude, and benevolence is sure to gather around him, friends who will be true and faithful. Honest industry will procure friends in any community and any part of the civilized world. Go to the men of business, worth, and influence and ask them who has their confidence and support. They will tell you the men who falter not by the wayside, who toil on in their callings against every barrier, whose eye is bent upward and whose motto is "Excelsior." These are the men to whom they give their confidence. But they shun the lazy, the indolent, the fearful and faltering. They would as soon trust the wind as such men. If you would win friends, be steady and true to yourself. Be the unfailing friend of your own purposes, stand by your own character and others will come to your aid. Though the earth quake and the heavens gather blackness, be true to your course and yourself. Quail not or doubt the result. Victory will be yours. Friends will come. A thousand arms of strength will be bared to sustain you.

First be sure that your trade, your profession, your calling in life is a good one. One that God and goodness sanctions. Then be true as steel to it. Think for it, plan for it, work for it and live for it. Throw in your mind, might, strength, heart, and soul into your actions for it and success will crown you her favored child. No matter whether your object is great or small, whether it is planting of a nation or a patch of potatoes, the same perseverance is necessary.

Everybody admires an iron determination and comes to the aid of him who directs it to good.

Perseverance will not only make friends, but it will make favorable circumstances. It will change the face of all things around us. It is silly and cowardly to complain of the circumstances that are against us. Clouds of darkness, evil forebodings, opposition, enemies, barriers of every kind will vanish before a stout heart and resolute energy of soul. The Alps stood between Napoleon and Italy which he desired to conquer. He scaled the mountain and descended upon his prey. His startling descent more than half conquered the country. He forced every circumstance into his favor. His greatest barrier proved a sure means of victory.

So a barrier once scaled affords a vantage ground for our future efforts. Opposing circumstances often create strength, both mental and physical. Labor makes us strong. Opposition gives us greater power of resistance. To overcome one barrier, gives greater ability to overcome the next. It is cowardice to grumble about circumstances. Some men always talk as though fate had woven a web of circumstances against them and it were useless for them to try to break through it. Away with such dastardly whining! It is their business to dash on in pursuit of their object against everything. Then circumstances will gradually turn in their favor and they will deem themselves the favored children of destiny.

Look at nature. She has a voice which is the voice of God teaching a thousand lessons of perseverance. The lofty mountains are wearing down by slow degrees. The ocean is gradually but slowly filling up by deposits from its thousand rivers. The Niagara Falls have worn back several miles through the hard limestone over which they pour their thundering columns of water, and will by-and-by drain the great lake which feeds their boiling chasm. The Red Sea and whole regions of the Pacific ocean are gradually filling up by the labors of a little insect so small as to be almost invisible to the naked eye. These stupendous works are going on before our eyes by a slow but sure process. They teach a great lesson of perseverance. Nature has but one voice on this subject, that is "Persevere!" and duty proclaims the same lesson. More depends upon an active perseverance than upon genius. Says a common sense author on this subject, "Genius unexerted is no more genius than a bushel of acorns is a forest of oaks." There may be epics in men's brains, just as there are oaks in acorns, but the tree must come out before we can measure it. We very naturally recall here, that large class of grumblers and wishers who spend their time in longing to be higher than they are. It should have been employed to advance themselves. They bitterly moralize on the injustice of society. Do they want a change? Let them then change! Who prevents them? If you are as high as your faculties will permit you to rise in the scale of society, why should you complain of men?

It is God who arranged the law of precedence. Impel Him or be silent! If you have capacity for a higher station, take it. What hinders you? How many men would love to go to sleep beggars and wake up Rothchilds or Astors? How many would fain go to bed dunces, to wake up as a Solomon? You reap what you have sown. Those who have sown dunce seed, vice seed, laziness seed, usually get a crop. Those who sow the wind reap a whirlwind. A man of mere "capacity undeveloped" is only an organized degradation with a shine on it. A flint and a genius that will not strike fire are no better than wet junk-wood. We have Scripture for it, that "a living dog is better than a dead lion!" If you would go up, go. If you would be seen, shine. At the present day, eminent position in any profession is the result of hard, unwearied labor. Men can no longer fly at one dash into eminent position. They have got to hammer it out by steady rugged blows. The world is no longer clay, but rather iron in the hands of its workers.

Work is the order of this day. The slow penny is surer than the quick dollar. The slow trotter will out-travel the fleet racer. Genius darts, flutters, and gets tired. Perseverance wears and wins. The all-day horse wins the race. The afternoon man wears off the laurels. The last blow finishes the nail.

Men must learn to labor and to wait if they would succeed. Brains grow by use as well as hands. The greatest man is the one who uses his brains the most and added most to his natural stock of power. Would you have fleeter feet? Try them in the race. Would you have stronger minds? Put them at rational thinking. Would you have greater success? Use greater and more rational and constant efforts. Does competition trouble you? Work away. What is your competitor but a man. Are you a coward, that you shrink from the contest? Then you ought to be beaten. Is the end of your labors a long way off? Every step takes you nearer to it. Is it a weary distance to look at? Ah, you are faint-hearted! That is the trouble with the multitude of youth. Youth are not so lazy as they are cowardly. They may bluster at first, but they won't "stick it out." Young farmer do you covet a homestead, nice and comfortable for yourself and that sweet one of your day-dreams? What hinders that you should not have it? Persevering industry with proper economy will give you the farm. A man can get what he wants if he be not faint-hearted. Toil is the price of success. Learn it, young farmer, mechanic, student, minister, physician, Christian. Learn it you former of character, you followers of Christ, you would-be men and women. You must have something to do and do it with all your might. You must harden your hands and sweat your brains. You must work your nerves and strain your sinews. You must be at it and always at it. No trembling, doubting, hesitating, flying the track. Like the boy on the rock, you cannot go back. Onward you must go. There is a great work for you all to do, a deep and earnest life-work, solemn, real and useful. Life is no idle game. No farce to amuse and be forgotten. It is a fixed and stern reality fuller of duties than the sky is of stars.

Pluck

THERE is seldom a line of glory written on the earth's face, but that a line of suffering runs parallel with it. Those who read the lustrous syllables of the one and stop not to decipher the spotted and worn inscription of the other, get the lesser half of the lesson earth has to give.

The hopelessness of any one's accomplishing anything without pluck is illustrated by an old East Indian fable. A mouse that dwelt near the abode of a great magician was kept in such constant distress by its fear of a cat. The magician, taking pity on it, turned it into a cat itself. Immediately it began to suffer from its fear of a dog. So the magician turned it into a dog. Then it began to suffer from fear of a tiger, and the magician turned it into a tiger. Then it began to suffer from its fear of huntsmen, and the magician in disgust said, "Be a mouse again! As you have only the heart of a mouse, it is impossible to help you by giving you the body of a more noble animal." And the poor creature again became a mouse.

It is the same with a mouse-hearted man. He may be clothed with the powers and placed in the position of a brave man, but he will always act like a mouse. Public opinion is usually the great magician that finally says to such a person "Go back to your obscurity again. You have only the heart of a mouse and it is useless to try to make a lion of you."

Many depend on luck instead of pluck. The P left off that word makes all the difference. The English say luck is all. "It is better to be born lucky than wise." The Spanish, "The worst pig gets the best acorn." The French, " A good bone never falls to a good dog." The German, "Pitch the lucky man into the Nile and he will come up with a fish in his mouth."

Fortune, success, and fame amid position are never gained but by piously, determinedly, bravely sticking, living to a thing till it is fairly accomplished. In short, you must carry a thing through if you want to be anybody or anything. No matter if it does cost you the pleasure, the society, the thousand pearly gratifications of life. No matter for these. Stick to the thing and carry it through. Believe you were made for the purpose, that no one else can do it. Put forth your whole energies. Be awake, electrify yourself. Go forth to the task. Only once learn to carry a thing through in all its completeness and proportion, and you will become a hero.

You will think better of yourself. Others will think better of you. The world in its very heart admires the stern, determined doer. It sees in him its best sight, the brightest object, its richest treasure. Drive right along then in whatever you undertake. Consider yourself amply sufficient for the deed and you will succeed.

Self-Reliance

GOD never intended that strong, independent beings should be reared by clinging to others, like the ivy to the oak for support. The difficulties, hardships, and trials of life are positive blessings. The obstacles are to be encountered on the road to fortune. They knit muscles and teach self-reliance.

Just as by wrestling with an athlete who is stronger, we increase our own strength and learn the secret of his skill. All difficulties come to us as Bunyan says of temptation, like the lion which met Samson. The first time we encounter them they roar and gnash their teeth, but once subdued we find a nest of honey in them. Peril is the very element in which power is developed. "Ability and necessity dwell near each other," said Pythagoras.

The greatest curse that can befall a young man is to lean, while his character is forming, on others for support. He who begins with crutches will generally end with crutches. Help from within always strengthens, but help from without invariably enfeebles its recipient. It is not in the sheltered garden or the hot-house, but on the rugged Alpine cliffs where the storms beat most violently that the toughest plants are reared. The oak that stands alone to contend with the tempest's blasts only takes deeper root and stands the firmer for ensuing conflicts. The forest tree, when the woodman's ax has spoiled its surroundings, sways and bends and trembles and perchance is uprooted. So it is with men. Those who are trained to self-reliance are ready to go out and contend in the sternest conflicts of life. While men who have always leaned for support on those around them, are never prepared to breast the storms of adversity that arise.

Many a young man and for that matter one who is older, halts at his outset on life's battlefield. He falters and faints for what he conceives to be a necessary capital for a start. A few thousand dollars, or hundreds, or "something handsome" in the way of money in his pocket. He imagines this to be about the only thing needful to secure his fortune.

The best capital in nine out of ten cases a young man can start in the world with is robust health, sound morals, a fair intelligence, a will to work his way honestly and bravely and if possible, a trade. Whether he follows it for a livelihood or not, he can always fall back on a trade when other paths are closed. Anyone who will study the lives of memorable men aside from the titled and inherited greats, will find a large majority of them rose from the ranks. They had no capital for a start. They did have intelligence, energy, industry, and a will to rise and conquer. In the mechanic and artisan pursuits, in commerce, in agriculture, and in the paths of literature, science and art, many of the greatest names have sprung from poverty and obscurity. Dr. Johnson made himself illustrious by his intellect and industry. So did Franklin and so have multitudes whose memories are renowned.

The grandest fortunes ever accumulated or possessed on earth were and are the fruit of endeavor that had no capital to begin with except energy, intellect, and a will. From Croesus down to Astor, the story is the same. Not only in the getting of the wealth, but also in the acquirement of various eminence. Those men have won most who relied most on themselves.

The path of success in business is invariably the path of common sense. Notwithstanding all that is said about "lucky hits," the best kind of success in every man's life is not that which comes by accident. The only "good time coming" we are justified in hoping for is that which we are capable of making ourselves. The fable of the labors of Hercules is indeed the type of all human doing and success. Every youth should be made to feel that if he would get through the world usefully and happily, he must rely mainly on himself and his own independent energies. Making a small provision for young men is hardly justifiable. It is of all things, the most prejudicial to themselves. They think what they have is much larger than it really is and they make no exertion. The young should never hear any language but this: "You have your own way to make and it depends on your own exertions whether you starve or not." Outside help is your greatest curse. It handcuffs effort, stifles aspiration, shuts the prison door on emulation and turns the key on energy.

The wisest charity is to help a man to help himself. To put a man in the way of supporting himself, gives him a new lease of life. It makes him feel young again, for it is very many times all the sick man needs to restore him to perfect health. People who have been bolstered up and levered all their lives are seldom good for anything in a crisis. When misfortune comes, they look around for somebody to cling to or lean on. If the prop is not there, down they go. Once down, they are as helpless as capsized turtles or unhorsed men in armor. They cannot find their feet again without assistance.

There are multitudes of such men. They are like summer vines which grow even ligneous, but stretch out a thousand little hands to grasp the stronger shrubs. If they cannot reach them, they lie disheveled in the grass, hoof-trodden, and beaten by every storm. It will be found that the first real movement upward will not take place until in a spirit of resolute self-denial, indolence, so natural to almost everyone is mastered. Necessity is usually the spur that sets the sluggish energies in motion. Poverty is more often a blessing to a young man than prosperity. While the one tends to stimulate his powers, the other inclines them to languor and disuse. Is it not very discreditable for the young man who is favored with education, friends, and all the outside advantages, which could be desired as means to worldly success to let those who stand in these respects at the beginning, far below him, gradually approach as the steady years move on and finally outstrip him in the race? It is not only discreditable, but disgraceful. A man's true position in society is that which he achieves for himself. He is worth to the world no more, no less. As he builds for society in useful work, so he builds for himself. He is a man for what he does, not for what his father or his friends have done. If they have done well and given him a position the deeper the shame, if he sink down to a meaner level through self-indulgence and indolence.

A child rightly brought up will be like a willow branch when broken off and touching the ground at once takes root. Bring up your children so that they will root easily in their own soil and not forever be grafted into your old trunk and boughs.

Labor

THERE is dignity in work. In toil of the hand, as well as toil of the head. Dignity to provide for the bodily wants of an individual life, as well as to promote some enterprise of world-wide fame. All labor that ends to supply man's wants, to increase his happiness, to elevate his nature, in a word all labor that is honest is honorable too. Labor clears the forest, drains the morass, and makes "the wilderness rejoice and blossom as the rose." Labor drives the plow, scatters the seeds, reaps the harvest, grinds the corn, and converts it into bread the staff of life. Labor, tending the pastures and sweeping the waters as well as cultivating the soil provides with daily sustenance the thousand and millions of the family of man. Labor gathers the gossamer web of the caterpillar, the cotton from the field, and the fleece from the flock and weaves it into raiment soft and warm and beautiful. The purple robe of the prince and the gray gown of the peasant being alike its handiwork. Labor molds the brick, and splits the slate, and quarries the stone, and shapes the column, and rears not only the humble cottage, but the gorgeous palace and the tapering spire and the stately dome. Labor, diving deep into the solid earth brings up its long-hidden stores of coal to feed ten thousand furnaces and in millions of homes to defy the winter's cold.

Labor explores the rich veins of deeply-buried rocks extracting the gold and silver, the copper and tin. Labor smelts the iron and molds it into a thousand shapes for use and ornament from the massive pillar to the tiniest needle. Labor forms the ponderous anchor to the wire gauze, the mighty fly-wheel of the steam engine to the polished purse ring or the glittering bead. Labor hews down the gnarled oak and shapes the timber, builds the ships, and guides it over the deep, plunging through the billows and wrestling with the tempest to bear to our shores the produce of every climate. Labor laughing at difficulties, spans majestic rivers, carries viaducts over marshy swamps, suspends bridges over deep ravines, pierces the solid mountain with the dark tunnel blasting rocks and filling hollows. While linking together with its iron but loving grasp, all nations of the earth. Labor verifies in a literal sense the ancient prophecy, "Every valley shall be exalted, and every mountain and hill shall be brought low." Labor draws forth its delicate iron thread and stretching it from city to city and province to province, through mountains and beneath the sea realizes more than fancy ever fabled. Labor constructs a chariot on which speech may outstrip the wind and compete with lightning, for the telegraph flies as rapidly as thought itself.

Labor the mighty magician, walks forth into a region of uninhabited waste. He looks earnestly at the scene so quiet in its desolation, then waving his wonder-working wand those dreary valleys smile with golden harvests. Those barren mountain slopes are clothed with foliage. The furnace blazes. The anvil rings. The busy wheel whirls round. The town appears. The mart of commerce, the hall of science, the temple of religion rear high their lofty fronts. A forest of masts merry with varied pennons, rise from the harbor. Representatives of far-off regions make it their resort. Science enlists the elements of earth and heaven in its service. Art awakening, clothes its strength with beauty. Civilization smiles. Liberty is glad. Humanity rejoices. Piety exults, for the voice of industry and gladness is heard on every side. Working men, walk worthy of your vocation! You have one able escutcheon. Disgrace it not. There is nothing really mean and low but sin. Stoop not from your lofty throne to defile yourself by contamination with intemperance, licentiousness or any form of evil. Labor allied with virtue may look up to heaven and not blush, while all worldly dignities prostituted to vice will leave their owner without a corner of the universe in which to hide his shame. You will most successfully prove the honor of toil by illustrating in your own persons its alliance with a sober, righteous, and godly life. Be you sure of this, that the man of toil who works in a spirit of obedient, loving homage to God, does no less than cherubim and seraphim in their loftiest flights and holiest songs.

Labor achieves grand victories. It weaves more durable trophies, it holds wider sway than the conqueror. His name becomes tainted and his monuments crumble. But labor converts his red battle-fields into gardens, and erects monuments significant of better things. Labor rides in a chariot driven by the wind. It writes with the lightning. It sits crowned as a king in a thousand cities and sends up its roar of triumph from a million wheels.

Labor glistens in the fabric of the loom. It rings and

sparkles from the steely hammer. It glories in shapes of beauty. It speaks in words of power. Labor makes the sinewy arm strong with liberty, the poor man's heart rich with content, crowns the swarthy and sweaty brow with honor, dignity, and peace.

Don't live in hope with your arms folded. Fortune smiles on those who roll up their sleeves and put their shoulders to the wheel. You cannot dream yourself into a character. You must hammer and forge yourself one. To love and to labor is the sum of living and yet, how many think they live who neither love nor labor?

The man or woman who thinks they are above labor and despise the laborer show a want of common sense. They forget that every article that is used is the product of more or less labor and that the air they breathe, the circulation of the blood in the veins are the result of the labor of the God of nature. There was a time when kings and queens stimulated their subjects to labor by example. Queen Mary had her regular hours of work and had one of her maids of honor read to her while she plied the needle. Sir Walter Raleigh relates a cutting reply made to him by the wife of a noble duke, at whose house he lodged overnight. In the morning, he heard her give directions to a servant in regard to feeding the pigs. On going into the breakfast room, he asked her if the pigs had all breakfasted. "All sir, but the strange pig I am about to feed," was the witty reply. Sir Walter was mute and walked up to the trough.

No man has the right to expect a good fortune, unless he go to work and deserve it. "Luck!" cried a self-made man, "I never had any luck, but by getting up at five every morning and working as hard as I could." No faithful workman finds his task a pastime. We must all toil or steal no matter how we name our stealing. A brother of the distinguished Edmund Burke was found in a revery. After listening to one of his most eloquent speeches in Parliament and being asked the cause, replied, "I have been wondering how Ned has contrived to monopolize all the talents of the family. But then I remember when we were at play, he was always at work."

The education, moral and intellectual, of every individual must be chiefly HIS OWN WORK. How else could it happen that young men who have precisely the same opportunities, should be continually presenting us with such different results and rushing to such opposite destinies? Difference of talent will not solve it because that difference is very often in favor of the disappointed candidate.

You will see issuing from the walls of the same college, sometimes from the bosom of the same family, two young men of whom the one shall be admitted to be a genius of high order. The other scarcely above the point of mediocrity. Yet you shall see the genius sinking and perishing in poverty, obscurity, and wretchedness. While on the other hand, you shall observe the mediocre plodding his slow but sure way up the hill of life. And he, gaining steadfast footing at every step and mounting at length to eminence and distinction. An ornament to his family and a blessing to his country.

Now, whose work is this? Manifestly their own. Men are the architects of their respective fortunes. It is the fiat of fate from which no power of genius can absolve you. Genius unexerted, is like the poor moth that flutters around a candle till it scorches itself to death.

What we have seen of men and of the world convinces us that one of the first conditions of enjoying life is to HAVE

SOMETHING TO DO. Something great enough to rouse the mind and noble enough to satisfy the heart. Then to give our mind and heart, our thought, toil, affections, to it. Labor for it. In the fine words of Robert Hall, "with an ardor bordering on enthusiasm," or as another sage expresses it, to "do it with all our might."

A life of full and constant employment is the only safe and happy one. If we suffer the mind and body to be unemployed, our enjoyments as well as our labors will be terminated. One of the minor uses of steady employment is that it keeps us out of mischief. For truly an idle brain is the devil's workshop, and a lazy man the devil's bolster. To be occupied is to be possessed as by a tenant, whereas to be idle is to be empty. And when the doors of the imagination are opened, temptation finds a ready access and evil thoughts come trooping in. It is observed at sea that men are never so much disposed to grumble and mutiny as when least employed. Hence an old captain, when there was nothing else to do would issue the order to, "scour the anchor."

Labor, honest labor is mighty and beautiful. Activity is the ruling element of life and its highest relish. Luxuries and conquests are the result of labor. We can imagine nothing without it. The most noble man of earth is he who puts his hands cheerfully and proudly to honest labor. Labor is a business and ordinance of God. Suspend labor and where are the glory and pomp of earth? The fruit fields and palaces and the fashioning of matter for which men strive and war. Let the labor-scorner look to himself, and learn what are the trophies. From the crown of his head to the sole of his foot, he is the debtor and worker of toil. The labor which he scorns has tricked him into the stature and appearance of a man. But where does he get the garments and equipment? Let labor answer. Labor that makes music in the mines and the furrow and the forge. Oh, scorn not labor, you man who never yet earned a morsel of bread! Labor pities you proud fool and laughs you to scorn. You shall pass to dust, forgotten. But labor will live on forever, glorious in its conquests and monuments.

Energy

THE longer we live the more we are certain the great difference between men, the feeble and the powerful, the great and the insignificant, is ENERGY. Invincible determination, a purpose once fixed, then death and victory! That quality will do anything that can be done in this world. No talents, no circumstances, no opportunities will make a two-legged creature without it.

Never suffer your energies to stagnate. There is no genius of life like the genius of energy and industry. All the traditions current among men that certain great characters have wrought their greatness, by an inspiration as it were, grows out of a sad mistake. There are no rivals so formidable as those earnest, determined minds which reckon the value of every hour and which achieve eminence by persistent application.

The difference between one man and another consists not so much in talent as in energy. If he applies persistence, he will inevitably head the more clever fellow without these qualities. Slow but sure wins the race. It is perseverance that explains how the position of boys at school is often reversed in REAL life. It is curious to note how some who were then so clever have since become so common-place. While others of whom nothing was expected, but sure in there pace have assumed the position of leaders of men. We remember as boys, we stood in the same class with one of the "dunces". One teacher after another had tried his skill on him and failed. Corporal punishment, the fool's cap, coaxing, and earnest entreaty proved fruitless. The experiment of putting him at the top of the class was tried. It was curious to note the rapidity with which he gravitated to the inevitable bottom, like a lump of lead passing through quicksilver. The youth was given up by many teachers and one pronouncing him "a stupendous booby". Yet slow though he was, he had an energy and a sort of beefy tenacity of purpose. This grew along with his muscles and his manhood. Strange to say, when he finally came to take part in the practical business of life he was found heading most of his school companions. He eventually left the greater number of them far behind. The tortoise in the right road will beat a racer in the wrong. It matters not though a youth go at a slower pace, if he is diligent. Quickness in part may even prove a defect, inasmuch as he who learns readily will often forget quite as readily. He finds no need of cultivating that quality of application and perseverance, which the slower youth is compelled to exercise to prove a valuable element in the formation of every character.

The highest culture is not obtained while at school or college so much, as by our own diligent, self-education when we have become men and women. Parents need not be in too great haste to see their children's talents forced into bloom. Let them watch and wait patiently, letting good example and quiet training do their work. Leave the rest to Providence. Let them see to it that the youth are provided with free exercise of his bodily powers, and a full stock of physical health. Set him fairly on the road of self culture. Carefully train his habits of application and perseverance. As he grows older if the right stuff is in him, he will be enabled vigorously and effectively to cultivate himself.

He who has heart has everything. He who does not burn, does not inflame. It is astonishing how much may be accomplished in self-culture by the energetic and the persevering, who are careful to avail themselves of opportunities. To use up the fragments of spare time, which the idle permit to run to waste. In study as in business, energy is the great thing. We must not only strike the iron while it is hot, but strike it until it is made hot.

Give us not men like weathercocks that change with every wind, but men like mountains who change the winds themselves. There is always room for a man of force and he makes room for many. You cannot dream yourself into a character. You must hammer and forge yourself one. Therefore, don't live in hope with your arms folded. Fortune smiles on those who roll up their sleeves and put their shoulders to the wheel. "I can't!" It is impossible!" said a foiled lieutenant to Alexander. "Begone!" shouted the conquering Macedonian in reply. "There is nothing impossible to him who will try." To make good his words, the haughty warrior not yet come to weep that there were no more worlds to subdue, charged with a phalanx the rock-crested fortress that had defied his timid officer, and the foe were swept down as with the bosom of destruction.

A man's character is seen in small matters. From even so slight a test, as the mode in which a man wields a hammer. His energy may in some way be inferred. Thus an eminent Frenchman hit off in a single phrase the characteristic quality of the inhabitants of a particular district, in which a friend of his proposed to buy land and settle. "Beware," said he, "of making a purchase there. I know the men of that department. The pupils who come from it to our veterinary school at Paris do not strike hard upon the anvil. They want energy. You will not get a satisfactory return on any capital you may invest there." A fine and just appreciation of character indicating the accurate and thoughtful observer. Strikingly illustrative of the fact that it is the energy of the individual man that gives strength to a state, and gives value upon the very soil he cultivates. It is a Spanish maxim that he who lost wealth, lost much. He who lost a friend, lost more. But he who lost his energies, lost all.

Courage

NOTHING that is of real worth can be achieved without courageous working. Man owes his growth chiefly to that active striving of the will. That encounter with difficulty which we call effort. It is astonishing to find how often results apparently impracticable are thus made possible. An intense purpose itself transforms possibility into reality. Our desires being often the precursors of the things which we are capable of performing. On the contrary the timid and hesitating find everything impossible, chiefly because it seems so. It is told of a young French officer how he used to walk about his apartment exclaiming, "I will be marshal of France and a great general." This ardent desire was the presentiment of his success. He did become a distinguished commander and he died a marshal of France.

Courage, by keeping the senses quiet and the understanding clear puts us in a condition to receive true intelligence. We are able to make just computations upon danger and pronounce rightly upon that which threatens us. Innocence of life, consciousness of worth, and great expectations are the best foundations of courage.

True courage is the result of reasoning. A brave mind is always able to resist attack. Resolution lies more in the head than in the veins. A just sense of honor and of infamy, of duty and religion will carry us further than all the force of mechanism.

To believe a business impossible, is the way to make it so. How many feasible projects have gone wrong through despondency or have failed by a cowardly imagination. It is better to meet danger than to wait for it. A ship on a lee shore stands out to sea in a storm to escape shipwreck.

Impossibilities, like vicious dogs, fly before him who is not afraid of them. Should misfortune overtake you, retrench, work harder, but never fly the track. Confront difficulties with unflinching perseverance. Should you then fail, you will be honored. But shrink, and you will be despised. When you put your hands to a work, let the fact of your doing so constitute the evidence that you mean to prosecute it to the end. Stand like a beaten anvil. It is the part of a great champion to be stricken and conquer.

"Trouble's darkest hour
Shall not make me cower
To the scepter's power
  Never, never, never,

"Then up my soul, and brace thee,
While the perils face thee;
In thyself encase thee
  Manfully for ever.

"Storms may howl around thee,
Foes may hunt and hound thee;
Shall they overpower thee?
  Never, never, never."

Courage, like cowardice, is undoubtedly contagious, but some persons are not at all liable to catch it. The attention of restless and fickle men turns to no account. Poverty overtakes them while they are flying so many different ways to escape it. What is called courage is sometimes nothing more than the fear of being thought a coward. The reverence that restrains us from violating the laws of God or man is not infrequently branded with the name of cowardice. The Spartans had a saying that he who stood most in fear of the law generally showed the least fear of an enemy. We may infer the truth of this from the reverse of the proposition. For daily experience shows us, that they who are the most daring in a bad cause are often the most pusillanimous in a good one.

Plutarch says courage consists not in hazarding without fear, but by being resolute in a just cause. An officer, after a very severe battle and being complimented on standing his ground firmly while under fire, replied, "Ah, if you knew how I was frightened you would compliment me more still." It is not the stolid or reckless man who exhibits the most noble bravery in the great battle of life. It is the man whose nerves and conscience are all alive. He looks before and behind. He weighs well all the probabilities of success or defeat and is determined to stand his ground. There is another fine anecdote apropos to this subject. A phrenologist examining the head of the Duke of Wellington, said, "Your grace has not the organ of animal courage largely developed." "You are right," replied the great man, "and except for my sense of duty, I should have retreated in my first fight." This first fight in India was one of the most terrible on record. O, that word "duty!" What is animal courage compared with it? Duty can create that courage or its equivalent, but that courage never can create duty. The Duke of Wellington saw a man turn pale as he marched up to a battery. "That is a brave man," said he, "he knows his danger and faces it."

To lead the forlorn hope in the field of courage, requires less nerve than to fight nobly and unshrinkingly the bloodless battle of life. To bear evil speaking and illiterate judgement with calmness, is the highest bravery. It is in fact, the repose of mental courage.

Physical courage which despises all danger will make a man brave in one way. Moral courage which despises all opinion will make a man brave in another. The former would seem most necessary for the camp, the latter for council. But to constitute a great man, both are necessary.

No one can tell who the heroes or who the cowards are until some crisis comes to put us to the test. And no crisis puts us to the test, that does not bring us up alone and single-handed to face danger. It is nothing to make a rush with the multitude even into the jaws of destruction. Sheep will do that. Armies might be picked from the gutter and marched up to make food for powder. But then some crisis singles one out from the multitude, pointing at him the particular finger of fate and telling him, "Stand or run." He faces about with steady nerve and with nobody else to stand behind, we may be sure the hero stuff is in him. When such crisis comes, the true courage is just as likely to be found in people of shrinking nerves or the weak and timid, as in the great burly people. It is a moral, not a physical trait. Its seat is not in the temperament, but the will. How courageous Peter and all those square-built fishermen of the sea of Galilee were at the Last Supper and in the garden of Gethsemane. Peter drew his sword and smote the officer! But when Christ looked down from his cross, whom did he see standing in focus. None of those stout fishermen, but a young man and a tenderhearted woman, John and Mary.

A good cause makes a courageous heart. They that fear an overthrow are half conquered. To be valorous, is not always to be venturous. A warm heart requires a cool head.

Though the occasions of high heroic daring seldom occur but in the history of the great, the less obtrusive opportunities for the exertion of private energy are continually offering themselves. With these, domestic scenes as much abound as does the tented field. Pain may be as firmly endured in the lonely chamber as amid the din of arms. Difficulties can be manfully combated. Misfortunes bravely sustained. Poverty nobly supported. Disappointments courageously encountered. Thus courage diffuses a wide and succoring influence and bestows energy, apportioned to the trial. It takes from calamity its dejecting quality and enables the soul to possess itself under every vicissitude. It rescues the unhappy from degradation and the feeble from contempt.

Economy

ECONOMY is the parent of integrity, of liberty, of ease, of cheerfulness, and of health. Profusion is a cruel and crazy demon that gradually involves her followers in dependence and debt. That is, it fetters them with "irons that enter into their souls."

A sound economy is a sound understanding brought into action. It is calculation realized. It is the doctrine of proportion reduced to practice. It is foreseeing contingencies and providing against them. Economy is one of three sisters of whom the other and less reputable two are greed and wastefulness. She alone keeps the straight and safe path, while greed sneers at her as profuse and wastefulness scorns at her as stingy. To the poor, she is indispensable. To those of moderate means, she is found the representative of wisdom. The loose change which many men and women throw away uselessly and sometimes even worse would often form the basis of fortune and independence. But when it is so recklessly squandered, it becomes their worst enemy. They will soon find nothing but expensive habits and perhaps a ruined character. Economy joined to industry and sobriety is a better outfit to business than a dowry.

We don't like stinginess. We don't like economy when it comes to rags and starvation. We have no sympathy with the notion that the poor man should hitch himself to a post and stand still while the rest of the world moves forward. It is no man's duty to make an iceberg of himself, to shut his eyes and ears to the sufferings of his fellows. To deny himself the enjoyment that results from generous actions, merely that he may hoard wealth for his heirs to quarrel about. There is an economy which is every man's duty who struggles with poverty. An economy which is consistent with happiness and which must be practiced, if the poor man would secure independence. It is almost every man's privilege and it becomes his duty to live within his means. Not to, but within them. This practice is of the very essence of honesty. For if a man does not manage honestly to live within his own means, he must necessarily be living dishonestly upon the means of someone else. If your means do not suit your ends, pursue those ends which suit your means. Men and women are ruined not by what they really need, but by what they think they want. Therefore, they should never go in search of their wants. If they are real needs, they will find them. For if they buy what they do not need, they will soon want what they cannot buy.

Wealth does not make the man we admit, and should never be taken into the account in our judgement of men. But competence should always be secured when it can be, by the practice of economy and self-denial only to a tolerable extent. It should be secured not for others to look upon or to raise us in the estimation of others, but to secure the consciousness of independence and the constant satisfaction which is derived from its acquirement and possession.

Simple industry and thrift will go far toward making a person of ordinary working faculty comparatively independent in his means. Almost every working man may be so, provided he will carefully hold dear his resources and watch the little outlets of useless expenditure. A penny is a very small matter, yet the comfort of thousands of families depends on the proper saving and spending of pennies. If a man allow the little pennies which are the result of his hard work to slip out of his fingers—some to the beershop, some this way and that—he will find that his life is little raised above one of mere animal drudgery. Instead let him take care of pennies by putting some weekly into a benefit society, insurance fund, savings-bank and confiding the rest to his wife to be carefully laid out, with a view to the comfortable maintenance and education of his family. He will soon find that his attention to small matters will abundantly repay him in increasing means, growing comfort at home, and a mind comparatively free from fears as to the future. If a working man have high ambition and possess richness of spirit, a wealth which far transcends all mere worldly possessions, he may not only help himself but be a profitable helper of others in his path through life.

When one is blessed with good sense and fair opportunities, this spirit of economy is one of the most beneficial of all gifts. It takes high rank among the minor virtues. It is by this mysterious power that the loaf is multiplied, that using does not waste, that little becomes much, that scattered fragments grow to unity and out of nothing comes the miracle of something! Economy is not merely saving, still less, extreme frugality. It is foresight and arrangement. It is insight and combination. It is a subtle philosophy of things by which new uses, new compositions are discovered. It causes inert things to labor, useless things to serve our necessities, perishing things to renew their vigor and all things to exert themselves for human comfort. Economy is generalship in little things. We know men who live better on a thousand dollars a year than others upon five thousand. We know very poor persons who bear about with them in everything, a sense of fitness and nice arrangement which makes their life artistic. There are day laborers who go home to more real comfort of neatness, arrangement, and prosperity in their single snug room than is found in the lordly dwellings of many millionaires. Blessings be on their good angel of economy which wastes nothing and yet is not sordid in saving. She lavishes nothing and is not frugal in giving. She spreads out a little with the blessings of taste upon it, which if it does not multiply the provision, more than makes it up in the pleasure given. Let no man despise economy.

There is no virtue so unduly appreciated as economy, nor is there one more truly worthy of estimation. A neglect of economy eventually leads to every misery of poverty and degradation, not infrequently to every variety of error and crime. Dr. Johnson asserted "that where there was no prudence, there was no virtue." Of all the maxims pronounced by that great moralist, perhaps no one was more just or more instructive. Even in that branch of prudence that directs us to take cognizance of our money affairs, the propriety of this maxim is very striking.

The progress of civilization has incurred a necessity of barter and exchange as the means of subsistence. Thus wealth, as the medium of acquiring all the comforts and luxuries of life has obtained high consideration among mankind. Philosophers may therefore scoff as much as they please at the value placed on riches, but they will never succeed in lessening the desire for their possession. When considered as the means of enjoying existence, it must be seen that it is only by the judicious expenditure of wealth that this end can be obtained. Pass a few years and the prodigal is penniless. How few under such circumstances directly or indirectly, are guilty of injustice and cruelty. Debts unpaid, friends deceived, kindred deprived of a rightful inheritance. Such are the consequences of profusion, and are they not positive acts of injustice and cruelty? Let those therefore who indignantly stigmatize the miser as a pest to society and in a fancied, honorable horror of miserly meanness are showing their noble spirit by running to an opposite extreme, reflect. Though the means are different the results of profusion are the same, exactly conducting the same crimes and misery. The taste of the age is so much more friendly to prodigality. The lavish expenditure of wealth by conducing to the gratification of society is so often unduly applauded, that it is an extreme likely to be rushed upon. But when the real consequences of its indulgence are fairly and dispassionately surveyed, its true deformity will be quickly perceived.

In short, economy appears to induce the exertion of almost every laudable emotion. A strict regard to honesty. A spirit of independence. A judicious prudence in providing for the wants. A steady benevolence in preparing for the claims of the future. Really, we seem to have run the circle of virtues; justice and contentment, honesty, independence, prudence, and benevolence.

Farm Life

AGRICULTURE is the greatest among the arts for it is first in supplying our necessities. It is the mother and nurse of all other arts. It favors and strengthens population. It creates and maintains manufacturing. It gives employment to navigation and materials to commerce. It animates every species of industry and opens to nations the surest channels of opulence. It is also the strongest bond of well-regulated society, the surest basis of internal peace, and the natural associate of good morals.

We ought to count among the benefits of agriculture the charm which the practice of it communicates to a country life. That charm which has made the country in our own view, the retreat of the hero, the safe house of the sage, and the temple of the historic spirit of poetry and art. The strong desire and longing after the country with which we find the bulk of mankind to be penetrated, points to it as the chosen abode of sublunary bliss. The sweet occupations of culture with her varied products and attendant enjoyments are a relief from the stifling atmosphere of the city. The monotony of subdivided employments, the anxious uncertainty of commerce, the vexations of ambition so often disappointed, of self-love so often mortified, of fictitious pleasures and unsubstantial vanities are cause for more relief.

Health, the first and best of all the blessings of life is preserved and fortified by the practice of agriculture. That state of well-being which we feel and cannot define. That self-satisfied disposition which depends on the perfect equilibrium and easy play of vital forces, turns the slightest acts to pleasure. It makes every exertion of our faculties a source of enjoyment. This inestimable state of our bodily functions is most vigorous in the country. If lost elsewhere, it is in the country we expect to recover it.

"In ancient times, the sacred plow employ'd
The kings, and awful fathers of mankind;
And some, with whom compared, your insect tribes
Are but the beings of a summer's day,
Have held the scale of empire, ruled the storm
Of mighty war, then, with unwearied hand,
Disdaining little-delicacies, seized
The plow and GREATLY INDEPENDENT LIVED."
                                    –THOMSON'S SEASONS

We deplore the disposition of young men to get away from their farm homes to our large cities. They are subject to difficulties and temptations which too often they fail to overcome.

Depend upon it, if you would hold your sons and brothers back from roaming away into the perilous centers, you must steadily make three attempts—to abate the task-work of farming, to raise maximum crops and profits, and to surround your work with the exhilaration of intellectual progress. You must elevate the whole spirit of your vocation for your vocation's sake till no other can outstrip it in what most adorns and strengthens a civilized state.

We have long observed and with unfeigned regret, the growing tendency of young men and lads yet early in their teens, to abandon the healthful and ennobling cares of the farm for the dangerous excitements and vicissitudes of city life and trade. Delightful firesides and friendly circles in the quiet rural districts are everyday sacrificed to this lamentable mania of the times. Young men favored with every comfort of life and not overworked, expect they may do far better than "to guide the ox or turn the stubborn glebe." With the merest trifle of consideration, their hands are withdrawn from the implements of agriculture and given to the office or workshop of the city and it generally proves vastly less agreeable or profitable, than they had anticipated. Disappointed and chagrined, they grow weary under the advance of

"Nimble mischance, that comes to swift of foot."

Where one is enabled to withstand the sweeping tide of temptation, five are submerged in its angry waves and hurried on to ruin. Every year finds hundreds, thousands, of such victims irrecoverably allied to the fallen and vicious of every class. From the smooth-tongued parlor gambler and rake, to the more degraded if not despicable, "Bowery Boy" and "Dead Rabbit." While the prison doors and the gates of hell close on many "lost ones" who had been saved, but for the foolish desertion of home and true friends. It has been well said that "for a young man of unstable habits and without religious principles, there is no place where he will be so soon ruined as in a large city."

Parents throughout the country have not failed to realize this startling truth, and to sorely mourn the strange inclination of their sons to encounter the snares and pitfalls of city residence and fashion. In brief, let the country lad be as well educated for the farm as his city cousin is for the bar or counting room. And by all possible means, let the farmer be led to properly estimate his high and honorable position in the community. "Ever remember," writes Goldthwait, "that for health and substantial wealth, for rare opportunities for self-improvement, for long life and real independence, farming is the best business in the world." History tells of one who was called from the plow to the palace, from the farm to the forum. And when he had silenced the angry tumults of a State, resumed again the quiet duties of a farmer. Of whose resting-place did Halleck write these beautiful lines?

"Such graves as his are pilgrim shrines,
　　Shrines to no code ar creed confined
The Delphian vales, the Palestines,
　　The Meccas of the mind."

He referred to Burns the plow-boy, afterward the national bard of Scotland. And Burns himself has left evidence, that he composed some of the rarest gems of his poetry while engaged in rural pursuits.

It would require volumes to enumerate the noble men who have imperishably recorded their exalted appreciation of rural life and enterprise. Every age has augmented the illustrious number. Our own immortal Washington was ever more enamored of the sickle than the sword, and unhesitating renounced agriculture "the most healthful, the most useful, and the most noble employment of man."

When we walk abroad in nature, we go not as artists to study her scenes, but as children to rejoice in her beauty. The breath of air, the blue of the unclouded sky, the shining sun and the green softness of the unflowered turf beneath our feet are all that we require to make us feel we are transported into a region of delights. We breathe and tread in a pure untroubled world. The fresh clear delight that breathes round our senses seems to bathe our spirits in the innocence of nature. It is not that we have prized a solitude which secludes us from the world of life. But the aspects on which we look, breathe a spirit. The characters we read speak a language, which mysterious and obscurely intelligible as they are, draw us on with an eager and undefined desire. Shapes and sounds of fear in naked crags, gulfs, precipices, torrents that have rage without beauty, desolate places. There is also that spirit of mind, an attractive power.

All speak in some way to our spirit and raise up in it a new and hidden emotion. Even when mingled with pain, it is glad to feel. For such emotion makes discovery to it of its own nature, and the interest it feels so strongly springs up from and returns to itself.

Of all occupations, that of agriculture is best calculated to induce love of country, and rivet it firmly on the heart. No profession is more honorable, none as conducive to health, peace, tranquility and happiness. More independent than any other calling it is calculated to produce an innate love of liberty. The farmer stands upon a lofty eminence and looks upon the bustle of cities, the intricacies of mechanism, the din of commerce, and brain-confusing, body-killing literature with feelings of personal freedom particularly his own. He delights in the prosperity of the city as his market place. He acknowledges the usefulness of the mechanic, admires the enterprise of the commercial man, and rejoices in the benefits that flow from the untiring investigations and developments of science. Then he turns his thoughts to the pristine quiet of his agricultural domain, and covets not the fame that accumulates around the other professions.

Success

TWENTY clerks in a store. Twenty hands in a printing office. Twenty apprentices in a shipyard. Twenty young men in a village. All want to get on in the world and expect to succeed. One of the clerks will become a partner and make a fortune. One of the compositors will own a newspaper and become an influential citizen. One of the apprentices will become a master builder. One of the young villagers will get a handsome farm and live like a patriarch. But which one is the lucky individual? Lucky! There is no luck about it. The thing is almost as certain as the Rule of Three. The young fellow who will out run his competitors is he who masters his business. It will be he who preserves his integrity, who lives cleanly and purely, who devotes his leisure hours to the acquisition of knowledge, who never gets into debt, who gains friends by deserving them and who saves his spare money. There are some ways to fortune shorter than this old dusty highway, but the staunch men of the community, the men who achieve something really worth having like good fortune and serene old age, all go on this road.

We hear a great deal about "good luck" and "bad luck." If a person has prospered in business, he is said to have had "good luck." If he has failed, he has had "bad luck." If he has been sick, good or bad luck is said to have visited him accordingly, as he got well or died. If he has remained in good health while others have been attacked by some epidemic disease, he has had the "good luck to escape that which others have had the "bad luck" to be seized. Good or bad luck is in most cases a synonym for good or bad judgement. The prudent, the considerate, and the circumspect seldom complain of ill luck.

We do not know anything which more fascinates youth than what we call brilliancy. Gradually however, this particular kind of estimation changes very much. It is no longer those who are brilliant, those who affect to do the most and the best work with the least apparent pains and trouble whom we most are inclined to admire. We eventually come

to admire labor and to respect it the more and it is pro-
claimed by the laborious man to be the cause of his success.

A great moral safeguard is the habit of industry. This
promotes our happiness. It leaves no cravings for those
vices which lead on and down to sin and its untold misery.
Industry conducts to prosperity. Fortunes may be won in a
day, it is true, but they may also be lost in a day. It is only the
hand of the diligent that makes one permanently rich. The
late Mr. Ticknor of Boston a model merchant and publisher,
in his last hours, spoke of the value of a steady pursuit of
one's legitimate business. He commented on the insane traffic in gold at the moment, as ruinous to the country and the
parties engaged in it. "The pathway of its track," said he, "is
strewn with wrecks of men and fortunes. But few have
failed of success who were honest, earnest, and patient." He
attributed his own success to his clinging of his resolution to
avoid all speculation and steadily pursuing the business of
his choice. He had been bred to the trade of a broker. But he
thought it as dangerous as the lottery and dice, and no young
man could fail to be warned by him who had seen the frenzy
that comes over the "Brokers' Board." "A Bable of conflict-
ing sounds." " A hot oven of excitement" is that board. It is
a moral storm which few can withstand long. How much
wiser is he who keeps out of this whirlpool, content with an
honest calling and reasonable gains.

Who are the successful men? They are those who when
boys, were compelled to work either to help themselves or
their parents. And who, when they were a little older were
under the stern necessity of doing more than their legitimate
share of labor. Who as young men, had their wits sharpened
by having to devise ways and means of making their time

more available than it would be under ordinary circumstances. Hence, in reading the lives of eminent men who have greatly distinguished themselves, we find their youth passed in self-denials of food, sleep, rest, and recreation. They sat up late, rose early to the performance of imperative duties, doing by daylight the work of one man and by night that of another. Said a gentleman the other day, now a private banker of high integrity who started in life without a dollar, "For years I was in my place of business by sunrise, and often did not leave it for fifteen or eighteen hours." Let not then any youth be discouraged if he has to make his own living, or even to support a widowed mother, or a sick sister, or unfortunate relative. For this has been the road to eminence, of many a proud name. This is the path which printers and teachers often tread. Thorny enough at times as others so beset with obstacles, as to be almost impassable. But the way was cleared, sunshine came, success followed and then the glory and renown.

The secret of one's success or failure in nearly every enterprise is usually contained in answer to this question. How earnest is he? Success is the child of confidence and perseverance. The talent of success is simply doing what you can do well and doing well whatever you do, without a thought of fame. Fame never comes because it is craved. Success is the best test of capacity. Success is not always a proper criterion for judging a man's character. It is certain that success naturally confirms us in a favorable opinion of ourselves. Success in life consists in the proper and harmonious development of those faculties which God has given us.

Be thrifty, that you may have wherewith to be charitable. He that labors and thrives spins gold.

We are familiar with people who whine continually at fate. To believe them, never was a lot so hard as theirs. Yet those who know their history will generally tell you, that their life has been but one long tale of opportunities disregarded or misfortunes otherwise deserved. Perhaps they were born poor. In this case, they hate the rich and have always hated them, but without ever having emulated their prudence or energy. Perhaps they have seen their rivals more favored by accident. In this event, they forget how many have been less lucky than themselves. So they squandered their little because as they say, they cannot save as much as others. Irritated at life, they grow old prematurely. Dissatisfied with everything, they never permit themselves to be happy. Because they are not born at the top of the wheel of fortune, they refuse to take hold of the spoke as the latter comes around. They lie stubborn in the dirt crying like spoiled children, neither doing anything themselves or permitting others to do it for them.

Some men make a mistake in marrying. They do not in this manner begin right. Have they their fortunes still to make? Too often instead of seeking one who would be a helpmate in the true sense of the term, they unite themselves to a giddy, improvident creature. With nothing but the face of a doll, and a few showy accomplishments. Such a wife they discover too late, neither makes home happy nor helps to increase her husband's means. At first thriftless, extravagant, and careless, she gradually becomes cross and reproachful. She envies other women, and reproches her husband because he cannot maintain her like them, the principal cause of his ill-fortune. The selection of a proper companion is one of the most important concerns of life. A well-assorted marriage assists instead of retarding a man's property. Choose a sensible, agreeable, amiable woman and you will have a prize "better than riches." If you do otherwise, then alas for you!

Treat everyone with respect and civility. "Everything is gained and nothing lost by courtesy." "Good manners secure success." Never anticipate wealth from any other source than labor. "He who waits for dead men's shoes may have to go a long time barefoot." And above all, "Nil desperandum," for "Heaven helps those who help themselves." If you implicitly follow these precepts, nothing can hinder you from accumulating. Let the business of everybody else alone and attend to your own. Don't buy what you don't want. Use every hour to advantage and study to make even leisure hours useful. Think twice before you throw away a shilling. Remember, you will have another to make for it. Find recreation in your own business. Buy low, sell fair, and take care of the profits. Look over your books regularly and if you find an error, trace it out. Should a stroke of misfortune come over your trade, retrench, work harder, but never fly the track. Confront difficulties with unceasing perseverance and they will disappear at last. If you should fail in the struggle, you will be honored. Shrink from the task and you will be despised.

Engage in one kind of business only and stick to it faithfully until you succeed, or until your experience shows that you should abandon it. A constant hammering on one nail will generally drive it home at last, so that it can be clinched. When a man's undivided attention is centered on one object, his mind will constantly be suggesting improvements of value. Improvements which would escape him if his brain were occupied by a dozen different subjects at once. Many a fortune has slipped through a man's fingers because he was engaging in too many occupations at a time. There is good sense in the old caution against having too many irons in the fire at once.

"At thy first entrance upon they estate," once said a wise man, "keep low sail, that thou mayst rise with honor. Thou canst not decline without shame. He that begins where his father ends, will end where his father began."

Everywhere is human experience and as frequently in nature is hardship the vestibule of the highest success. That magnificent oak was detained twenty years in its growth upward, while its roots took a great turn around a boulder by which the tree was anchored, to withstand the storms of centuries.

In our relationship with the world a cautious circumspection is of great advantage. Slowness of belief and a proper distrust are essential to success. The credulous and confiding are ever the dupes of knaves and imposters. Ask those who have lost their property how it happened, and you will find in most cases it has been owing to misplaced confidence. One has lost by endorsing, another by crediting, another by false representations. All of which, a little more foresight and a little more distrust would have prevented. In the affairs of this world men are not saved by faith, but by the want of it.

Those who are eminently successful in business who achieve greatness or notoriety in any pursuit, must expect to make enemies. Whoever becomes distinguished is sure to be a mark for the malicious spite of those who are bitter, by the merited triumph of the more worthy. The opposition which originates in such despicable motives is sure to be of the most unscrupulous character. They hesitate at no iniquity and descend to the shabbiest littleness. Opposition, if it is honest and manly, is not in itself undesirable. It is the whetstone by which highly spirited natures are polished and sharpened. He that has never known adversity is but half acquainted with others or with himself. Constant success shows us but one side of the world. For as it surrounds us with friends who will tell us only our merits, so it silences those enemies from whom alone we can learn our defects.

Honesty

THE first step toward greatness is to be honest, says the proverb. But the proverb fails to state the case strong enough. Honesty is not only the first step toward greatness, it is greatness itself.

It is with honesty, in one example, as with wealth. Those that have the thing care less about the credit of it than those that don't have it. What passes as open honesty is often masked as malaise. He who says there is no such thing as an honest man, you may be sure is dishonest himself. When any one complains as Diogenes did, that he has to hunt the street with candles at noon-day to find an honest man, we are apt to think that his nearest neighbor would have the same difficulty. If you think there isn't an honest man living, you had better for appearance sake, put off saying it until you are dead yourself. Honesty is the best policy, but those who do honest things merely because they think it good policy are not honest. No man has ever been too honest. Cicero believed that nothing is useful that is not honest. "He that walketh uprightly, walketh surely. But he that perverted his ways shall be known." There is a chemistry in an honest heart which transmutes other things to its own quality. The truth of the good old maxim that "Honesty is the best policy," is upheld by the daily experience of life.

Uprightness and integrity being found as successful in business as in everything else. As Hugh Miller's worthy uncle used to advise him, "In your dealings give your neighbor the cast of the bank, "good measure, heaped up, and running over" and you will not lose it in the end."

Honesty is the best policy. But no man can be upright amid the various temptations of life, unless he is honest for honesty's sake. You should not be honest from the low motive of policy, but because you feel better for being honest. The latter will hold you fast. Let the element set as it will, let storms blow ever so fiercely, the former is but a cable of pack-thread which will snap apart. In the long run, character is better than capital. Most of the great American merchants whose revenues outrank those of princes, owe their colossal fortunes principally to a character of integrity and ability. Lay the foundations of a character broad and deep. Build them on a rock and not on sand. The rains may then descend, the floods rise and the winds blow, but your house will stand. But establish a character for loose dealings and lo, some great tempest will sweep it away.

The religious tradesman complains that his honesty is a hindrance to his success. That the tide of custom pours into the doors of his less scrupulous neighbors in the same street, while he himself waits for hours idle. My brother, do you think that God is going to reward honor, integrity, and high-mindedness with THIS WORLD'S COIN? Do you expect He will pay spiritual excellence with plenty of custom? Now consider the price man has paid for his success, perhaps mental degradation and inward dishonor. His advertisements are all deceptive. His treatment of his workmen tyrannical. His cheap prices made possible by inferior articles. Sow that man's seed and you will reap that man's harvest. Cheat, lie, advertise falsely, be unscrupulous in your assertions, custom will come to you! But if that price is too dear let him have his harvest, and take yours. Yours is a CLEAR CONSCIENCE, a pure mind, rectitude within and without. Will you part with that, for his? Then why do you complain? He has paid his price. You do not choose to pay it.

Some in their passion for sudden accumulation, practice secret frauds and imagine there is no harm in it so long as they are not detected. In vain will they cover up their transgressions. God sees it to the bottom. Let them not hope, they will always keep it from man. The birds of the air sometimes carry the tale abroad. In the long web of events, "be sure your sin will find you out." He who is carrying on a course of latent corruption and dishonesty, be he a president of some mammoth corporation or engaged only in private transactions is sailing in a ship like that fabled one of old. As he comes nearer and nearer to a magnetic mountain, every nail will at last be drawn out of that ship. All faith in God and all trust in man will eventually be lost. He will get no reward for his guilt. The very winds will sigh for his iniquity. "A beam will come out of the wall," and convict and smite him.

Strict honesty is the crown of one's early days. "Your

son will not do for me," was once said to a friend of mine. "He took pains, the other day, to tell a customer of a small blemish in a piece of goods." The salesboy is sometimes virtually taught to declare that goods cost such and such a sum. That they are strong, fashionable, perfect, when the whole story is false. So is the tear of a God-inspired truthfulness not seldom brushed from the cheek of innocent-hearted children.

We hope and trust these cases are rare. But even one such house as we allude to, may ruin the integrity and the fair fame of many a lad. God grant our young men to feel that "an honest man is the most noble work of God," and under all temptations, to LIVE as they feel.

The possession of the principle of honesty is a matter known most intimately to the man and God, and fully only to the latter. No man knows the extent and strength of his own honesty, until he has passed the fiery ordeal of temptation. Men shudder at the dishonesty of others at one time in life. Then sailing before the favorable wind of prosperity and adversity overtakes them, their honesty too often flies away on the same wings with their riches. What they once viewed with holy horror, they now practice with shameless impunity. Others at the commencement of a prosperous career, are quite above any tricks in trade. But their love of money increases with their wealth, their honesty relaxes, and they become hard honest men. Then hardly honest, and finally, confirmed in dishonesty.

On the great day of account it will be found that men have erred more in judging of the honesty of others, than in any one thing else not even religion excepted. Many who have been condemned and had the stigma of dishonesty fixed upon them, because misfortune disabled them from paying their just debts, will stand acquitted by the Judge of the quick and the dead, not those men who covered dishonest hearts and actions undetected by man.

It is our earnest desire to eradicate the impression so fatal to many a young man, that one cannot live by being perfectly honest. You must have known men who have gone on for years in unbroken prosperity and yet, never adopted that base motto, "All is fair in trade." You must have seen too, noble examples of those who have met with losses and failures, and yet risen from them all with a conscious integrity. Those who were sustained by the testimony of all around them that though unfortunate, they were never dishonest. When we set before you such examples and show you not only that "honesty is the best policy," but that it is the very keystone of the whole arch of manly and Christian qualities, it cannot be that every ingenuous heart does not respond to the appeal. Heaven grant all such to feel that "an honest man is the most noble work of God," and to live as they feel.

Character

THERE is a structure which everybody is building, young and old, each one for himself. It is called character. Every act of life is a stone. If day by day we are careful to build our lives with pure, noble, upright deeds, at the end will stand a fair temple honored by God and man.

Our minds are given us, but our characters we make. Our mental powers must be cultivated. The seed is not the tree, the acorn is not the oak, neither is the mind a character. God gives the mind, man makes the character. The mind is the garden, the character is the fruit. The mind is the white page, the character is the writing we put on it. A subtle thing is a character. A constant work is its formation. Whether it is good or bad, it has been long in its growth and is the aggregate of millions of little mental acts. A good character is a precious thing, above rubies, gold, crowns, or kingdoms, and the work of making it is the most noble work on earth.

A person can have no character before he has had actions. Great actions carry their glory with them as the ruby wears its colors. Whatever your condition or calling in life, keep in view the whole of your existence. Act not for the little span of time allotted you in this world, but act for eternity.

Every man should aim at the possession of a good character as one of the highest objects of his life. The very effort to secure it by worthy means will furnish him with a motive for exertion. Character is like stock in trade. The more of it a man possesses, the greater his facilities for adding to it. Character is power and influence. It makes friends, creates funds, draws patronage and support and opens a sure and easy way to wealth, honor, and happiness.

Truthfulness is a corner-stone in character and if it is not firmly laid in youth, there will be ever after a weak spot in the foundation.

The value of character is the standard of human progress. The individual, the community, the nation tells its standing, advancement, its worth, wealth and glory in the eye of God by its estimation of character. Wherever character is made a secondary object, sensualism and crime prevail. He who enters upon any study, pursuit, amusement, pleasure, habit, or course of life without considering its effect upon his character is not an honest man. Just as a man prizes his character, so is he. This is the true standard of a man.

Principle and Right

WE OFTEN judge unwisely. We approve or condemn men by their actions. But it so happens that many a man whom we condemn, God approves. Many a one whom we approve, God condemns. Here it often happens that we have saints in prisons and devils in priestly robes. We often view things under false sight and pass our judgements accordingly. But God judges from behind the veil, where motives reveal themselves like lightnings on a cloud.

Now right and might lie in motive. Personally they answer the question, "Ought I?" and "Can I?" We all have good and bad in us. The good would do what it ought to do. The bad does what it can do. The good dwells in the kingdom of right. The bad sits on the throne of might. Right is a loyal subject. Might is a royal tyrant. Right is the foundation of the river of peace. Might is the mother of war and its abominations. Right is the evangelic of God that proclaims the "acceptable year of the Lord." Might is the scourge of the world that riots in carnage, groans, and blood. Right is the arm of freedom made bare and beautiful in the eyes of all the good in heaven and earth. Might is the sword of power unsheathed in the hand of oppression. Right gains its victories by peace. Might conquers only by war. Right strengthens its army by the increase of all its conquered. Might weakens its force by every victory, as a part of its power must stand guard over its new-made subjects. Right rules by invitation. Might by compulsion. Right is from above. Might from below. Right is unselfish. Might knows nothing but self.

Some men are honest when they think it policy to be honest. They smile when it is policy though they design to stab the next minute. Men of policy are honest when it is convenient and plainly profitable. When honesty costs nothing and will pay well, they are honest. But when policy will pay best, they give it the slip at once. Principle, right, and honesty are always and everywhere eternally best. It is hard to make honesty and policy work together in the same mind. Honesty will not stay where policy is permitted to visit. They have nothing in common.

There are men who choose honesty as a soul companion. They live in it, with it, and by it. They embody it in their actions and lives. Their words speak it. Their faces beam it. Their actions proclaim it. Their hands are true to it. They believe it is of God. When God looks about for his jewels, these are the men his eye rests on well pleased. They are the martyrs. Some at the stake, some in stocks, some in prison, some before judges as criminals, some on gibbets and some on the cross. They smile on their foes. They have peace within. They are strong and brave in heart.

THE DEPARTURE.

FOR THE ROYAL PATH OF LIFE.

Greed

THE MISER starves himself, knowing that those who wish him dead will fatten on his hoarded gains. He submits to more torture to lose heaven than the martyr does to gain it. He serves the worst of tyrannical masters more faithfully than most Christians do the best Master. He worships this world, but repudiates all its pleasures. He endures all the misery of poverty through life that he may die in the midst of wealth. He cheats himself for money. He is the father of more misery than the prodigal, that while he lives he heaps them on himself and those around him. He is his own and the poor man's enemy.

His mind is never expanded beyond the circumference of the almighty dollar. He thinks not of his immortal soul, his accountability to God or of his final destiny. He covets the wealth of others, revels in extortion, stops at nothing to gratify his ruling passion that will not endanger his dear idol.

Banish all inordinate desires after wealth. If you gain an abundance be discreetly liberal, judiciously benevolent, and if your children have arrived at their majority attend to your will.

Temperament

GOOD temper is like a sunny day, it sheds its brightness on everything. No trait of character is more valuable than the possession of good temper. Home can never be made

happy without it. It is like flowers springing up in our pathway, reviving and cheering us. Kind words and looks are the
outward demonstration. Patience and forbearance are the
sentinels within.

If man has a quarrelsome temper, let him alone. The
world will soon find him employment. He will soon meet
with some one stronger than himself who will repay him
better than you can. A man may fight duels all his life if he
is disposed to quarrel. How sweet the serenity of habitual
self-command! How many stinging self-reproaches it
spares us! When does a man feel more at ease with himself? When he has passed through a sudden and strong
provocation WITHOUT SPEAKING A WORD OR IN
UNDISTURBED GOOD HUMOR! When on the contrary,
does he feel a deeper humiliation than when he is conscious
that anger has made him betray himself by word, look, or
action? Nervous irritability is the greatest weakness of
character. It is the sharp grit which aggravates friction and
cuts out the bearings of the entire human machine. Nine out
of every ten men we meet are in a chronic state of annoyance. The least untoward thing sets them in a ferment.
There are people, many people always looking out for
slights. They cannot carry on the daily relationships of the
family without finding that some offense is designed. They
are as touchy as hair triggers. If they meet an acquaintance
who happens to be preoccupied with business, they attribute
his abstraction in some mode, personal to themselves and
take offense accordingly. They lay on others the fruit of
their irritability. Indigestion makes them see impertinence
in every one they come in contact with. Innocent persons
who never dreamed of giving offense are astonished to find

some unfortunate word mistaken for an insult. To say the least, the habit is unfortunate. It is far wiser to take a more charitable view of our fellow beings and not suppose that a slight is intended, unless the neglect is open and direct. After all, life takes its hues in a great degree from the color of our own mind. If we are frank and generous, the world will treat us kindly. If on the contrary we are suspicious, men learn to be cold and cautious to us. Let a person get the reputation of being "touchy," and everybody is under restraint. In this way, the chances of an imaginary offense are vastly increased.

Do you not find in many households women or men who are jealous, exacting, and have a temper that will be swayed by nothing? Many sermons tell us to be meek and humble, but you don't hear many tell you to live in your families to growl, bite, and worry one another. All that a man expects to be in heaven, he ought to try to be from day to day with his wife and children and members of his family.

Like flakes of snow that fall unperceiving upon the earth, the seemingly unimportant events of life succeed one another. As the snow gathers together, so our habits are formed. No single flake that is added to the pile produces a sensible change. No single action creates, however it may exhibit a man's character. Solomon said, "He that is slow to wrath is of great understanding, but he that is hasty of spirit exalted folly."

Our advice is to keep cool under all circumstances if possible. We should learn to command our feelings and act prudently in the ordinary concerns of life. This will better prepare us to meet sudden emergencies with calmness and fortitude. Our best antidote is implicit confidence in God.

Anger

IT does no good to get angry. Some sins have a seeming compensation or apology, but anger has none. A man feels no better for it. It is really a torment and when the storm of passion has cleared away, it leaves one to see that he has been a fool. He has made himself a fool in the eyes of others.

Sinful anger when it becomes strong is called wrath. When it makes outrages, it is fury. When it becomes fixed, it is termed hatred. When it intends to injure any one, it is called malice. All these wicked passions spring from anger. The continuance and frequent fits of anger produce an evil habit in the soul. There is a propensity to be angry which oftentimes ends in anger, bitterness, and gloom.

Anger is such a headstrong and impetuous passion that the ancients call it a short madness. There is no difference between an angry man and a madman while the fit continues because both are void of reason and blind for that season. It is a disease that is no less dangerous than deforming to us. It swells the face, it agitates the body, and inflames the blood. As the evil spirit mentioned in the Gospel threw the possessed into the fire or the water, so it casts us into all kinds of danger. It too often ruins or subverts whole families, towns, cities, and kingdoms. It is a vice that very few can conceal. If it does not betray itself by such external signs as paleness of the countenance and trembling of the limbs, it is more impetuous within and by gnawing in the heart injures the body and the mind very much.

No man is obliged to live so free from passion as not to show some resentment. It is rather stoical stupidity than virtue, to do otherwise. Anger may glance into the breast of a wise man, but rest only in the bosom of fools. Fight hard against a hasty temper. Anger will come, but resist it strongly. A spark may set a house on fire. A fit of passion may give you cause to mourn all the days of your life. Never revenge an injury. If you are conscious of being in a passion keep your mouth shut, for words increase it. Many a person has dropped dead in a rage. Fits of anger bring fits of disease. If you would demolish an opponent in argument, first make him as mad as you can. Dr. Fuller used to say that the heat of passion makes our souls to crack and the devil creeps in at the crevices. Anger is a passion, the most criminal and destructive of all passions. The only one that not only bears the appearance of insanity, but often produces the wildest form of madness. It is difficult indeed sometimes to mark the line that distinguishes the bursts of rage from the bursts of frenzy. Similar are its movements and too often equally similar are its actions. What crime has not been committed in the paroxysms of anger? Has not the friend murdered his friend? The son massacred his parent? The creature blasphemed his Creator? When the nature of this passion is considered, what crime may it not commit? Is it not the storm of the human mind which wrecks every better affection? Anger wrecks reason and conscience. As a ship driven without helm or compass before the rushing gale, is not the mind borne away without guide or government by the tempest of unbounded rage?

A passionate temper renders a man unfit for advice, deprives him of his reason, robs him of all that is either great or noble in his nature. It makes him unfit for conversation, destroys friendship, changes justice into cruelty and turns all order into confusion. Says Lord Bacon: "An angry man who suppresses his passions, thinks worse than he speaks. An angry man that will chide, speaks worse than he thinks." A wise man hath no more anger than is necessary to show that he can apprehend the first wrong, nor any more revenge than justly to prevent a second. One angry word sometimes raises a storm that time itself cannot allay. There are many men whose tongue might govern multitudes, if he could only govern his tongue. He is the man of power who controls the storms and tempests of his mind. He that will be angry for anything will be angry for nothing. As some are often incensed without a cause, so they are apt to continue their anger lest it should appear to their disgrace to have begun without occasion. If we do not subdue our anger it will subdue us. It is the second word that makes the quarrel. Anger is not warranted that hath seen two suns. One long anger and twenty short ones have no very great difference. Our passions are like the seas agitated by the winds. As God hath set bounds to the seas, so should we to our passions—so far shall thou go and no farther.

Angry and easily angered men are as ungrateful and unsociable as thunder and lightning, being in themselves all storm and tempests. But quiet and easy natures are like fair weather, welcome to all and acceptable to all men. They gather together what the other disperses and reconcile all whom the other incenses. They have the good will and the good wishes of all other men so they have the full possession of themselves. They have all their own thoughts at peace and enjoy quiet and ease in their own fortunes.

But how is it with the angry? Who thinks well of an ill-tempered, churlish man who has to be approached in the most guarded and cautious way? Who wishes him for a neighbor or a partner in business? He keeps all about him in nearly the same state of mind as if they were living next door to a hornet's nest or rabid animal. To prosperity in business, one gets along no better for getting angry. What if business is perplexing and everything goes "by contraries!" Will a fit of passion make the wind more propitious, the ground more productive, the market more favorable? Will a bad temper draw customers, pay notes, and make creditors better natured? If men, animals, or senseless matter cause trouble, will getting "mad" help matters? Will it make men more subservient, brutes more docile, wood and stone more tractable? An angry man adds nothing to the welfare of society. He may do some good, but more hurt. Heated passion makes him a firebrand and it is a wonder that he does not kindle flames of discord on every hand.

In moments of cool reflection the man who indulges in anger, views with deep regret, the desolations produced by a summer storm of passion. Friendship, domestic happiness, self-respect, the esteem of others and sometimes property are swept away by a whirlwind, perhaps a tornado of anger. We have more than once seen the furniture of a house in a mass of ruin the work of an angry moment. We have seen anger make wives miserable, alienate husbands, ruin children, derange all harmony and disturb the quiet of a whole neighborhood. Anger like too much wine hides us from ourselves, but exposes us to others.

Some people seem to live in a perpetual storm. Calm weather can never be reckoned upon in their company. Suddenly when you least expect it and without any reason, the sky becomes black and the wind rises. There is a growling thunder and pelting rain. You can hardly tell where the tempest came from. An accident for which no one can be rightly blamed, a misunderstanding which a moment's calm thought would have terminated. A chance word which meant no evil, a trifling difficulty which good sense might have removed at once, a slight disappointment which a cheerful heart would have borne with a smile. All of these can bring on earthquakes and hurricanes. What men want of reason for their opinions, they are apt to supply and make up in rage. The most irreconcilable enmities grow from the most intimate friendships. To be angry with a weak man, is to prove that you are not very strong yourself. It is much better to reprove than to be angry secretly. Anger, says Pythagoras, begins with folly and ends with repentance.

Be not angry that you cannot make others as you wish them to be, since you cannot make yourself what you wish to be.

He that is angry with the just reprover kindles the fire of the just avenger. Bad money cannot circulate through the veins and arteries of trade. It is a great pity that bad blood can circulate through the veins and arteries of the human frame. It seems a pity that an angry man, like the bees that leave their stings in the wounds they make, could inflict only a single injury. It may be so, for anger has been compared to a rain which in falling upon its victims breaks to pieces. Since anger is useless, disgraceful, without the least apology and found "only in the bosom of fools," why should it be indulged at all?

Obstinacy

A STUBBORN man does not hold opinions, they hold him. When he is once possessed of an error it is like a devil, only cast out with great difficulty. Whatsoever he lays hold on like a drowning man, he never loosens though it but help to sink him the sooner. Narrowness of mind is the cause of stubbornness. We do no easily believe what is beyond our sight. There are few, very few who will admit themselves in a mistake. Obstinacy is a barrier to all improvement. Whoever perversely resolves to adhere to plans or opinions be they right or wrong, because such plans or opinions have been already adopted by him, raises an impenetrable bar to conviction and information. To be open to conviction speaks a wise mind, an amiable character. Human nature is so frail and so ignorant, so liable to misconception that none but the most incredibly vain can pertinaciously determine to abide by self-suggested sentiments, unsanctioned by the experience or judgement of others. Only the most foolish, can be satisfied with the extent of their knowledge. The wiser we are the more we are aware of our ignorance. Whoever resolves not to alter his ideas, shuts himself out from all possibility of improvement and must die as he lives, ignorant or uninformed.

In morals perhaps, obstinacy may be more plausibly excused and under the misnomer of firmness, be practiced as a virtue. But the line between obstinacy and firmness is strong and decisive. The smallest share of common sense will suffice to detect it. There is little doubt that few people pass this boundary without being conscious of the fault.

It will probably be found that those qualities which come under the head of weakness of character rather than vice, render people most intolerable as companions and assistants. It is astonishing to see how this practice of making difficulties on every occasion, grows into a confirmed habit of mind. What disheartenment it causes. The savor of life is taken out of it when you know that nothing you propose to do, suggest, hope for or endeavor will meet with any response but an enumeration of difficulties that lie in the path you wish to travel. The difficulty-monger is to be met with not only in domestic and social life, but also in business. It occurs not infrequently in business relations, that the chief approve of anything that is brought to him by his subordinates. Of all disagreeable people, the obstinate are the worst.

Society is often dragged down to low standards by two or three who propose in every case, to fight everything and every idea of which they are not the instigators.

When a new idea is brought to such persons instead of drawing out of it what good they can, they seek to get the bad ever ready to heap a mountain of difficulties upon it.

But there are situations, in which the proper opinions and mode of conduct are not evident. In such cases, we must maturely reflect before we decide. We must seek for the opinions of those wiser and better acquainted with the subject than ourselves. We must candidly hear all that can be said on both sides. Then and only then can we in such cases, hope to determine wisely. But the decision once adopted, we must firmly sustain and never yield, but to the most unbiased conviction of our former error.

Hypocrisy

THERE is no folly in the world so great as to be a hypocrite. The hypocrite is hated of the world for seeming to be a Christian. He is hated by God for not being one. He hates himself and he is even despised by Satan for serving him and not acknowledging it. Hypocrites are really the best followers and the greatest dupes that Satan has. They serve him better than any other, but receive no wages. They study more to enter into religion than that religion should enter into them. They are zealous in little things, but cold and remiss in the most important. They are saints by pretension, but Satans in intention. They testify, they worship only to answer their wicked purposes. They stand as angels before their sins so as to hide them. A scorpion thinks when its head is under a leaf it cannot be seen, so the hypocrite. The false saints think when they have hoisted up one or two good works that all their sins therewith are covered and hid.

Let us ask ourselves seriously and honestly, "What do I believe after all? What manner of man am I after all? What sort of a show should I make after all, if the people around me knew my heart and all my secret thoughts? What sort of show do I already make in the sight of Almighty God, who sees every man exactly as he is?" Oh that poor soul, though it may fool people and itself, it will not fool God!

Hypocrisy shows love, but is hatred. It shows friendship, but is an enemy. It shows peace, but is at war. It flatters, it curses, it praises, it slanders. It always has two sides of a question. It possesses what it does not pretend to and pretends to what it does not possess.

Men are afraid of slight outward acts which will injure them in the eyes of others, while they are heedless of the damnation which throbs in their souls in hatreds, jealousies, and revenges.

They are more troubled by the outburst of a sinful disposition than by the disposition itself. It is not the evil, but its reflex effect upon themselves that they dread. It is the love of approbation and not the conscience that enacts the part of a moral sense, in this case. If a man covet, he steals. If a man have murderous hate, he murders. If a man brood dishonest thoughts, he is a knave. If a man harbor sharp and bitter jealousies, envies, hatreds though he never express them by his tongue or shape them by his hand, they are there. Society to be sure, is less injured by the cherished thoughts of evil in his own soul, as by the open commission of it. For evil brought out ceases to disguise itself, and seems as hideous as it is. But evil that lurks and glances through the soul, avoids analysis and evades detection.

Pretension! Profession! How haughtily they stride onto the kingdom of the lowly Redeemer and take the highest seats, put on robes of sanctity, sing the hymns of praise, and utter aloud to be heard of men, the prayers which the spirit ought to breath in silent and childlike confidence into the ear of the listening and loving Father! How they build high domes of worship with velvety seats and golden alters and costly plate and baptismal fonts by the side of squalid want and ragged poverty! How their mocking prayers mingle with the cry of beggary, the curse of blasphemy, the wail of pain and the lewd laugh of sensuality! How mournfully their organ chants of praise bought with sordid gold, go up from the seats of worldliness and pride, and how reproachfully the tall steeples of cathedrals and synagogues and churches look down on the oppression and pride and selfishness which assemble below them. The slavery, poverty, and intemperance which pass and repass their marble foundations! Oh, shade of religion, where art thou? Spirit of the lowly bleeder on Calvery, hast thou left this world in despair? Comforter of the mourning, dweller with the sinful, how long shall these things be? Religion is made a show-bubble. Pride is her handmaid and selfishness her leader. What a tawdry show they make! Who believes the substance is equal to the show, the root as deep as the tree is high, the foundation as firm as the structure is imposing? Nowhere does show more wickedly become the dominion of substance than in the realm of religion. In the world, we might expect to see hypocrisy. But the true religion is above the world. "MY kingdom is not of this world," said its Founder. It has a world of its own. It is built on substance. But men have sought to make it a world of show, to carry the deception and Pharisaic of this world up into the Redeemer's world and pass them off there for the golden reality that shall be admitted to heaven. Poorly will hypocrisy pass at the bar of God. No coin but the true one passes there. No gilding will hide the hollowness of a false soul. No tawdry displays will avail with that eye whose glance like a sword, pierces to the heart. All is open there. All hypocrisy, vanity. Worse than vanity, it is sin. It is a gilded lie, a varnished cheat. It is proof of the hollowness within, the sign of corruption. Yet more it is itself corrupting, a painted temptation. It lures men away from the truth. It wastes their energies on a shadow. It wins their affections to fading follies and gives them a disrelish for the real, the substantial, and enduring. Who can expect that God will not hide in every hollow show intended to deceive, a sharp two-edged sword that shall cut with disappointment and pierce with inward wasting want?

Fretting and Grumbling

MANY very excellent persons whose lives are honorable and whose characters are noble, pass numberless hours of sadness and weariness of heart. The fault is not with their circumstances nor with their general characters, but with themselves that they are miserable. They have failed to adopt the true philosophy of life. They wait for happiness to come instead of going to work and making it. While they wait they torment themselves with borrowed troubles, with fears, forebodings, morbid fancies and moody spirits. Then they are all unfitted for happiness, under any circumstances. Sometimes they cherish unchaste ambition, covet some fancied or real good which they do not deserve and could not enjoy if it were theirs. Wealth they have not earned, honors they have not won, attention they have not merited. Love which their selfishness only craves.

Sometimes they undervalue the good they do possess. They throw away the pearls in hand for some beyond their reach and often less valuable. They trample the flowers about them under their feet. They long for some never seen, but only heard or read of. They forget present duties and joys in future and far-off visions. Sometimes they shade the present with every cloud of the past. Although surrounded by a thousand inviting duties and pleasures, revel in sad memories with a kind of morbid relish for the stimulus of their misery. Sometimes forgetting the past and present, they live in the future. Not in its probable realities, but in its most improbable visions and unreal creations, now of good and then of evil. They wholly unfit their minds for real life and enjoyments. These morbid and improper states of mind are too prevalent among some persons. They excite that nervous irritability which is so productive of pining regrets and fretful complaints. They make that large class of fretters who enjoy no peace themselves nor permit others to enjoy it. In the domestic circle, they fret their life away. Everything goes wrong with them because they make it so. The smallest annoyances chafe them as though they were unbearable aggravations. Their business and duties trouble them as though such things were not good. Pleasure they never seem to know because they never get ready to enjoy it. Even the common movements of Providence, are all wrong with them. The weather is never as it should be. The seasons roll badly. The sun is never properly tempered. The climate is always charged with a multitude of vices. The winds are everlastingly perverse, either too high or too low blowing dust in everybody's face or not fanning them as they should. The earth is ever out of humor, too dry or too wet, too muddy or dusty. The people are just about like it. Something is wrong all the time and the wrong is always just about them. Their home is the worst of anybody's. Their street and their neighborhood is the most unpleasant to be found. Nobody else has so many annoyances as they. Their lot is harder than falls to common mortals. They have to work harder and always did. They have less and always expect to. They have seen more trouble than other folks know anything about.

They are never so well as their neighbors and they always charge all their unhappiness upon those nearest connected with them. They never dream that they are themselves the authors of it all. Such people are to be pitied. Of all the people in the world, they deserve most our compassion. They are good people in many respects, very benevolent, very conscientious, very pious, but very annoying to themselves and others. As a general rule, their goodness makes them more difficult to cure of their evil. They cannot be led to see that they are at fault. Knowing their virtues, they cannot see their faults. They do not perhaps, overestimate their virtues. But they fail to see what they lack, and this they always charge upon others, often upon those who love them best. They see other's actions through the shadow of their own fretful and gloomy spirits. Hence it is that, they see their own faults as existing in those about them. Like a defect in the eye produces the appearance of a corresponding defect in every object toward which it is turned. This defect in character is more generally the result of vicious or improper habits of mind than any constitutional idiosyncrasy. It is the result of the indulgence of gloomy thoughts, morbid fancies, inordinate ambition, habitual melancholy, a complaining, fault finding disposition.

A fretting man or woman is one of the most unlovable objects in the world. A wasp is a comfortable house-mate in comparison. It only stings when disturbed. But an habitual fretter buzzes if he doesn't sting, with or without provocation. Children and others cease to respect the authority or obey the commands of a complaining, worrisome, exacting parent or companion. They know that "barking dogs don't bite," and fretters don't strike.

If we are faultless, we should not be so much annoyed by the defects of those with whom we associate. If we were to acknowledge honestly that we have not virtue enough to bear patiently with our neighbors' weaknesses, we should show our own imperfection and this alarms our vanity.

He who frets is never the one who mends, heals or repairs evils. He discourages, enfeebles and too often disables those around him, who but for the gloom and depression of his company would do good work and keep up brave cheer. When the fretter is one who is beloved whose nearness of relation is to us, it makes his fretting seem almost like a personal reproach. Then the misery of it becomes indeed insupportable. Most men call fretting a minor fault and not a vice. There is no vice except drunkenness, which can so utterly destroy the peace, the happiness of a home. We never knew a scolding person that was able to govern a family. What makes people scold? Because they cannot govern themselves. How can they govern others? Those who govern well are generally calm. They are prompt and resolute, but steady.

It is not work that kills men, it is worry. Work is healthy. You can hardly put more on a man than he can bear. Worry is rust upon the blade. It is not the revolution that destroys the machinery, but the friction. Fear secretes acids, but love and trust are sweet juices. The man or woman who goes through the world grumbling and fretting is not only violating the laws of God, but sins against the peace and harmony of society.

There are two things about which we should never grumble. The first is that which we cannot help and the other that which we can help.

Fault Finding

NEVER should we employ ourselves to discover the faults of others, but look to our own. You had better find out one of your own faults than ten of your neighbor's. When a thing does not suit you, think of some pleasant quality in it. There is nothing so bad as it might be. Whenever you catch yourself in a fault-finding remark, say some approving one in the same breath and you will soon be cured. Since the best of us have too many infirmities to answer for, says Dean Swift, we ought not to be too severe on those of others. Therefore if our brother is in trouble, we ought to help without inquiring over-seriously what produced it.

Those who have the fewest resources in themselves seek the food of their self-love elsewhere. The most ignorant people find most to laugh at in strangers. True worth does not exult in the faults and deficiency of others. There are some who seem to purposely treasure up things that are disagreeable. The tongue that feeds on mischief, the babbling, the tattling, the sly whispering, the impertinent meddling, all these tongues are trespassing on the community constantly. Slander can swallow perjury like water, turn truth into falsehood, good into evil and innocence into crime.

Beecher says: "When the absent are spoken of, some will speak gold of them, some silver, some iron, some lead, and some always speak dirt. They have a natural attraction toward what is evil and think it shows penetration in them. As a cat watching for mice does not look up though an elephant goes by, so they are so busy mousing for defects that they let great excellences pass them unnoticed. I will not say that it is not CHRISTIAN to make beads of others' faults and tell them over every day. I say it is INFERNAL. If you want to know how the devil feels, you do know if you are such a one."

What a world of gossip would be prevented, if it were only remembered that a person who tells you the faults of others intends to tell others of your faults. Everyone has his faults. Every man his ruling passion. The eye that sees all things sees not itself. To a sensitive, affectionate mind every act of finding fault is an act of pain. It is only when we have become callous to the world that we are able to play with unconcern the parts of persecutors and slanderers. He who is first to condemn will be often the last to forgive.

Envy and Slander

ENVY'S memory is nothing but a row of hooks to hang up grudges on. Some people's sensibility is a mere bundle of aversions and you hear them display and parade it. Not in the things and persons they are attached to, but those they "cannot bear."

It began with Satan. When he fell, he could see nothing to please him in Paradise. He envied our first parents in innocence, therefore tempted them to sin. Envy is always degrading or misrepresenting things which are excellent. Point out a pious person and ask the envious man what he thinks of him. He will say he is a hypocrite or deceitful. Praise a man of high education or great abilities and he will say he is too proud of his attainments. Mention a beautiful woman and he will slander her chastity. In this way, he depreciates every pleasing object. To envy a man, is to allow him to be superior. The brightness of prosperity that surrounds others, pains the eyes of the envious man more than the meridian rays of the sun. It brings into action jealousy, revenge, falsehood, and the basest passions of the fallen nature of man.

Envy seeks to elevate itself by the degradation of others. It detests the sound of another's praise and deems no renown that must be shared.

And what produces envy? The excellence of another. Humiliating deduction! Envy is only the expression of inferiority. The homage paid to excellence. Envy is unquestionably a high compliment, but a most ungracious one. An envious man pines as much at the manner in which his neighbors live, as if he maintained them. Some people as much envy others a good name as they want it themselves. Envy is fixed on merit. Like a sore eye, is offended with anything that is bright. Envy increases in exact proportion with fame. The man that makes a character, makes enemies. Virtue is not secure against envy. Evil men will lessen what they are not able to imitate. If a man is good, he is envied. If evil, himself is envious. Envious people are doubly miserable in being afflicted with others' prosperity and their own adversity.

Envy is a weed that grows in all soils and climates. It is no less luxuriant in the country than in the court. It is not confined to any rank of men or extent of fortune. It rages in the breasts of all degrees. Envy keeps all sorts of company and wiggles itself into the liking of the most contrary natures and dispositions. Yet it carries so much poison and venom

with it, that it alienates the affections from heaven and raises rebellion against God. It is worth our utmost care to
watch it in all its disguises and approaches. That if we do
discover it in its first entrance, to dislodge it before it procures a shelter or retiring place and conceals itself.

Slander with its forked tongue is charged with poison. It
searches all corners of the world for victims. It sacrifices the
high and the low, the king and the peasant, the rich and the
poor, the matron and maid, the living and the dead. It
delights most in destroying worth and corrupting innocence.

It is a melancholy reflection upon human nature to see
how small a matter will put the ball of scandal in motion. A
mere hint, a significant look, a mysterious countenance.
Then directing it to a particular person, often gives an alarm-
ing force to it. A mere interrogatory is converted into an
affirmative assertion. The cry of mad dog is raised and the
mass join in the chase. So a mortal wound is inflicted on the
innocent and meritorious, perhaps by one who had no ill-will
or desire to do harm.

There is a sad propensity in our fallen nature to listen to
the retailers of petty scandal. With many it is the spice of
conversation, the exhilarating gas of their minds. Without
any intention of doing essential injury to a neighbor, a careless remark relative to some minor fault may be seized by a
babbler. As it passes through the babbling tribe, each one
adds to its bulk and gives its color a darker hue, untill it
assumes the magnitude and blackness of base slander. Few
are without visible faults. Most persons are sometimes
inconsistent. Upon the faults and mistakes, petty scandal
delights to feast. Envy and jealousy can start the blood-
hound of suspicion. An unjust and unfavorable innuendo is

started against a person of unblemished character. It gathers force as it is rolled through Babbletown. It soon assumes the dignity of a problem. Before truth can get her shoes on, a deep and damning stain has been stamped on the fair fame of an innocent victim by an unknown hand. The source is more difficult to find than that of the Nile.

Deal tenderly with the absent. Say nothing to inflict a wound on their reputation. They may be wrong and wicked, yet your knowledge of it does not oblige you to disclose their character except to save others from injury. Then, do it in a way that bespeaks a spirit of kindness for the absent offender. Be not hasty to credit evil reports. They are often the result of misunderstanding or of evil design. They may proceed from an exaggerated or partial disclosure of facts. Wait and learn the whole story before you decide. Then believe just what evidence compels you to and no more. Even then take heed not to indulge the least unkindness, else you dissipate all the spirit of prayer for them and unnerve yourself for doing them good. We are nearer the truth in thinking well of people than ill. Human nature is a tree bearing good as well as evil, but our eyes are wide open to the latter and half closed to the former. Believe but half the ill and credit twice the good said of your neighbor.

An injurious rumor once attached to a person's name, will remain beside it a blemish and doubt forever. Especially is this true of the fair sex, many of whom have from this cause withered and melted in their youth like snow in the spring, only to shed tears of sadness over the world's unkindness and "man's inhumanity to man."

There is a natural inclination in almost all persons to pelt others with stones. Our right hands ache to throw them.

There is such wicked enjoyment in seeing the victims dodge and flinch and run. This is human nature in the rough. There are so many who never get out of the rough. There are multitudes of respectable people who get exquisite pleasure in making others smart.

If Christ possesses us wholly and we have been transformed by His spirit, there is no disposition to stone our neighbor even if at fault. It is not in the genius of Christianity to do it. It is a cancer in the soul that must be cut out, burned out or purged out of the blood or it will kill.

Pride

HE that is proud eats himself up. Pride is his own glass, his own trumpet, his own chronicle. Whatever praises itself in the deed, devours the deed in praise. Pride is like an empty bag and who can stand such a thing upright? It is hollow and heartless. Like a drum, makes more noise from its very emptiness. What is there in us to induce such a sentiment? Who can say with truth, "I am better than my neighbor?" Some shrewd philosopher has said, that if the best man's faults were written on his forehead they would make him pull his hat over his eyes! Ah, there is so much good in those who are evil, and so much that is bad in the best. It ill becomes us to judge our neighbors harshly or set ourselves up to saints at their expense. Let those who feel above their fellows, view the heights above themselves and realize their littleness. For as there is none so vile, but that a more vile hath been known, so there is no saint, but a more holy one can be named.

When one asked a philosopher what the great God was doing, he replied, "His whole employment is to lift up the humble and to cast down the proud." And indeed, there is no one sin which the Almighty seems more determined to punish than this. The examples of God's displeasure against it are most strikingly exhibited in the history of Pharaoh, Hezekiah, Haman, Nebuchadnezzar, and Herod.

Pride is generally the effect of ignorance. Pride and folly attend each other. Ignorance and pride keep constant company. Pride joined with many virtues chokes them all. Pride is harmful to happiness. It is told of the French family of the Duke de Levis that they have a picture in their pedigree in which Noah is represented going into the ark, and carrying a small trunk on which is written, "Papers belonging to the Levis family." Pride is the mist that vapors round insignificance. We can conceive of nothing so little or ridiculous as pride. It is a mixture of insensibility and ill-nature in which it is hard to say which has the largest share. Pride is as loud a beggar as want and a great deal more saucy. Knavery and pride are often united. Pride breakfasted with Plenty, dined with Poverty and supperd with Infamy. Pride would rather at any time go out of its way, than come behind.

Pride must have a fall. Solomon said, pride goeth before destruction. Of all human actions, pride the most seldom obtains its end. While it aims at honor and reputation, it reaps contempt and derision. Pride and ill-nature will be hated in spite of all the wealth and greatness in the world. Civility is always safe, but pride creates enemies. As liberality makes friends of enemies, so pride makes enemies of friends. Say Dean Swift: "If a proud man makes me keep my distance, the comfort is, he at the same time keeps his." Proud men have friends neither in prosperity because they know nobody, nor in adversity because nobody knows them. There is an honest pride such as makes one ashamed to do an evil act. Its such a degree of self-esteem as makes one above doing an injury to anyone. But it is the pride which sets one above his fellows, that we deprecate. That spirit which demands homage to itself as being better and greater than others. In the name of good sense, how can anyone feel that way when it is realized that the entire life of a man is but a moment in the scale of eternity. That in a few short days at most, we must all go from here. When the soul is about to depart, what does it matter whether a man die on a throne or in the dust?

Pride is a virtue, let not the moralist be scandalized. Pride is also a vice. Pride like ambition is sometimes virtuous and sometimes vicious, according to the character in which it is found. The object to which it is directed. As a principle, it is the parent of almost every virtue and every vice. Everything that pleases and displeases in mankind. As the effects are so very different, nothing is more easy to discover even to ourselves, whether the pride that produces them is virtuous or vicious. The first object of virtuous pride is rectitude and the next independence. Pride may be allowed to this or that degree or a man could not keep his dignity. In gluttony there must be eating, in drunkenness there must be drinking. It is not the eating or drinking that must be blamed, but the excess. So in pride.

There is an eternal war with want on one hand and proud ambition on the other. This trying to be "somebody," and forgetting that it is not necessary to be goldwashed. To have a silver spoon in one's mouth, in order to reach that good in life's journey. There are plenty of "somebodies" among the honest poor and plenty of "nobodies" among the dainty rich. Pride and poverty are the most ill-assorted companions that can meet. They live in a state of continual warfare and the sacrifices they exact from each other, like those claimed by enemies to establish a hollow peace, only serve to increase their discord.

Proud persons in general think of nothing but themselves. They imagine that all the world thinks about them too. They suppose that they are the subject of almost every conversation and fancy every wheel which moves in society has some relation to them. People of this sort desire to know what is said of them. As they have no conception that any but great things are said of them, they are extremely solicitous to know them.

Pride and charity are two parallels never put asunder. Charity feeds the poor, so does pride. Charity builds a hospital, so does pride. In this they differ, charity gives her glory to God, pride gives her glory to man.

Likeness begets love, yet proud men hate each other. Pride makes us esteem ourselves. Vanity makes us desire the esteem of others. It is just to say that a man is too proud to be vain. The pride of wealth is contemptible. The pride of learning is pitiable. The pride of dignity is ridiculous. To be proud of knowledge, is to be blind in the light. To be proud of authority, is to make your rise your downfall. The sun appears largest when about to set, so does a proud man swell most magnificently just before an explosion.

No two feelings of the human mind are more opposite than pride and humility. Pride is founded on a high opinion of ourselves, humility on the consciousness of the want of merit. Pride is the offspring of ignorance. Humility is the child of wisdom. Pride hardens the heart. Humility softens the temper and disposition. Pride is deaf to the clamors of conscience. Humility listens with reverence to the monitor within. And finally, pride rejects the counsels of reason, the voice of experience, and the dictates of religion. While humility with a docile spirit, thankfully receives instruction from all who address her in the garb of truth.

It was pride that changed angels into devils. It is humility that makes men as angels. The best way to humble a proud man is to take no notice of him. Men are sometimes accused of pride, merely because their accusers would be proud themselves if they were in their places. There are those who despise pride with a greater pride. To quell the pride of even the greatest, we should reflect how much we owe to others and how little to ourselves.

When a man's pride is thoroughly subdued, it is like the sides of Mount AEtna. It was terrible while the eruption lasted and the lava flowed, but when that is past and the lava is turned into soil, it grows vineyards and olive trees up to the very top.

Manners

MANNERS are different in every country, but true politeness is everywhere the same. Manners which take up so much of our attention, are only artificial helps which ignorance assumes in order to imitate politeness. Politeness is the result of good sense and good nature. He who assumes airs of importance exhibits his credentials of insignificance. There is no policy like politeness. A good manner is the best thing in the world to get a good name or to supply the want of it. Good manners are a part of good morals and it is as much our duty as our interest to practice in both. Good manners is the art of making those around us easy. Whoever makes the fewest persons uneasy, is the best bred man in the company. Good manners should begin at home. Good manners is the result of much good sense, some good nature, and a little self-denial for the sake of others.

Good manners are not learned so much as acquired by habit. We must be courteous, agreeable, civil and kind at home. Then it will become a kind of second nature everywhere. A course rough manner at home results in a habit of roughness, which we cannot lay off if we try. The most agreeable persons in company are those who are the most agreeable at home. Home is the school for all the best things.

Good manners are an essential part of life-education. The art of being agreeable is to be well pleased with all company and to be entertained with them, rather than to bring entertainment to them. If a man have common sense and something friendly in his behavior, it puts at ease men's minds more than those without this disposition. Social courtesies should emanate from the heart, for remember always that the worth of manners consists in their being the sincere expression of feelings. Like the dial of the watch, they should indicate that the work within is good and true.

One of the most marked tests of character is the manner in which we conduct ourselves toward others. It pleases others because it indicates respect for their personality. It also gives tenfold more pleasure to ourselves. Every man may to a large extent, be a self-educator in good behavior as in anything else. He can be civil and kind if he will, though he may have not a penny to his name.

If dignity exists in the mind, it will not be wanting in manners. It is difficult to like a man who, though he may not pull your nose, habitually wounds your self-respect. He takes pride in saying disagreeable things to you. There are others who are dreadfully condescending. They cannot avoid seizing upon every small opportunity of making their greatness felt.

Agreeable manners contribute wonderfully to a man's success. Take two men possessing equal advantages in every other respect, but let one be kind, obliging and conciliating. The other disobliging, rude, harsh and insolent and the one will become rich while the other will starve.

A person it is true may be superficially polite, but the very conditions of his obligations to others is necessary in mind and soul. Therefore, in word and deed be polite.

Wit

GENUINE good humor can be compared to a kaleidoscope. Every time it is shaken, it presents new and beautiful figures. He who endeavors to oblige the company by his good-nature never fails of being beloved. He who strives to entertain it by his good sense never fails of being esteemed. But he who is continually aiming to be witty, it is his misfortune. For we seldom admire the wit, when we dislike the humor. Wit and wisdom may be found in the same person, but when the former is flashy its glare hides the latter.

Wit loses its respect with the good when seen in company with malice. To laugh at the joke which plants a thorn in another's breast, is to become a principal in the mischief. Let your wit rather serve you for a buckler to defend yourself with a humorous reply, than a sword to wound others. Remember that a word cuts deeper than a sharp weapon, and the wound it makes is longer curing. Let those who have it endeavor to control it, and those who don't make better use of the sense they have.

Truth

GOD is the Author of truth, the devil the father of lies. If the telling of a truth shall endanger your life, the Author of truth will protect you from the danger.

The ancient Persians instructed their children only in three things, to manage a horse, to shoot dexterously with the bow, and TO SPEAK THE TRUTH. This show of importance it was to fix this virtuous habit on the minds of youth. Truth is the foundation of all knowledge and the cement of all society. Truth is a standard according to which all things are to be judged. When we appeal to it, it should be with sincerity of purpose and honesty of feeling. The soul open to what is honest, right, and true. Our only desire should be to judge of things as they really are. Candidly and truly to acknowledge and receive them as such. For this is truth, the perception and representation of things as they are.

Truth, divine in nature and pure before heaven is the

foundation of all human excellence. The keystone of all sincere affection, the seal of true discipleship with the Good Shepherd. It is impossible to love one in whose truthfulness we cannot confide. Truth or silence should be our alternative.

Woe to falsehood! It affords no relief to the breast like truth. It gives us no comfort, pains him who forges it, and like an arrow misdirected, flies back and wounds the archer. A contract with truth must be to love, cherish, and obey her not only till death, but beyond it. This is a union that must survive not only death but time, the conqueror of death. There is nothing which all mankind admire so much as simple truth. It exhibits at once a strength of character and integrity of purpose in which all are willing to confide.

Which one of the painters or sculptors will or can give us a correct and faithful delineation and embodiment of truth?

How may we place it upon our alters and in our halls in public and private places? That truth may be honored and worshiped in every home and in every heart!

No idea can be formed of the important effect truth would produce. The most perfect confidence would not be the least of its benefits and the most perfect inward tranquility. Exaggeration is but another name for falsehood. To exaggerate, is to pass the bounds of truth. How can those bounds be passed without entering upon the precincts of falsehood? There can be but a true or a false representation. There can be no medium. What is not true must be false.

Nothing can be more easy than to speak truth. The unwise, the poor, the ignoble, the youthful, can all equally practice it. Nothing can be more difficult than to speak falsely. The wise, the rich, the great, the aged have all failed in their attempts. Can there be offered a more obtainable, a more gratifying, a more noble object of emulation to the youthful heart? A parent can do no better than to teach always to tell the truth by being truthful!

Patience

No man in any condition of life can pass his days with tolerable comfort without patience. It is of universal use. Without it prosperity will be continually disturbed, and adversity will be clouded with double darkness. He who is without patience will be uneasy and troublesome to all with whom he is connected, and will be more troublesome to himself than to any other. The loud complaint, the querulous temper and fretful spirit, disgrace every character. We weaken the sympathy of others and estrange them from offices of kindness and comfort. But to maintain a steady and unbroken mind amid all the shocks of adversity, forms the highest honor of man. Afflictions, supported by patience and surmounted by fortitude, give the last finishing stroke to the heroic and the virtuous character.

Patience is the guardian of faith, the preserver of peace, the cherished of love, the teacher of humility. Patience governs the flesh, strengthens the spirit, sweetens the temper, stifles anger, extinguishes envy and subdues pride. Patience bridles the tongue, restrains the hand, tramples on temptations, endures persecutions, and consummates martyrdom.

Patience produces unity in the church, loyalty in the state, harmony in families and societies. She comforts the poor and moderates the rich. She makes us humble in prosperity, cheerful in adversity and is unmoved by reproach. She teaches us to forgive those who have injured us and to be the first in asking the forgiveness of those whom we have injured. She delights the faithful and invites the unbelieving. She adorns the woman and approves the man. Patience is beautiful in either sex and every age.

Patience has been defined as the "courage of virtue," the principle that enables us to lessen pain of mind or body. An emotion that does not so much add to the number of joys, as it tends to diminish the number of sufferings. If life is to abound with pains and troubles by the errors and crimes of man, it is no small advantage to have a faculty that enables us to soften these pains and to improve these troubles. How powerful and extensive the influence of patience to judge, but from experience. Those who have known most bodily pain can best testify its power. Impatience in fact, by inducing restlessness and irritation, not only doubles every pang and prolongs suffering, but often creates the trials to be endured. In pains of the body this is the case, but more potently is it so in all mental affliction.

We must be satisfied to work energetically with a purpose and wait the results with patience. Buffon has even said of patience that it is genius. The power of great men consisting in their power of continuous working and waiting. All progress of the best kind is slow. But to him who works faithfully and in the right spirit, be sure that the reward will be vouchsafed in its own good time. We must continually apply ourselves to right pursuits and we cannot fail to advance steadily, though it may be unconsciously.

Always have a good stock of patience laid by, and be

sure you put it where you can easily find it. Cherish patience as your favorite virtue, always keep it about you. You will find use for it more often than all the rest. You can do anything if you will only have patience. Water may be carried in a sieve, if you only wait till it freezes. Those who at the commencement of their career meet with less applause than they deserve, frequently gain more than they deserve at the end of it.

He has made a good progress in business that has thought well of it beforehand. Some do first and think afterwards. That is done soon enough which is done well. Soon ripe, soon rotten. He that would enjoy the fruit must not gather the flower. Patience affords us a shield to defend ourselves, and innocence denies us a sword to defend others. Knowledge is power, but it is one of the slowest because one of the most durable of agencies. Continued exertion and not hasty efforts, leads to success. What cannot be cured must be endured. How poor are they who have not patience!

Contentment

"Poor and content is rich, and rich enough'
But riches endless is as poor as winter
To him that always fears he shall be poor."

EVERY man either is rich or may be so, though not all in one and the same wealth. Some have abundance and rejoice in it. Some a competency and are content. Some have nothing and have a mind desiring nothing. He that has most, wants something. He that has least, something is supplied.

Wherein, the mind that is made rich, may well possess him with the thought of wanting more. Who whistles out more content than the small farmer or sings more merrily than the cobbler? Content dwells with those who are out of the eye of the world, whom she has never trained with her ornaments, her toils, or her lures. Wealth is like learning, in that our greater knowledge is only a larger sight of our wants. Desires fulfilled only teach us to desire more. We that at first were pleased after gaining that desire, have now become unfulfilled.

We knew a man who had health and riches and several houses all beautiful and ready furnished. He would often trouble himself and family to be moving from one house to another. Being asked by a friend why he moved so often from one house to another, replied: "It was to find content in some of them." But his friend knowing his temper told him, "If he would find content in any of his houses, he must leave himself behind. For content will never dwell, but in a meek and quiet soul."

We sometimes go along the street to see how few people there are whose faces look as though any joy had come down and sung in their souls. We can see lines of thought, care, and fear. Money lines, shrewd, grasping lines, but how few happy lines. The rarest feeling that ever lights the human face is the contentment of a loving soul. Sit on the steps of the Exchange on Wall Street and you will behold a drama which is better than a thousand theaters, for all the actors are real. We can find a score of handsome faces where we can find one happy face. An eccentric wealthy man stuck up a board in a field on his estate. He painted the following: "I will give this field to any man contented." He soon had an applicant. "Well sir, are you a contented man?" "Yes sir, very." "Then what do you want with my field?" The applicant did not stop to reply.

True it is that whoever would have this jewel of contentment, must come with minds divested of all ambitious and covetous thoughts or they are never likely to obtain it. The foundation of content must spring up in a man's own mind. He has little knowledge of human nature to seek happiness by changing anything, but his own disposition.

He will waste his life in fruitless efforts and multiply the griefs which he purposes to remove. No man can tell whether he is rich or poor by turning his ledger. It is the heart that makes a man rich. He is rich or poor according to what he is, not according to what he has.

Enjoy the present, whatever it may be and be not desirous for the future. If you take your foot from the present standing and thrust it forward to tomorrow's event, you are in a restless condition. It is like refusing to quench your present thirst by fearing you will want to drink the next day. Let your trouble tarry, till its own day comes. Enjoy the blessings of this day and the evils of it bear patiently, for this day is ours. We are dead to yesterday and not yet born to tomorrow. A contented mind is the best blessing a man can enjoy in this world. If in the present life his happiness arises from the subduing of his desires, it will arise in the next from the gratification of them.

Contentment is felicity. Few are the real wants of man. Like a majority of his troubles, they are more imaginary than real. Some well persons want to be better, take medicine and become sick in good earnest. Some have wealth, want more and enter into some new business they don't understand and become poor. Many who are surrounded by all the substantial comforts of life become discontented because a wealthier neighbor sports a carriage, his lady has a Brussels carpet and mahogany chairs, entertains parties or makes more show in the world than they. Like a monkey, they attempt to imitate all they see that is deemed fashionable. They make a dash for contentment. They dash out their comfortable store of wealth, sometimes close the farce with a tragedy and dash their brains out with a blue pill. They covet, they wish and wishes are as prolific as rabbits. One imaginary want, like a stool pigeon, brings flocks of others. The mind becomes so overwhelmed that it loses sight of all the real comforts in possession.

Contentment consists not in adding more fuel, but in taking away some fire. Not in multiplying wealth, but in subtracting men's desires. Worldly riches, like nuts, tear men's clothing in getting them, spoil the teeth in cracking them, but fill not the belly in eating them. Alexander saw Diogenes sitting in the warm sun and asked what he should do for him. He desired no more than that Alexander would stand out of his sunshine and not take from him what he could not give. A quiet and contented mind is the supreme good. It is the utmost happiness a man is capable of in this world. The maintaining of such uninterrupted tranquility of spirit is the very crown and glory of wisdom. Nature teaches us to live, but wisdom teaches us to live contented.

Contentment is opposed to fortune and opinion. It is the wealth of nature for it gives everything we either want or need. The discontents of the poor are much easier allayed than those of the rich. Solon being asked by Croesus, who in the world was happier than himself though he was poor, was a good man and content with what he had. He died in a good old age. No line holds the anchor of contentment so fast as a good conscience.

Those who are content with a little deserve much. Those who deserve much are far the more likely persons to be contented with a little. Contentment is more often made of cheap materials than of dear ones. Shakespeare's shepherd said: "Sir, I am a true laborer, I earn what I wear; owe no man hate; envy no man's happiness; glad of other men's good, contented with my farm." Be contented with enough. You may butter your bread until you are unable to eat it. Enough is as good as a feast. When you feel dissatisfied with your circumstances, look at those beneath you. John Quincy Adams said, "It is only necessary to possess honors to know how little they contribute to happiness. I would rather be shut up in a very modest cottage, with my books, my family and a few old friends, dining on bacon and hominy and let the world roll by, than to occupy the most high places which human power can give."

Cheerfulness

GOD bless the cheerful person, man, woman, child, young, old, illiterate, educated, handsome, or homely. Over and above every other social trait, stands cheerfulness. What the sun is to nature, what the stars are to night, what God is to the stricken heart which knows how to lean on Him are cheerful people in the house and by the wayside. Man recognizes the magic of a cheerful influence in woman more quickly and more willingly than the potency of dazzling genius, commanding worth, or even beauty.

If we are cheerful and contented, all nature smiles with us. The air seems more balmy, the sky more clear, the ground has a brighter green, the trees have a richer foliage, the flowers a more fragrant smell, the birds sing more sweetly and the sun, moon, and stars all appear more beautiful.

Cheerfulness! How sweet in infancy, how lovely in youth, how saintly in age! There are a few noble natures whose very presence carries sunshine which means pity for the poor, sympathy for the suffering, help for the unfortunate and kindness toward all. How such a face enlivens every other face it meets and carries into every company liveliness, joy, and gladness! But the scowl and frown begotten in a selfish heart and manifesting itself in daily almost hourly fretfulness, complaining, fault-finding, angry criticisms, spiteful comments on the motives and actions of others. How they thin the cheek, shrivel the face, sour and sadden the countenance! No joy in the heart, no nobility in the soul, no generosity in the nature. The whole character as cold as an iceberg, as hard as Alpine rock, as arid as the wastes of Sahara! Reader, which of these countenances are you cultivating? If you find yourself losing all confidence in human nature, you are nearing an old age of vinegar, of wormwood and of gall. Not a mourner will follow your solitary coffin, not one tear-drop shall ever fall on your forgotten grave.

Look at the bright side. Keep the sunshine of a living faith in the heart. Do not let the shadow of discouragement and despondency fall on your path. However weary you may be, the promises of God will like the stars at night never cease to shine, to cheer and to strengthen. Learn to wait as well as labor. The best harvests are the longest in ripening. It is not pleasant to work in the earth plucking the ugly tares and weeds, but it is as necessary as sowing the seed. The harder the task the more need of singing. A hopeful spirit will discern the silver lining of the darkest cloud. Behind all the planning and doing with its discouragements and hindrances, shines the light of Divine promise and help. You are God's workers. It is for you to be faithful. He gives the increase.

Be cheerful, for it is the only happy life. The times may be hard, but it will make them no easier to wear a gloomy and sad countenance. It is the sunshine and not the cloud that makes the flower. There is always that before and around us which should fill the heart with warmth. The sky is blue ten times where it is black once. You have troubles, it may be, so have others. None are free of them, perhaps it is as well that none should be. They give sinew and tone to life, fortitude and courage to man. That would be a dull sea and the sailor would never get skill where there was nothing to disturb the surface of the ocean. It is the duty of everyone to extract all the happiness and enjoyment he can without and within him. And above all, he should look on the bright side of things. What if things do look a little dark? The lane will turn and the night will end in broad day. In the long run, the great balance rights itself. What is ill, becomes well. What is wrong, becomes right. Men are not made to hang down heads or lips. Those who do, only show that they are departing from the paths of true common sense and right. There is more virtue in one sunbeam than a whole hemisphere of cloud and gloom. Cultivate what is warm and genial not the cold and repulsive, the dark and morose. Don't neglect your duty. Live down prejudice.

We always know the cheerful person by their hearty "good morning." Dear reader, don't forget to say it. Say it to your parents, your brothers and sisters, your schoolmates, your teachers and associates. Say it cheerfully and with a smile. It will do you good and do your friends good. It is of all kind, cheerful greetings, that cheer the discouraged, rest the tired one and somehow make the wheels of time run more smoothly. Be liberal, and let no morning or evening pass that you do not help at least to brighten it by your smiles and cheerful words.

The cheerful are busy. When trouble knocks at your door or rings the bell, he will generally retire if you send him word "Engaged." Active minds are seldom troubled with gloomy forebodings. These come up only from the stagnant depths of a spirit unstirred by generous impulses or the blessed necessities of honest toil.

What shall we say by way of commending that sweet cheerfulness of a mother, wife, sister or daughter they bring to the home. Amid the weariness and cares of life, the troubles of family, the thoughts and toils of thrift, order, and comfort, the women are there amid the varieties of temper, crosslines of taste and inclination found in a large household. To maintain a heart full of good nature and a face always bright with cheerfulness, this is a perpetual festivity. Its that exhaustless patience and self-control, kindness, and tact which spring from good sense and brave purpose. Its real exhibition is in the dark background of real adversity. When the strong man has bowed himself and his brow is knit and creased, then we see the whole life of the household hang on the women. With solitudes of her own, she has an eye or an ear for everyone but herself. She is suggestive of remedies, hopeful in extremities, helpful in kind words and affectionate smiles, morning, noon, or night. The medicine, the light, the heart of a whole household. God bless that bright, sunny face!

There is enough in this world to complain about and find fault with if men have the disposition. We often travel on a hard and uneven road, but with a cheerful spirit and a heart to praise God for his mercies, we may walk therein with great comfort and come to the end of our journey in peace.

Let us try to be like the sunshiny member of the family who has the inestimable art to make all duty seem pleasant, all self-denial and exertion easy and desirable, even disappointment not so blank and crushing. They are like a bracing, crisp, frosty atmosphere throughout the home, without a suspicion of the element that chills and pinches. You have known people within whose influence you felt cheerful, amiable, and hopeful, equal to anything! Oh! for that blessed power and for God's grace to exercise it rightly! I do not know a more enviable gift than the energy to sway others to good. To diffuse around us an atmosphere of cheerfulness, piety, truthfulness, generosity and over-looking insults. It is not a matter of great talent. Not entirely a matter of great energy, but rather of earnestness and honesty and of that quiet, constant energy like a soft gentle rain penetrating the soil. It is rather a grace than a gift. We all know where all grace is to be had freely for the asking.

Happiness

WRITERS of every age have endeavored to show that pleasure is in us and not in the object offered for our amusement. If the soul is happily disposed, everything becomes capable of affording entertainment and distress will almost want a name.

The fountain of content must spring up in the mind and he who seeks happiness by changing anything but his own disposition, will waste his life in fruitless efforts. He will multiply the griefs he purposes to remove.

Man is in all respects constituted to be happy. Hence, it is that he sees goodness around him in proportion to the goodness that is within him. It is also for this reason that when he calls the evil that is within him, outside of him, it also appears so. If man therefore chooses that which does not seem to him good, he can in a measure enjoy it. Goodness and truth leaves something to be re-enjoyed in memory and after life, while falseness and evil leaves regret, disappointment and suffering.

A great part of the unhappiness of men arises not so much from their situations or circumstances as from their pride, vanity, and ambitious expectations. In order to be happy, these dispositions must be subdued. We must always keep before our eyes such views of the world as shall prevent our expecting more from it than it is designed to afford. We destroy our joys by devouring them beforehand with too eager expectation. We ruin the happiness of life when we attempt to raise it too high. Mendedemus was told one day that happiness was to have whatever we desire. "Yes," said he, "but it is a much greater happiness to desire nothing but what we have."

The idea has been transmitted from generation to generation that happiness is one large and beautiful precious stone. A single gem so rare that our search after it is vain effort, fruitless and hopeless. It is not so. Happiness is a mosaic composed of many smaller stones. Each taken apart and viewed singly may be of little value, but when all are grouped together and judiciously combined and set they form a pleasing and graceful whole. A costly jewel.

Trample not under foot the little pleasures. A gracious Providence scatters in the daily path while you are in eager search after some great and exciting joy. We can adorn the head, but we cannot satisfy the heart. Happiness is in us, not in things. We talk of wealth, fame, and power as undeniable sources of enjoyment. Limited fortune, obscurity, and insignificance as incompatible with happiness. Le Droz who wrote a treatise on happiness, describes the conditions necessary for it as consisting of the greatest fortitude to resist and endure the ills and pains of life, united with the most keen sensibility to enjoy its pleasures and delights.

There is little real happiness on earth because we do not look in the right place. We look where it is not, in outward circumstance and external good. We neglect to look where alone it dwells, in the chambers of the heart and soul.

Hope

THE poet Hesiod tells us that the misery of all mankind were included in a great box and that Pandora took off the lid, by which means all of them came abroad, only hope remained at the bottom. Hope is the principal antidote that keeps our heart from bursting under the pressure of evils. It is that flattering mirror that gives us a prospect of some greater good. Some call hope the manna from heaven that comforts us in all extremities. Others call hope the pleasant flatterer that caresses the unhappy with expectations of happiness for the future. When all other things fail us, hope stands by us to the last. Hope gives freedom to the captive when chained to the oar, health to the sick, victory to the defeated, and wealth to the beggar.

True hope is based on energy of character. A strong mind always hopes and has always cause to hope. It knows the mutability of human affairs and how slight circumstance may change the whole course of events, such a spirit rests upon itself. It is not confined to partial views or to one particular object. If at last all should be lost, it has saved itself. Its own integrity and worth. Hope awakens courage while despondency is the last of all evils. It is the abandonment of good. The giving up of the battle of life with dead nothingness. He who can implant courage in the human soul is the best physician.

Earthly hope like fear is confined to this dim spot on which we live, move, and have our being. It is excluded from heaven or hell. It is a dashing blade with a great estate in expectancy. When put in earthly hopes possession, produces instant death. It draws large drafts on experience, payable in the future and is seldom able to liquidate them. Hope is always buoyant and like Old Virginia, never dies. It answers well for breakfast, but makes a bad supper. Like a balloon we know where it starts from, but can make no calculation when, where, and how it will land us. Hope is a great calculator, but a bad mathematician. Hopes problems are seldom based on true data. Their demonstration is more often fictitious than otherwise. It builds cities and towns on paper. It suspends earth in the air and plays with bubbles like a child with soap suds. It is bold as Caesar and ever ready to attempt great feats, if it should be to storm the castle of despair.

When all other emotions are controlled by events, hope alone remains forever buoyant and undecayed under the most adverse circumstances, "unchanged, unchangeable." Causes that affect with depression every other emotion, appear to give fresh elasticity to hope. No oppression can crush it. Under every weight, it rebounds. No disappointments can annihilate its power, no experience can deter us from listening to its sweet illusions. It seems a counterpoise for misfortune, an equivalent for every endurance. Who is there without hope? The fettered prisoner in his dark cell, the diseased sufferer on his bed of anguish, the friendless wanderer on the unsheltered waste. Each cherishes some latent spark of this pure and ever-living light. Like the beam of heaven, it glows with indestructible brilliance to the heart of man, what light is to the eye, cheering, blessing, and invigorating.

A true hope we can touch somehow, through all the lights and shadows of life. It is a prophecy fulfilled in part. God's earnest-money paid into our hand. He will be ready with the whole when we are ready for it. The sunlight on the hill top when the valley is dark as death. The spirit touching us all through our pilgrimage. When we know that the end is near, it will take us on its wings and soar away into the blessed life. We may expect that the fulfillment will be entirely equal to the hope. That the old glamour will come over us again and beckon us on forever as the choicest blessing Heaven has to give. We know of no condition in any life trying to be real and true, in which this power will not do for us, just what we have seen it doing for the man who has to wait on the seasons for his daily bread.

We can cherish a sure hope about our future and the future of those who hope with us. A sunny, eager look toward the fulfillment of all the promises God has written on our nature. We may be all wrong in our thoughts of the special form in which our blessings will come. We can never be wrong about the blessing. It may be like the mirage shifting from horizon to horizon as we plod wearily along. The soul is bound to find at last the resting place and the spring. There is many a father in the world today trying hard to get his head above water who will sink, but his boys will swim and reach the firm land. They will think of him with infinite tenderness while he perhaps, is watching them from above. Their success may be one of the elements of his joy in Heaven. The setting of a great hope is like the setting of the sun. The brightness of our life is gone, shadows of the evening fall behind us, the world seems but a dim reflection itself, a broader shadow. We look forward to the coming night. The soul withdraws itself, then stars arise and the night is holy.

Hope has sunshine in its eye, encouragement on its tongue and inspiration in its hand. Rich and glorious is hope and faithfully should it be cultivated. Let its inspiring influence be in the heart of every youth. It will give strength and courage. Let hope's cheerful words fall ever from his tongue, and his bright smile play ever on its countenance. Cultivate well this ever shining flower of the spirit. It is the evergreen of life that grows at the eastern gate of the soul's garden.

Hopes and fears checker human life. He who wants

hope is the poorest man living. Our hopes and fears are the mainsprings of all our religious endeavors. There is no one whose condition is so low but that he may have hopes, nor is anyone so high as to be out of the reach of fears. Hopes and disappointments are the lot and entertainment of human life. The one serves to keep us from presumption, the other from despair. Hope is the last thing that dies in man, yet it is of good use to us. While we are traveling through this life, it conducts us in an easier and more pleasant way to our journey's end. When faith, temperance, the graces, and other celestial powers left the earth, hope was the only one left behind. Hopes enchantments never die. Hope gilds the future. Hope cheers and rouses the soul. Hope and strive is the way to thrive. The man who carries a lantern in a dark night can have friends all around him. They will walk safely by the help of its rays and not be defrauded. He has the God-given light of hope and can help many others in this world's darkness. Not to his own loss, but to their precious gain.

Hope is an anchor to the soul both sure and steadfast that will steady our frail bark while sailing over the ocean of life, then will enable us to outride the storms of time, a hope that reaches from earth to Heaven. This hope is based on faith and keeps our earthly hopes from running riot into forbidden paths. The cable of this hope cannot be sundered until death and the prisoner goes free. To live without it, is blind infatuation. To die without it, eternal ruin.

Kindness

MORE hearts pine away in secret anguish for the want of kindness from those who should be their comforters. A word of kindness is a seed which, when dropped by chance, springs up a flower. A kind word and pleasant voice are gifts easy to give. Be liberal with them. They are worth more than money. "If a word or two will render a man happy," said a Frenchman," he must be a wretch indeed, who will not give it." It is like lighting another man's candle with your own, which loses none of its brilliancy by what the other gains." If all men acted on that principle the world would be much happier than it is. Kindness is like a calm and peaceful stream that reflects every object in its just proportion. The violent spirit like troubled waters, renders back the images of things distorted and broken. It communicates to them that disordered motion which arises from its own agitation. Kindness makes sunshine wherever it goes. It finds its way into hidden chambers of the heart and brings forth golden treasures. Harshness on the contrary, seals them up forever. Kindness makes the mother's lullaby sweeter than the song of the lark. It makes the care-laden brow of the father and man of business less severe in their expression. Kindness is the real law of life. The link that connects earth with heaven, the true philosopher's stone. All it touches it turns to virgin gold. The true gold where we purchase contentment, peace, and love. Write your name by kindness, love, and mercy on the hearts of the people you come in contact with year by year and you will never be forgotten.

In the relationship of social life it is by little acts of watchful kindness recurring daily and hourly. The opportunities of doing kindness, if sought for, are forever coming up. It is by words, by tones, by gestures, by looks that affection is won and preserved.

How sweet are the affections of kindness! How balmy the influence of that regard which dwells around the fireside. Where virtue lives for its own sake, and fidelity regulates and restrains the thirst for admiration. Where distrust and doubt dim not the luster of purity. Where solicitude, except for the preservation of an unshaken confidence, has no place. The gleam of suspicion or jealousy never disturbs the harmony and tranquillity of the scene. Paternal kindness and devoted affection blossom in all the freshness of eternal spring! It matters not if the world is cold, if we can turn to our own dear circle for the enjoyment for which the heart yearns. Lord Bacon beautifully says: "If a man be gracious to strangers it shows he is a citizen of the world, and his heart is no island cut off from other lands, but a continent that joins them."

There is nothing like kindness in the world. It is the very principle of love. It flows from the heart to soften and gladden and should be encouraged in all our relationship with our fellow beings. It is impossible to resist continued kindness.

Home enjoyments, home affections, home courtesies, cannot be too carefully or steadily cultivated. They form the sunshine of the heart. They bless and sanctify our private circle. They become a source of calm delight to the man of business after a day of toil. They teach the merchant, the trader, the working man that there is something purer than the gains of industry. Home kindness twines around the heart, calls forth its best emotions and resources. It enables us to be more virtuous, more upright, more Christian in all our relations of life. We see in the little ones around us the elements of gentleness, of truth, and the beauty of loyalty and religion. A day of toil is robbed of many of its cares by the thought that in the evening we may return home and mingle with the family household. There our experience teaches us, we may find confiding and loving souls who look up to and lean on. To whom, we also may look for counsel and encouragement.

We say to our friends cultivate the home virtues, the household beauties of existence. Endeavor to make a little circle of domestic life a cheerful, an intelligent, a kindly and a happy one. Whatever may go wrong in the world of business and trade, however arduous may be the struggle for fortune or fame, let nothing mar the purity of giving and receiving love. Let nothing throw into its harmonious existence, the apple of discord.

Life is made up not of great sacrifices or duties, but of little things. Where smiles and kindness and small obligations, given habitually, are what win and preserve the heart and secure comfort.

Give no pain. Breathe not a sentiment or say a word. Give not the expression of the countenance that will offend another, nothing that would send a thrill of pain to his heart. We are surrounded by sensitive hearts which a word or a look might fill to the brim with sorrow. If you are careless of the opinions of others, remember they may be of a constitution different from yours. Never by word or sign, cast a shadow on a happy heart or throw aside the smile of joys.

Many lose the opportunity of saying a kind thing by

waiting to weigh the matter too long. Our best impulses are
too delicate to endure much handling. If we fail to give
them expression the moment they rise, they effervesce,
evaporate and are gone. If they do not sour they become
flat, losing all life and sparkle by keeping. Speak promptly
when you feel kindly.

Deal gently with the stranger. Remember the severed
cord of affection, and beware not to wound by a thoughtless
act or a careless word. The stranger! He may have lived in
an atmosphere of love as warm as that we breathe. Alone
and friendless now, he treasures the images of loved ones
far away. Speak gently. Like a clinging vine torn from its
support, the stranger's heart begins to twine its tendrils
around the first object which is presented to it. Is love so
cheap a thing in this world, or have we already so much that
we can lightly cast off the instinctive affections? Oh, do
not! To some souls an atmosphere of love is as necessary
as the vital air to the physical system. A person of such a
nature may clothe one in imagination with all the attributes
of goodness, and make his heart's sacrifices at the shrine.
Let us not cruelly destroy the illusion, by unkindness! Let
the name of stranger be ever sacred, whether honored guest
at our fireside or a servant in our kitchen. When we find
ourselves far from friends and dear associations of home,
may some kind, angel-hearted being cause our heart to thrill
with unspoken gratitude. Then, we will find again the bread
long "cast upon the waters."

Our friends we must prize and appreciate while we are
with them. It is a shame not to know how much we love our
friends or how good they are, till death. We must seize with
joy all our opportunities. Our duties we must perform with

pleasure. Our sacrifices we must make cheerfully. Knowing that he who sacrifices most, is the most noble. We must forgive with an understanding of the glory of forgiveness. Use the blessings we have, realizing how great are small blessings when properly accepted.

Kindness is stored away in the heart like rose-leaves in a drawer, to sweeten every object around them. Little drops of rain brighten the meadows and little acts of kindness brighten the world. We can conceive of nothing more attractive than when the heart is filled with the spirit of kindness. Certainly nothing so embellishes human nature as the practice of this virtue. A sentiment so genial and so excellent ought to be emblazoned on every thought and act of life. The principle underlies the whole theory of Christianity, and in no other person do we find it more happily exemplified than in our Savior. Who, while on earth went about doing good. And how true it is that

> "A little word in kindness spoken,
>   A motion, or a tear,
> Has often heal'd the heart that's broken,
>   And made a friend sincere!"

Friendship

PURE, impartial friendship is a bright flame emitting none of the smoke of selfishness and seldom is worthy among men. Its origin is divine, its operations heavenly, and its results lifts the soul. Deception is a propensity deeply rooted in human nature and the hobby horse on which some ride through life. The heart is deceitful above all things; who can know it? We should be extremely careful who we confide in and then we will often find ourselves mistaken. Let adversity come, then we may know more of our friends. Many will probably show that they were sunshine friends and will escape as for their lives, like rats from a barn in flames! Ten to one, those who have enjoyed the most sunshine will be first to forsake, condemn, and reproach. Friendship based entirely on self ends in desertion the moment the selfish ends are accomplished or frustrated.

Wherever it is watered with the dews of kindness and affection, there you may be sure to find friendship. Allied in closest companionship with its twin-sister charity, it enters the abode of sorrow and wretchedness and causes happiness and peace. It knocks at the lonely and disconsolate heart and speaks words of encouragement and joy. Its all-powerful influence hovers over contending armies and unites the deadly foes in the closest bonds of sympathy and kindness. Its eternal and universal fragrance dispels every thought of envy and purifies the mind with a holy and priceless contentment, which all the pomp and power of earth could not bestow. Friendship, true friendship can only be found to bloom in the soil of a noble and self-sacrificing heart. There it has a perennial summer, a never-ending season of happiness and joy to its possessor, casting a thousand rays of love and hope and peace all around.

No one can be happy without a friend, and no one can know what friends he has until he is unhappy.

It has been observed that a real friend is somewhat like a ghost or apparition, much talked of, but hardly ever seen. Though this may not be exactly true, it must be confessed that a friend does not appear every day. He who in reality has found one ought to value them and be thankful. Where persons are united by the bonds of genuine friendship, there is nothing more conducive to happiness. It supports and strengthens the mind, alleviates the pain of life and renders the present state more comfortable.

What a blessing it is to have a friend to whom one can speak fearlessly on any subject. With whom, one's deepest thoughts come simply and safely. Oh, the comfort of feeling safe with a person. Having to neither weigh the thoughts or measure the words, but pouring them all right out just as they are. Chaff and grain together, certain that a faithful hand will take and sift them. A friend will keep what is worth keeping and then with the breath of kindness, blow the rest away.

If any form a friendship just for what they can gain by it, it is not true friendship. It must be free from any such self-ish view and only design mutual benefit as each may require. Again, it must be unreserved.

Friends must study to please and oblige each other in the most delicate, kind, and liberal manner. In poverty and trouble, as well as in riches or prosperity. The benevolence of friends is also manifested in overlooking each other's faults and with sincere kindness admonish each other when they do amiss. Upon the whole, the purse, the heart, and the house ought to be open to a friend and in no case can we shut them out.

The first law of friendship is sincerity. He who violates this law will soon find himself destitute of what he so erring-ly seeks to gain. The deceitful heart of such a one will soon betray itself and feel the contempt due to insincerity. The world is so full of selfishness that true friendship is seldom found. The envious man seeks to gain the applause of others for an unholy usage, by which he may have a seat of pre-eminence for himself. Self-love, the spring of motion, acts upon the soul. All are fond of praise and many are dishonest in the use of means to obtain it. It is often difficult to distinguish between true and false friendship.

Courtship and Marriage

ALL the blessedness and happiness of the married state depend on its truthfulness. Marriage is not necessarily a blessing. It may be the most bitter curse. It may sting like an adder and bite like a serpent. Its bower is as often made of thorns as of roses. It blasts as many sunny expectations as it realizes. Every improper marriage is a living misery, an undying death. Its bonds are grated bars of frozen iron. It is a spirit prison, cold as the dungeon of ruin. An ill-mated human pair, is the most woeful picture of human wretchedness that is presented in the book of life. Yet, such pictures are plentiful. Every page we turn gives us a view of some such living bondage. But a proper marriage, a true interior soul-linked union is a living picture of blessedness unrivaled in beauty. A true marriage is the soul's Eden. It is the portal of heaven. It is the visiting place of angels. It is the charm of a spirit in captivation with all imaginable beauty and loveliness. It is a constant peace offering that procures a continual sweetness. It is not given to words to express the refinement of pleasure, the delicacy of joy, and the abounding fullness of satisfaction that those feel whom

"SUMMER HOURS."

FOR THE ROYAL PATH OF LIFE.

God has joined in a high marriage of spirit. Such a union is the highest school of virtue, the soul's convent where the fires of purity are kept continually burning.

Marriage should be made a study. Every youth both male and female should so consider it. It is the grand social institution of humanity. Its laws and relations are of momentous importance to the human race.

Shall it be entered blindly, in total ignorance of what it is, what its conditions of happiness are?

"Marriage is a lottery," exclaim so many men and women you meet. And why is it so? Simply because courtship is a grand scheme of deception. Is it not so? Who courts honestly? Some it is true, but few indeed. It is conducted something like this: A young man and woman meet at a party, ball, school, or church. The young man sees something in the lady that attracts his attention. It may be her pretty face, her golden curls, her flashing eyes, her delicate hand or slender waist, or curve of her neck, or graceful carriage, or more likely, the plumage in which the bird shines. He looks again and again and without one particle of sense or reason for it, his attraction rises into enchantment. He seeks an introduction. They dream and sing and make verses about each other and meditate ways and means to appear captivating at the next meeting. Then it arrives, they meet all wreathed in smiles and shining beautiful things. How can it be otherwise than that their fascination shall become absolute adoration now? The afternoon and evening are spent together, each in perfect delight. The lovers talk about flowers, stars, poetry, and give hints and signs and tokens till each understands the other's enchantment. They are engaged and get married.

Married life now comes and ushers in its morning glory and they are happy as a happy pair can well be, for a while. But "life is real," and character is real and love is real. When life's reality comes, they find things in each other's characters that perfectly startle them. Every day reveals something new and something unpleasant. The courtship character fades away and with it the courtship love. Now comes disappointment, sorrow, regret. They find that their characters are entirely dissimilar. Married life is a burden full of cares, vexations, and disappointments. Yes, marriage is a lottery. They know it. Some may get prizes and some may not. No one knows before he draws whether he will draw a blank or a prize. This is their conclusion. They did not court in the right way! They courted by impulse and not by judgement. It was a process of wooing and not of discovery. It was an effort to please and not a search for companionship. It was done with excitement and not with calmness and deliberation. It was done in haste and not with cautious prudence. It was a vision of the heart and not a solemn reality. It was conducted by feeling and not by reason. It was managed as to be a perpetual pleasure and intoxicating delight, and not a trying ordeal for the enduring realities of solid and stubborn life. It was a yielding up of everything and not a firm maintaining of everything that belongs to the man or woman. In almost every particular, it was false and was followed by evil consequences. All similar courting is not good. They voluntarily blind themselves and then blind each other. They "go it blind" till their eyes are opened in marriage. It is necessary for the youth of both sexes to be perfectly HONEST in their relations with each other. To always exhibit, their true character and nature. Dishonesty,

is a greater barrier even than ignorance, to a proper understanding of the real character of those whom we plan to
marry. Some men and women are not true to themselves.
They put on false characters. They assume airs not their
own. They shine in borrowed plumes. They practice every
deception for the concealment of their real characters. They
study to appear better than they are. They appear in each
other's society to be the embodiment of goodness and sweetness. They are full of human weaknesses and frailties.

The object of courtship is the choice of a companion. It
is not to woo. It is not to charm, gratify, or please, simply for
the present pleasure. It is not for the present sweets of such
an intimate and confiding relation. It is simply and plainly
for the selection of a life companion. One who must bear,
suffer, and enjoy life with us in all its frowns and smiles, joys
and sorrows. One who can walk through all the intricate and
irregular changes in the course of life. Now how shall
courtship be conducted to make marriage a certainty and not
a lottery? This is the question.

This is a companion. One who is kindred in soul with us.
Who is already united to us by the ties of spiritual harmony.
The union is the object of the courtship to discover.
Courtship then is a voyage of discovery. A court of inquiry,
established by mutual consent of the parties. To see in and to
what extent, there is harmony existing. If in all these, they
honestly agree and find a deep and thrilling pleasure in their
agreement. If, they find their union gives a charm to their
social relations. If now, they feel that their hearts are bound
as well as their sentiments in a holy unity. That for each
other they would live, and labor and make every personal
sacrifice with gladness. That without each other they would

not know how to live, it is their privilege and their duty to form a marriage union. It will not be a lottery. They know what they are to give and what they are to get. They will be married in the full blaze of light and love. They will be married for a happy, virtuous, and useful union to bless themselves and the world with a living type of heaven.

Flirting and Bachelors

THE affections are too tender and sacred to be trifled with. He who does it is a wretch. He should be ranked among thieves, robbers, villains, and murderers. He who steals money steals trash, but he who steals affections without a return of similar affections, steals that which is more dear than life and more precious than wealth. His theft is robbery of the heart. Flirting is a horrid outrage on the most holy and exalted feelings of the human soul and the most sacred and important relation of life. It had and still has, its origin in the basest lust. The refined soul is always disgusted with it. Its demoralizing in its tendency and low in its character. The whole tendency of such lightness is to cause the marriage relation to be lightly esteemed and courtship to made fun of. How can courtship be anything else than a grand game of hypocrisy where flirting is practiced? Let all your dealings be frank, honest, and noble.

Marriage has a great refining and moralizing tendency. Nearly all the crime is committed by unmarried men. When a man marries early and uses prudence in choosing a suitable companion, he is likely to lead a virtuous, happy life. In an unmarried state, all alluring vices have tendency to draw him away. Many prisons are filled with unmarried men. Marriage renders a man more virtuous and more wise. In nine cases out of ten, where married men become drunkards or commit crimes against the peace of the community, the foundation of these acts were done while they were single, or where the wife was an unsuitable match. Marriage changes the current of a man's feelings and gives him a center for his thoughts, his affections, and his acts.

If it were intended for man to be single, there would be no harm in remaining so. Men and women should marry and live as they were designed to live.

Marriage is a school and exercise of virtue. Though marriage have cares, single life has desires which are more troublesome and dangerous. The single life may have more privacy of devotion, yet marriage has more variety and is an exercise of more graces. Marriage is the duty of parents and the charity of relations. Here, kindness is spread abroad and love is united and made firm as a center. Marriage is the nursery of heaven. Marriage has in it more safety than the single life. It has more cares, it is more merry and more sad. It is fuller of sorrow and fuller of joys. It lies under more burdens, but is supported by all the strength of love and charity which makes those burdens delightful. Marriage is the mother of the world and preserves kingdoms, and fills cities, and churches, and heaven itself. Marriage is that state of good things to which God has designed the present constitution of the world.

We advise every man to get married. The chances are better by fifty per cent, all through life, in every respect. There is no ready hand and kind heart for the bachelor. No one to cheer him in his loneliness and bereavement. There is none in whose eyes he can see himself reflected, and from whose lips he can receive the unfailing assurances of care and love. He may be courted for his money. He may eat and drink and revel. He may sicken and die in a hotel or a garret with plenty of attendants about him, but he will never know the comforts of the domestic fireside.

A man who avoids marriage on account of the cares of wedded life, cuts himself off from a great blessing for fear of a trifling annoyance. Bachelors, there cannot be a home where there is no wife. To talk of a home without love, we might as well expect to find an American fireside in one of the pyramids of Egypt.

There is a world of wisdom in the following: "Every schoolboy knows that a kite would not fly unless it had a string tying it down. It is just so in life. The man who is tied down by a half-dozen blooming responsibilities will make a higher and stronger flight than the bachelor. Having nothing to keep him steady, he is floundering in the mud. If you want to ascend in the world, tie yourself to somebody."

Matrimony

MARRIAGE is to a woman, at once the happiest and sad-dest event of her life. It is the promise of future bliss. She quits her former home, her parents, her companions, her occupations, and her amusements. Everything, on which she had before depended for comfort, affection, kindness, and pleasure. The parents by whose advice she had been guided, the sister she had dared impart thought and feeling, the brother who had played with her at counseling and being counseled, and the younger children to whom she had been the mother and playmate. All are forsaken in one instant. Every former tie is loosened, the spring of every hope and action is changed. Yet, she flies with joy into the untrodden paths before her buoyed up by the confidence of requited love. She bids a fond and grateful good-by to the life that is past and turns excited hopes and joyous anticipations of the happiness to come. Then woe to the man who can blast such hopes! Who can cowardlike, break the illusions that have won her and destroy the confidence which his love inspired.

There is no one thing more lovely in this life, more full of the divinest courage, than when a young girl from her past life and happy childhood is taken. When she rambled over every field and moor around her home. When a mother anticipated her wants, and soothed her cares. When brothers and sisters grew from merry playmates, to loving, trustful friends. When shes taken from the Christmas gatherings, and summer festivals in the garden, and the secure backgrounds of her childhood.

Wedlock indissoluble, except by an act of God. A sacrament whose solemnity reaches to eternity will always hold its rank in literature as the most impressive fact of human experience in dramatic writing. Whether of the stage or closet, the play or the novel, it must be so.

A judicious wife is always snipping off from her husband's moral nature like little twigs growing in the wrong direction. She keeps him in shape by continual pruning. If he says anything silly or absurd, she will find means of preventing him. By far, the chief part of all common sense there is in the world belongs unquestionably to woman. The wisest things which a man commonly does are those which his wife counsels him to do.

It would surely be, that intellectual beings were intended by their Creator to go through the world together. United not only in hand and heart but in principals, in views, and in dispositions. At the same time, both pursuing one common and noble end to their development and the happiness of those around them. Mutually correcting, sustaining, and strengthening each other. Each finding a candid, but severe judge in the understanding, and a warm and partial advocate in the heart of his and her companion. To be secure from the follies, misunderstandings, and evils of the world in the arms of each other. Being as one, in the inestimable joy of undisturbed confidence and unrestrained intimacy.

If there be a passion in the human heart which tends to lift us out of egotism and self and teaches us to love another, it is love. It purifies and warms the whole mortal being as we hold it and cherish it. For even when the active life of man is employed in such grave pursuits, and the love of his early years seem to him like a dream of romance, there is still love. That love having lifted him once out of egotism into sympathy, does but pass into new forms and development. It has locked his heart to charity and benevolence. It gives a smile to his home and rises up in the eyes of his children.

Nothing delights one more than to enter the neat little home of the young couple, without any resources but their own knowledge of industry. Where they have joined heart and hand, and are engaged to share together the responsibilities, duties, interests, trials and pleasures of life while putting their house in order. This is the true domestic pleasure. Health, contentment, love, abundant and bright prospects, are all here.

It has become a prevalent sentiment that a man must acquire his fortune before he marries. That the wife have no sympathy or share with him in the pursuit of it, in which most of the pleasure truly consists. That the young married couple must set out with as large and expensive an establishment as is becoming to those who have been wedded for twenty years. This is unhappy. It fills the community with bachelors who are waiting to make their fortunes. It destroys the true economy and design of the domestic institution. It encourages inefficiency among females who are expecting to be taken in by fortune and passively sustained, without care or concern on their part.

The Creator found that it was not good for man to be alone. Therefore, he made woman from man to be a "helpmate for him." For many ages history has shown that "the permanent union of one man with one woman establishes a relation of affections and interests, which can in no other way be made to exist between two human beings." To establish this relation was one of the great designs of God in giving the rite to man. By establishing this relation, marriage becomes to him an aid in the stern conflict of life. This is often proved in practical life. Many men have risen from obscurity to fame who have freely and gratefully acknowledged that for the sympathy and encouragement of his wife, he owed very much of his achieved success.

While men say they cannot marry because the girls of this generation are too extravagant, the fault by no means is altogether with the girls. In the first place, men admire the elegant costumes in which many ladies appear. What is the natural effect of this? In the second place, men are too proud themselves to commence their married life in a quiet, economical way. They are not willing to marry until they have money enough to continue all their own private luxuries and support a wife in style. If both men and women would be true to the best feelings of their hearts, and careless of what the world would say, pure and happy homes would be more abundant. A man to succeed well in life, needs the influence of a mindful woman and her sympathy to sweeten the cup of life.

Woman's influence is the best anchor of society. This influence is due not exclusively to the fascination of her charms, but chiefly to the strength, uniformity, and consistency of her attributes. These are maintained with so much fortitude and heroism and under so many sacrifices, that with these endowments and qualifications, their power is irresistible.

Sometimes we hear the them recall the happiness of their earlier years and blame folly and rashness of choice. They warn those that are coming into the world against the same infatuation. But it is to be remembered, that the days which they so much wish to call back are the days of youth. The days of novelty and improvement, of ardor and of hope, of health and vigor of body, of cheery lightness of heart. It is not easy to surround life with any circumstances in which youth would not be delightful!

There is no misery so distressful as the desperate agony of trying to keep young when one cannot. We know an old bachelor who has attempted it. He is a fast young man of fifty. He plies innocent young girls with the pretty compliments, the same as in his twenties. His fashion of talking to young girls has changed in thirty years, and more out of date than a two-year old bonnet.

"I wish that I had married thirty years ago," said another old bachelor. I wish I had a wife and half-dozen children around me, and bring along with them the affection which we would have had by being early acquainted. But as it is in my present state, there is not a person in the world I care a straw for. The world is even with me, for I don't believe there is a person in it who cares a straw for me."

Let young men and women disregard totally all considerations of wealth, beauty, external accomplishments, fashion, connections in society, and every mere selfish and worldly end in seeking a wife or husband. But look into the mind and heart, before you think of marrying. If they cannot love you for yourself alone, and what goes to make up your character, then shun marriage. What is set forth, every one consider to make the choice in marriage to the right end. Wealth cannot bring happiness and is ever in danger of taking to itself wings. Beauty cannot last long, where there is grief at the heart.

We are not inclined to wonder why marriage is sometimes unhappy, some making matches for their children.

There are those who throw themselves into the arms of someone they do not love, after rejection from another. Some who have squandered their own money. Some because their houses are continually filled with company. Some want to live like other people. Some because they are sick of themselves. Those where the contract of matrimony begins on such principles, should neither wonder that it has ended in disappointments. To marry with uncertainty, is a sad tale. It is proved for the worse because they did not KNOW each other.

Marriage is the seal of man's earthly well-being or woe. No event is to be compared, for its interest and its immeasurable results. Why are so many unhappy in this union, never indeed truly married? Because they rush into its sacred temple, either deluded or unsanctioned by God and good principles. Custom, convenience, proximity, passion, vicious novels, silly companions intoxicate the brain. The step is taken without one serious thought.

Women have so little the power of choice that it is not perhaps fair to say that they are less likely to choose well then men. But I am persuaded that they are more frequently deceived in the attachments they form, and their opinions concerning men are less accurate. I would also say there are more good wives in the world than there are good husbands.

Marriage offers the most effective opportunities for spoiling the life of another. Nobody can debase, harass, and ruin a woman so fatally as her own husband. Nobody can do so much to chill a man's aspirations, to paralyze his energies as his wife. A cheerful wife is a rainbow in the sky when her husband's mind is tossed on the storms of anxiety and care. A man is what his wife makes him. Make marriage a matter of moral judgement.

We do not believe in marriage without love. Respectability is all very well, but it does not take the place of affections. It is said that in such matches love comes after marriage. We have no doubt that it often does, but we think love should precede as well as follow matrimony. No. If you do not love, do not marry. Singleness is blessedness compared to marriage without affection.

Ladies, do not rely upon common report or the opinion of friends, but upon personal knowledge of the individual's life and character. How can another know what you want in a companion? You alone know your own heart. If you do not know it, you should not marry. No one else can tell what fills you with pleasing and grateful emotions. It is for you to KNOW who asks for your hand, who has your heart, and who links life with yours. If you know him who can make true answer to your soul's love, whose soul is kindred with yours, whose life answers to your ideal demeanor, you know who presents a true spirit as husband and father. If you only fancy that he is right, or believe and hope, you have a poor foundation on which to build future happiness. Do not as you value life and its comforts, marry a man who is naturally cruel. If his nature delights in torture he will not spare his wife, or his helpless children.

Do not marry a man who pays overly much attention to his clothes or appearance. There is in such a character nothing of true dignity. Nothing that commands respect or insures even a decent standing in the community. His very attitude and gait tell the stranger who he is though he passes him silently on the street. To unite your destiny with such a man, would but disgrace your character. Look with disgust on what is called the "fast man." Those who frequent the bar-room, only to drench themselves in "fire-water." They are filled with conceit, large talk and big sounding oaths. His highest ambition is to sport a fast horse, to swear roundly, and wear flashy garments. They look with contempt on their elders and equals who toil in some honest occupation and regard labor as a badge of disgrace.

A habit of industry once formed is not likely to ever be

lost. We would regard your prospects for life far better, if you would marry a man of very limited property. One with an honest vocation and a habit of working, rather than united with one who had never been taught to exercise his own powers toward wealth.

Perhaps no folly holds so strong a place in a woman's mind as, that she can cause change in a man's heart and mind from her love alone. So if he is a little fast, after marriage he will settle down into a sensible husband. History too often repeats the failure of such beliefs. She will find a husband with a strong will and too selfish for any control. You cannot reclaim those who have not the power to reclaim themselves. Beware! The deepest rascal has the finest clothes and the smoothest tongue. Yet, young women are continually willing to marry those who are in the habit of indulging in drunkenness. A rich and fashionable young man has no trouble getting to the alter, even though he is hardly sober long enough to pronounce the marriage vows. A man or woman who marries a person addicted to drinking liquors is attaching to themselves a dead weight that will drag them down to the same level.

Says Jeremy Taylor "a happy wedlock is a long falling in love." Marriage is very gradual, a fraction of us at a time. The real ministers that marry people are the slow years. They are the joys and sorrows shared, our children on earth, and the angels in heaven. The years of toils and burdens borne in company. These are the ministers that really marry us. The real marriage service isn't anything printed or said: it is the true heart service which each yields to the other. Year in and year out, when the bridal ring is getting sadly worn. Let this heart service be performed, and even if marriage was a lottery to begin with, this would go far to redeem it and make it a marriage of coequal hearts and minds.

When the honeymoon is over, then begins the business of adapting. If they find that they do not love as they thought, they should double their attentions to one another and let nothing in the way to separate them. Life is too precious to be thrown away in secret regrets or open differences. Renew the attentions of earlier days. Draw your hearts closer together. Talk things over. Acknowledge your faults to one another. Decide that you will be all in all to each other. My word for it, you shall find in your relation the sweetest joy earth has for you. There is no other way for you to do it. If you are happy at home, you will be happy anywhere. The conviction that he or she is attached for life in an undesirable marriage and no way to escape, has lost life.

It is a great thing for two fragile natures to live as one for life long. What human will or wisdom cannot do, God can do with his Providence uniting those who DEVOUTLY try to do the work of life and enjoy its goods together. For them there is in store a respect and affection, a peace and power all unknown in the hey-day of young romance.

The marriage institution is the bond of social order. If treated with respect, care, and discretion it greatly enhances individual happiness and consequently, general good. There are causes that have stripped the marriage institution of its ancient simplicity and rendered its pure stream turbid in places. Among the Patriarchs, the young pair made the match, and the girl always made her choice, an indispensable pre-requisite to a happy union.

How to secure happiness to married life is the question.

The prime difficulty in most cases is the entire thoughtlessness, the want of consideration, and common sense and practical wisdom. Many married people have a vague notion that happiness comes of itself. They wait for certain dreams to be fulfilled by beatific realities. Happiness does not come of its own accord, nor by accident. It is not a gift, but an attainment. Circumstances may favor it, but cannot create it.

Love on both sides and all things equal in outward circumstances, are not all the requisites of domestic happiness. Human nature is frail and multiform in its passions. The honeymoon gets a dash of vinegar now and then when least expected. People are apt to marry faultless, but faults are there and will come out.

We exhort you who are husbands to love your wife, even as you love yourself. Give honor to her as the delicate vessel. Respect her heart and mind. Continue through with the same attention and manly tenderness, which in youth, gained her affections.

We exhort you who are wives to be gentle and gracious to your husband. Let the influence which you possess over him, arise from the mildness of your manners and the discretion of your conduct. Keep yourself presentable, but more attentive with cheerfulness and good humor. You will lighten his cares and chase away the vexations of the world by rendering your home a pleasant refuge.

To both husbands and wives we say: "Preserve a strict guard over your tongues that you not utter anything rude, contemptuous, or severe. Guard your tempers that you not appear sullen or gloomy. Expect not, too much from each other. If any offence arise, forgive it. Think not that a human being can be exempt from faults."

In conclusion we would say, that marriage is one of God's first blessings. Although it involves many weighty responsibilities, it is a gem in the crown of life. Man and wife are equally concerned to avoid all offences of each other in the beginning of their conversation. And by age and consolidation, they can endure the storms and the loud noise of the tempest. The hearts of the man and the wife are endeared and accepting by mutual confidence and experience.

Love

LOVE is such a giant power that it seems to gather strength from obstructions and at every difficulty rises to higher might. It is all dominant, all conquering. There is no hope of resisting it, for it outreaches the most vigilant, submerges everything, acquiring strength as it proceeds. Ever growing, even growing out of itself. Love is the light, the majesty of life. That principle to which, after all our struggling, writhing, and twisting all things must be resolved. Take love away and what becomes of the world? It is a barren wilderness!

Love is of such a refining, elevating character that it expels all that is mean and base. It bids us to think great thoughts, do great deeds, and changes our common clay into fine gold. Love illuminates our path, dark and mysterious as it may be, with torchlights lit from the one great light. Poor, weak, and inexpressive are words, when sought to strew as with stars the path, the expression of love's greatness and power.

There is another love. That which blends hearts in blissful unity. It makes willing separation of the son from his father's house, and the daughter from all the sweet endearments of her childhood home. They go out together and rear for themselves an alter around which clusters all cares and delights, the anxieties and sympathies of family relationship. This love is to be pure, unselfish, and discreet. It constitutes the chief usefulness and happiness of human life. This love is indeed heaven on earth.

Love is the sun of life. It is the sun of the soul. Life without love is worse than death. The love which does not lead to labor will soon die out. The thankfulness which does not embody itself in sacrifices is already changing to gratitude. Love is not ripened in one day, nor in many, nor even in a human lifetime. It is the oneness of soul with soul, in appreciation and perfect trust. To be blessed, it must rest in that faith in the Divine which underlies every other emotion. To be true, love must be eternal as God himself.

> Love is blind, and lovers cannot see
> The pretty follies that themselves commit.

Remember that love is dependent on forms. Courtesy guards and protects courtesy of heart. Men and women should not be judged by the same rules. There are many radical differences in their affectionate natures.

> Man's love is of man's life a thing, a part;
> Tis woman's whole existence.

Woman loves or abhors, and man admires or despises. Woman's love is stronger than death. Misfortune cannot suppress it. Enmity cannot alienate it. Temptation cannot enslave it. It is the guardian angel of the nursery and the sick bed. It gives an affectionate concord to the partnership of life and interest. Circumstances cannot modify it. It ever remains the same to sweeten existence, to purify the cup of life on the rugged pathway to the grave. Her love melts to moral pliability the brittle nature of man.

The love of a woman is always silent. Even when fortunate, she scarcely breathes it to herself. When she feels unloved, she buries it in the recesses of her heart and there lets it brood among the ruins of her peace. With her, the desire of the heart has failed.

The affection that links together man and wife is a far holier and a more enduring passion than the enthusiasm of young love. Talk not to us of the absence of love in wedlock. It burns with a steady and brilliant flame, shedding an influence upon existence. It is a million times more precious and delightful than the cold dreams of philosophy. Domestic love! Who can measure its height or its depth? Who can estimate its preserving and purifying power?

The love that has nothing but beauty to sustain it soon withers and dies. The love that is fed with presents, always requires feeding. Love and love only, is the loan of love. The purest joy we can experience in one we love, is to see that person a source of happiness to others. When you are with the person loved, you have no sense of being uninspired. This humble and trivial circumstance is the great test. It is the only sure and abiding test of love. When two souls come together, each seeking to magnify the other, each helps the other. When these two souls come together, they are lovers.

Husband and Wife

AS HUSBAND and wife it is your high and solemn duty to make each other as happy as it is in your power. The husband should have as his object and rule of conduct, the happiness of his wife. Of that happiness, the confidence in his affection is the chief element. The proofs of this affection on his part, constitutes his chief duty. An affection that is not lavish of caresses only, as these were the only demonstrations of love, but of that respect which distinguishes love as a principle, from that brief passion. A respect which consults the judgement as well as the wishes of the one beloved. To consider her worthy of being taken to the heart, as well as being admitted to all the counsels of the heart. He must often forget her or be useless to the world. She is most useful to the world by remembering him. From the tumultuous scenes which agitate many of his hours, he returns to the calm scene where peace awaits him and happiness is sure because she is there. Her smile is peace and her presence is happiness to his heart.

An unkind word or look or an unintentional neglect, sometimes leads to thoughts which ripen into the ruin of body and soul. A spirit of forbearance, patience, and kindness, and a determination to keep the chain of love bright are likely to develop corresponding qualities. It will make the rough places of life smooth and pleasant. Have you ever considered that either of you have the power to make the other utterly miserable? And when the storms and trials of life come, for they will come, how much either of you can do to calm, to elevate, to purify, the troubled spirit of the other and substitute sunshine for the storm? Then you are determined to outdo each other in making personal sacrifices, to live by the spirit of the Savior. You have laid a foundation for happiness which is not likely to be shaken by the joys or sorrows, the prosperity and adversity, the riches and poverty, or by the frowns or flattery of the world. There is a place on earth where gloomy passions have no empire, where pleasure and innocence live constantly together. Cares and labors are delightful. Every pain is forgotten in reciprocal tenderness. There is an equal enjoyment of the past, the present, and the future. It is the house of a wedded pair, but of a pair who in wedlock are still lovers.

Married life will not go itself, or if it does it will not keep on the right track. It will turn off at every turn or impediment. It needs a couple of good conductors who understand the engineering of life. Good watch must be kept up by a constant addition of the fuel of affection. The boilers must be kept full and the machinery in order and all hands at their posts. If not, there will be a smashing up, or life will go hobbling or jolting along. There is wearing and tearing, breaking and bruising, leaving some heads and hearts to get well the best way they can. It requires skill, prudence, and judgement to lead this life well. These must be tempered with forbearance, charity, and integrity.

The young are likely to hang too many garlands about the married life. If it is wisely entered and truthfully lived, it is more beautiful than any have imagined. It is the true life which God has designed for his children. It is the hallowed home of virtue, peace, and bliss.

The warmest hearted and most unselfish women soon learn to accept quiet trust and the loyalty of a loving life, as the calmest and happiest condition of marriage. The men who are sensible enough to rely on the good sense of such wives, sail round as admirers, both for true affection and comfortable tranquillity.

Allow the young wife to remember, that her husband is under a certain amount of bondage all day. That his interests compel him to look pleasant under all circumstances. That he offend none and to say no hasty word. Then she will see that when he reaches his own fireside, he wants most of all to have this strain removed. He wants to be at ease. This he cannot be if he is continually afraid of wounding his wife's sensibilities, by forgetting some outward and visible token of his affection for her. She pays him a poor compliment by fretting for what is unreasonable to desire, and deeply wrongs herself.

Make a home. Beautify and adorn it. Cultivate all the charms within it. Sing songs of love in it. Bear your portion of work and pain, sorrow and joy in it.

Get daily lessons of strength and patience there. Shine like a star on the face of the darkest night over it. Tenderly, rear the children. Set the home interests to feed the mind, feed the soul, strengthen the love. Strengthen charity, truth, and all holy and good things within its walls.

Love in marriage cannot live nor subsist unless it be mutual. Where love cannot be, there can be left of wedlock nothing but the empty husk of an outside matrimony, as undelightful and unpleasing to God as any other kind of hypocrisy.

Wedded love does not die all at once. A hasty word casts a shadow on it and the shadow darkens with the sharp reply. A little thoughtlessness misconstrued, a little unintentional neglect, a word misinterpreted. Through such small avenues, discord gains admittance to the heart and then welcomes continual discord. Something malicious is felt, but not acknowledged. Love becomes silent, confidence is chilled, and noiselessly but surely, the work of separation goes on until the two are left as isolated as the pyramids. There is nothing left of the union but the legal form, the dead trunk of a tree. A tree whose branches once tossed in the bright sunlight and whose sheltering leaves trembled with the music of singing birds. It now affords no shade for the traveler.

In the true wife, the husband finds not affection only, but companionship. A companionship with which no other can compare. The family relation gives retirement with solitude and society without the rough intrusion of the world. It plants in the dwelling, a friend who can bear his silence without weariness. One who can listen to the details of his interests with sympathy. One who can appreciate his repetition of events, important because they come from the heart. Common friends are linked to us by a slender thread. We must retain them by ministering in some way to their interest or their enjoyment. What a luxury it is to feel, at home, there is a true and affectionate being in whose presence one can through off restraint without danger to dignity. One to confide without fear of treachery, or to be sick or unfortunate, without being abandoned. If in the outside world you grow weary of human selfishness, your heart can safely trust in one whose indulgences overlook defects.

The treasure of a wife's affection like the grace of God is given, not bought. Gold is power. It can sweep down forests, raise cities, build roads and deck houses. It can collect troops of flatters and inspire awe and fear. But alas, wealth can never purchase love. Bonaparte's greatest conquest was the unbought heart of Josephine. His sweetest and most priceless treasure was her outraged, but unchanged love. Is man overwhelmed by disappointment and mortified by reproaches? There is one who can hide her eyes even from his faults. Who like her Father in heaven, can forgive and love him still.

Books to young married people abound with advice to the WIFE to control her temper, and never utter complaints when the husband comes home fretful or unreasonable. Would not the advice be as excellent and appropriate that the HUSBAND conquer his fretfulness and forbear his complaints? Should he not also consider his wife's ill- health, fatiguing cares, and the thousand disheartening influences of domestic routine?

Husbands! Think on your duty. Have you joined with her in her endeavors? Have you helped open the minds of your children and give them good moral lessons? Have you helped to strengthen them with advice, kindness, and good books? Have you spent time with her for intellectual, moral, and social qualities? Have you looked on her as an immortal being as well as yourself?

There is a picture where hearts are united for mutual happiness and improvement. Where a kind voice cheers in the hour of trouble. Where the shade of anxiety is chased from the brow. Where sickness is soothed, and love, hope, and faith burn bright. For such there is a great reward, both here and hereafter, in spiritual happiness and growth. Draw each others thoughts from business and lead them to the regions of the beauty in art and nature, and the true and divine in sentiment.

How often it happens that a married man, after having been away from home all day and the wife toiled at duties, goes again to some place of amusement, leaving her to toil on alone, uncheered and unhappy! How often it happens that her kindest offices pass unobserved and unrewarded, even by a smile. Her best efforts are condemned by the fault-finding husband! How often it happens, even when the evening is spent at home, that it is employed in silent reading, or some other way that does not recognize the wife's right to share in the enjoyments! Yet, she left all to join her destiny with yours to make your home happy. She has done all that woman's ingenuity could devise to meet your wishes and to lighten the burdens which might press upon you.

A loving wife is to a man, wisdom, courage, strength, hope, and endurance. No condition is hopeless. Let woman know that she ministers at the very fountain of life and happiness. It is her hand that ladles out with overflowing cup its soul refreshing waters, or casts the branch of bitterness which makes them poison and death. Her ardent spirit breathes the breath of life into all enterprise.

Her patience and constancy are mainly instrumental in carrying forward to completion the best human designs. Her moral sensibility is the unseen power which is ever at work to refine society. The nearest glimpse of heaven that mortals ever get on earth, is that domestic circle which her hands have trained to intelligence, virtue, and love. Her influence pervades and is the center.

Last of all, let it be remembered that the husband is bound by the divine law to treat his wife as an immortal being. He is to have regard for their moral and spiritual welfare. In that remarkable hour that witnessed the formation of

the marriage union, the era of separation was anticipated by
the solemn vow "till death shall they part."

Joy

JOY is a prize unbought, and is most free and pure in its
flow when it comes unsought. You must carry it with you,
else it is not there. You must have it in you as the music of
a well-ordered soul, the fire of a holy purpose. An
unchanging state of joy is not possible on earth as it is now,
because evil and error are here. The soul must have its midnight hour as well as its sunlight seasons of joy and gladness. Still, the mercy of the Lord is shown as much in the
night as in the day. It is only in the night that we can see the
stars. The most noble spirits are those which turn to heaven
not in the hour of sorrow, but in that of joy. Like a lark they
wait for the clouds to disperse, that they may soar up into
their native element.

He who selfishly hoards his joys thinking to increase
them, is like a man who looks at his granary and says, "Not
only will I protect my grain from mice and birds, but neither
the ground, nor the mill shall have it." So in the spring, he
walks around his little pit of corn and exclaims, "How waste-
ful are my neighbors, throwing away whole handfuls of
grain!" But autumn comes, and while he has only his few
poor bushels, their fields are yellow with an abundant harvest. "There is that scatters, and yet increases."

Those who joy in wealth grow greedy. Those who joy in
their friends, too often lose their noble spirit. Those who joy

in sensuousness, lose dignity of character. Those who joy in literature, often become narrow minded. Those who joy in liberty, that all should do as they would be done to, possess the happiest of joys. It is a solid joy no one can barter away.

He who to the best of his power has secured the final stake, has a perennial fountain of joy within him. He is satisfied with himself. Those who are not satisfied, borrow from without. Joy from without is false, precarious, and short.

Joy from circumstances may be gathered from without, but it must soon wither and become offensive. Joy from within is like smelling the rose on the tree. It is lasting and immortal. Happy are the moments when sorrow forgets its cares and misery its misfortunes. When peace and gladness spring up on the wings of hope, and the light of contentment dawns once more on the disconsolate, unfortunate, and unhappy heart.

Our whole life is temperate between sweet and sour. We must all look for a mixture of both. There are joys which long to be ours. God sends ten thousand truths which come about us like birds seeking inlet. But we are shut up to them, and so they bring us nothing. They sit and sing awhile upon the roof and then fly away.

Beauty

WE doubt not that God is a lover of beauty. He fashioned the worlds in beauty when there was no eye to behold them, but His own. All along the wild old forest He carved the forms of beauty. Every cliff, mountain, and tree is a statue of beauty. Every hill, dale, and landscape is a picture of beauty. Every diamond, rock, and pebbly beach is a mine of beauty. All through the expanses of the universe are scattered the life-gems of beauty. Shall we say then, He is not a lover of beauty?

There is beauty in the songsters of the air, the symmetry of their bodies, the wing so light and expert in fanning the breeze. The graceful neck and head, their tiny feet and legs all so well fitted for their native element. More than this, their sweet notes that awaken delight in every heart that loves to rejoice. Who can range the sunny fields and shady forests on a bright summer's day and listen to the melody of a thousand voices chanting their Maker's praise, and not feel the soul melt with joy and gratitude for the scene? The universe is its temple. Those who are alive to it, cannot lift their eyes without feeling themselves encompassed with it on every side. This beauty is so precious, the enjoyments it gives are so refined and pure. It is so congenial with our most tender and noble feelings as to be akin to worship. It is painful to think of the multitude as living in the midst of it and living almost blind to it as if, instead of this fair earth and glorious sky, they were tenants of a dungeon. An infinite joy is lost to the world by the want of culture of this spiritual endowment.

The highest style of beauty to be found in nature, pertains to the human form, as animated and lighted up by the intelligence within. It is the expression of the soul that constitutes this superior beauty. The beauty of spirit, mind, heart, and life. It is a beauty which perishes not. This beauty is such as the angels wear. It is a child. It forms the washed white robes of the saints. It wreathes the countenance of every doer of good. It adorns every honest face. It shines in the virtuous life. It molds the hands of charity. It sweetens the voice of sympathy. It sparkles on the brow of wisdom. It flashes in the eye of love. It breathes in the spirit of piety. It is the beauty of the heaven of heavens. It is that which may grow by the hand of cultivation in every human soul. It is the flower of the spirit which blossoms on the tree of LIFE. Every soul may plant and nurture it in its own garden. This is the capacity for beauty that God has given to the human soul, and this beauty placed within the reach of us all. We may all be beautiful. Oh, there is a power in interior beauty that melts the hardest heart!

Woman, we regard as the most perfect type of beauty on earth. To her we ascribe the highest charms, belonging to this wonderful element so profusely mingled in all God's works. The earth gives us no form more perfect, no features more symmetrical, no style more chaste, no movements more graceful, no finish more complete. Our artists ever have and ever will, regard the woman form of humanity as the most perfect earthly type of beauty.

Beauty has a wonderful, charming gift of pleasure. It will win admiring eyes, favor, and draw hearts. It will pave the way to esteem. It will throw an air of agreeableness into the manner of all who approach. All this beauty will do, before it puts forth a single effort to win the esteem and love of others.

Plato says, beauty is a privilege of nature. Theocritus says, a delightful prejudice. Cameades, a solitary kingdom. Aristotle affirmed that beauty was better than all the letters of recommendation in the world. Homer, that it was a glorious gift of nature. Beauty has been called the "power and aims of

woman." A beautiful woman is a natural queen in the universe of love, where all hearts pay a glad tribute to her reign.

Beauty reproduces what it reflects. Women of beauty
change not with the features, which fades with years. It is
the beauty of expression. It is the only kind of beauty which
can be relied upon for the permanent influence with the
other sex. The love that has nothing but beauty to sustain it,
soon withers away. A pretty woman pleases the eye. A good
woman, the heart. The one is a jewel, the other a treasure.
Invincible fidelity, good humor, and complacency of temper,
outlive all the charms of a fine face and cause age to be
invisible. That is TRUE BEAUTY which has not only a substance, but a spirit. A beauty that we must intimately know
to justly appreciate.

Beauty is a dangerous gift for both its possessor and its
admirer. Beauty of countenance which is the light of the
soul shining through the face, is independent of features or
complexion. It is the most attractive as well as the most
enduring charm. Nothing but talent and amiability can
bestow it, no statue or picture can rival it, and time cannot
destroy it.

Music

THE rapturous charm of music! What power it has to
soften, melt, unchain in its spirit chords of subduing harmony! Truly there is power in music, an almost authorita-
tive power. It will tyrannize over the soul. Music will force
the soul to bow down and worship. It will wring adoration

from it and compel the heart to yield its treasures of love. Every emotion, from the most reverent devotion to the wildest gushes of joy, it holds subject to its imperative will. It calls the religious devotee to worship, the patriot to his country's altar, the freeman to his temple of liberty, the friend to the altar of friendship, and the lover to the side of his beloved. It elevates, empowers, and strengthens them all. The human soul is a mighty harp and all its strings vibrate to the sound of music.

Who does not know the softening power of music, especially the music of the human voice? It is like the angels whispering kind words in the hour of trouble. Who can be angry when the voice of love speaks in song? Who hears the harsh voice of selfishness, and brutalizing passion, when music gathers up her love notes to salute the ear with a song? Sing to the wicked man, sing to the disconsolate, sing to the sufferer, sing to the old, and sing to the children. Music will inspire them all.

The human voice is the most perfect musical instrument ever made. It had the most skillful Maker. The voice should be cultivated to sing the tones of love to God and man. In the social circle and around the fireside, it should sing the voice of love and at the altar of God, it should pour forth praise.

How early should children be taught to sing? What is sweeter than the songs of innocent children, so refining, refreshing, and so suggestive of heaven? Music sweetens the cup of bitterness, softens the hand of want, lightens the burden of life, makes the heart courageous, and the soul cheerfully devout. Into the soul of childhood and youth, it pours a tide of redeeming influence. Its first and direct effect is to stir his mental being to activity, to awaken strong emotions, to move among the powers with energy, holy aspiration and beauty. Music moves through the soul to elevate, refine, and spiritualize. No lethargy can exist in the soul that is pouring forth a tide of music. The souls very recesses are all astir. Everything within becomes active, the perceptions acute, the affections warm, the moral sensibilities will quicken. When we think how much the world wants awakening, we can think of no power better calculated to do it than that which dwells in the melodies of music. Let every body become musicians, and surely they would become LIVING SOULS.

Besides music being powerful, universal, the voice of love, and the type of the infinite, it is venerable for its age. The first account of it on record was at the laying of the foundations of the earth, when the "morning stars," delighted with the promise of a new planet, "sang together and all the sons of God shouted for joy." As soon as the earth was made, its rocky spires thrown up, its forest harps strung, its ocean organs tuned, it raised its everlasting anthem to swell the chorus of the skies.

A song can sooth and uplift. At times, a song is as good as a prayer. When the heart is right, it is the spirit of thanksgiving. In the soul touched with pain, music finds a place it may sing its best. Music is healthful. There is no better cure for BAD HUMORS. No medicine more pleasant to take. We know of nothing more genial and heart warming than to hear the whole family join in a song. They will love each other and their home better for it. Songs learned in childhood are like birds nesting, their notes will be heard and loved in later years. The voice of song by a mother to her little one, may in later days be a voice to recall them from ruin.

No family can afford to do without music. It is a luxury and an economy. Music is the alleviator of sorrow and a spring of enjoyment. It is a protection against vice and an excitement to virtue. When rightly used, its effects, physically, intellectually, and morally are very good. Make home attractive. Music affords a means of doing this. "Music has charms to soothe the savage breast." Show us the family where good music is cultivated, where parents and children often mingle their voices together in song, and we will show you one where peace, harmony, and love prevail.

Music can be acted as well as sung. The heart may make music when the lips are silent. A simple word may be full of music and stir the pulses to new and better emotions, the soul to higher joys! If only sounds were music! Some there are who cannot sing, yet whose natures are the finest harps, (unheard by mortal ears) and continually ascending. Some there are who cannot speak, or hear, and yet their sympathies and comprehensions are beautiful with the instinct of melody. There is sacred music that leads the soul to communion with God. The world needs music and the poor cry aloud for it.

Honor

To be ambitious of true honor, of the true glory and perfection of our natures is the very best principle and incentive of virtue. To be ambitious of titles, of place, of ceremonial respects and civil pageantry is as vain and little as the things we court.

True honor defined by Cicero, are those being fit to give praise who are themselves praiseworthy. The ancient Romans worshipped virtue and honor. They built two temples which were so seated, that none could enter the temple of honor without passing through the temple of virtue.

The way to be truly honored, is to be illustriously good. Maximilian the German emperor, replied to one who desired his letter patent to ennoble him, saying, "I am able to make you rich. But virtue must make you noble." The king of Sparta ruled his country by obeying it. A single good quality cannot render a man accomplished. But a succession of fine features and good qualities, can make true honor.

The man of honor is internal, the person of honor an external. A person of honor may be a profane libertine, promiscuous, proud, insult people, and defraud his creditors. But it is impossible for a man of honor, to be guilty of any of these.

Among the ancient Greeks and Romans, honor was more sought after than wealth. Times are changed. Now, wealth is the surest passport to honor. Respectability is endangered by poverty. "Rome, was Rome no more" when the imperial purple had become an article of traffic, and when gold could purchase with ease the honors that patriotism and valor could once secure only with difficulty.

There is no true glory, no true greatness, without virtue. Without it, we abuse all the good things we have whether they are great or little, false or real. Riches make us either covetous or prodigal. Fine palaces make us despise the poverty. Valor can sometimes turn brutal and unjust.

Real honor and real esteem are not difficult to be obtained in the world. But they are best won by actual worth and merit, rather than by art and intrigue. Seek not to be honored in any way except in your own spirit, within yourself.

Thinkers

THINKERS rise upon us like new stars, a few in a century. The multitude follow them by instinct. They adopt their theories and accept their thoughts at sight. So it is. Men swallow whole what they eat, wheat or chaff, meat or bone, nut or shell. They do not chew their mental food.

They do not examine the facts they learn. They do not digest their knowledge. If they did, every one would be making his OWN use of his knowledge, forming his OWN conclusions and working out his OWN kind and degree of culture.

To perceive accurately and to think correctly is the aim of all mental training. Heart and conscience are more than the mere intellect. Some say that a man never feels till he sees, and when the object disappears, the feeling ceases. We cannot exaggerate the importance of clear, correct thinking. We should eat, drink, sleep, walk, exercise body and mind, to this end. If we do not, we are over reached by the crafty, and trodden under foot by the strong.

The appetite for learning often grows weak with the inability to digest it. Thought is to the brain, what gastric juice is to the stomach, a solvent to reduce whatever is received to a condition where all that is wholesome may be digested and that alone. To learn merely for the sake of learning is like eating merely for the taste of food. The stomach is to the frame what memory is to the mind. It is as unwise to cultivate the memory at the expense of the mind, as it would be to enlarge the capacity of the stomach by eating more food than the frame requires or needs. Learning is healthfully digested by the mind when it reflects upon what is learned. All leisure should not be devoted to reading, but a part reserved for reflecting and arranging in the mind what is read. It is far better to read with care, a few well selected volumes.

A child indeed, like a machine, may be made to perform certain functions by external means. But it is only when he begins to think, that he rises to the dignity of a rational being. It is not reading, but thinking that gives you a possession of knowledge. A person may see, hear, read and learn whatever he pleases and as much, but he will know little beyond that which he has thought over and made the property of his mind. Take away thought from the life of man and what remains? You may glean knowledge by reading, but you must separate the chaff from the wheat by thinking.

Think before you speak and consider before you promise. Take time to deliberate and advise, but take no time in executing your resolutions. Do nothing today that you will repent of tomorrow. In the morning think of what you have to do, and at night ask yourself what you have done. Seek not the thoughts that are too hard for you. Strive not in a matter that concerns you not. Evil thoughts are dangerous enemies, and should be stopped even as they enter our minds. Fill the heart and head with good thoughts, that there be no room for bad ones.

Some complain that they cannot find words for their thoughts. The real trouble is, they cannot find thoughts for their words. It is not the depth of thought which makes obscure to others, the work of thinkers. Thoughts are but dreams till their effects are tried. The best thoughts are ever swiftest, the duller lag behind. A thought must have its own way of expression or it will have no way at all. The thought that lives is only the deed struggling into birth. It is with our thoughts as with flowers, those that are simple in expression carry their seed with them.

Too many yield to the opinions of others, without asking or meditating upon their bearing. Often the masses are enslaved to opinion, especially political matters. This may be necessary in some countries where a few rule, but not in our country where all may be taught to think. Books are so cheap now that the poorest can have access to the channels of thought. Books should only be used as an impetus to set the mind in motion and to pry deeper and farther into nature's hidden recesses and realms of truth.

No man need fear that he will exhaust his substance of thought, if he will only draw his inspiration from actual human life. In human life, God pours depths and endless truths. The thinker is but a writer endeavoring to report the discourse of God. Shall a child on the banks of the Amazon fear lest he should drink up the stream?

Benefactors

WE die but leave an influence behind us that survives. The echoes of our words are evermore repeated and reflected along the ages. It is what man was, that lives and acts after him. What he said, sounds along the years like voices amid the mountain gorges. What he did, is repeated after him in ever multiplying and never ceasing reverberations. Every man has left behind him influences for good or evil that will never exhaust themselves. The sphere in which he acts may be small, or it may be great. It may be his fireside, or it may be a kingdom, a village, or a great nation. It may be a parish, or broad Europe. But act he does, ceaselessly and forever. His friends, his family, his successors in office, his relatives are all receptive of an influence. A moral influence which he has transmitted and bequeathed to mankind. Either a BLESSING which will repeat itself in showers of benedictions, or a CURSE which will multiply itself in ever accumulating evil.

Every man is a missionary forever, for good or for evil, whether he intend and design it or not. He may be a blot, radiating his dark influence outward to the very ends of society, or he may be a blessing, spreading influence over the length and breadth of the world. But a BLANK he cannot be. The seeds sown in life springs up in harvests of blessings or harvests of sorrow. Whether our influence is great or small, whether it is for good or evil, it lasts. Our influence lives somewhere within some limit, and is operative wherever it is. The grave buries the dead dust, but the character walks the world and distributes itself, as a prayer or a curse among the families of mankind.

The tree falls in the forest. But in the lapse of time, it is turned to coal. It lights our fires that burn brighter because it grew and fell. The coral insect dies, but the reef it raised breaks the surge on the shores of great continents, or formed an isle in the middle of the ocean. They wave with harvests for the good of man. We live and we die. But the good or evil that we do, lives after us, and is not "buried with our bones."

The babe that perished on the breast of the mother, like a flower that bowed its head and drooped amid the death frosts of time. That babe not only in image, but in its influence, still lives and speaks in the chambers of the mother's heart.

The friend with whom we took counsel is removed from the outward eye. But the lessons that he taught, the grand sentiments that he spoke, the deeds of generosity by which he was characterized, the morals and likeness, still survive and appear to us in memory, being dead and yet speaking eloquently and in the midst of us.

What we do is transacted on a stage of which all in the universe are spectators. What we say is transmitted in echoes that will never cease. What we are is influencing and acting on the rest of mankind. Neutral we cannot be. Living we act and dead we speak. The whole universe is the mighty company forever looking and listening. And all nature the tablets, forever recording the words, the deeds, the thoughts, the passions of mankind!

Since our earthly life is so brief, "and the night will soon come when the murmur and hum of our days shall be silent evermore," it were well to have milestones by the way, pointing to a better land.

If we would be numbered among the earth's benefactors, we must often be oblivious of ourselves and learn well the lesson contained in the "Golden Rule." And be still further protected in the two great commandments, Love God and love your neighbor as yourself.

Go forth then into the spheres that you occupy, the

employments, the trades, the professions of social life. Go forth into the high places, or into the lowly places of the land. Whatever sphere you fill, carry into it a holy heart and you will radiate around you life, power, and influence.

Trials of Life

MAN must be willing to take life as it comes. To mount the hill when the hill swells, and to go down the hill when it lowers. He must be willing to walk the plain when it stretches before him, and to ford the river when it rolls over the plain. "I can do all things through Christ who strengthens me."

The best of people will meet now and then with disappointments. They are inherited by mortality. It is however, the better philosophy to take things calmly and endeavor to be content with our lot. We may at least add some rays of sunshine to our path, if we earnestly endeavor to dispel the clouds of discontentment that may arise in us. And by so doing, we the more fully enjoy the bountiful blessing that God gives to his most humble creatures. The thoughts of the mind should go out and reach after the higher good. In this manner, we may improve ourselves till our thoughts are good companions that will lead us along the path of virtue. Thus we many grow better within, while the cares of life, the crosses and losses and disappointments lose their sharp thorns, and the journey of life is made comparatively happy and pleasant.

Much material good must be resigned if we would attain

Engraved & Printed by Illman Brothers

TRIALS OF LIFE.

FOR THE ROYAL PATH OF LIFE.

to the highest degree of moral excellence. Many spiritual joys will be foregone, if we resolve at all risks to win great material advantages. To strive for a high professional position, and yet expect to have all the delights of leisure. To labor for vast riches, and yet to ask for freedom from anxiety and care, and all the happiness which flows from a contented mind. To indulge in sensual gratification, and yet demand health, strength, and vigor. To live for self, and yet look for the joys that spring from a virtuous and self-denying life, is to ask for impossibilities.

God knows what keys in the human soul to touch in order to draw out the most perfect harmonies. They may be the minor strains of sadness and sorrow. They may be the loftier notes of joy and gladness. God knows where the melodies of our natures are and what discipline will bring them forth.

Sickness/Tears/Sorrow

SICKNESS may bring a share of blessings with it. Stores of human love and sympathy it reveals. Constant affectionate care is ours. Kindly greetings from friends and associates. This very loosening of our hold on life, calls out such wealth of human sympathy that life seems richer than before. Then it teaches humility. Our absence is scarcely felt or noticed. Our place is filled and all moves on without us.

What important people we imagine ourselves to be! We think that we alone are the life of the circle in which we move. In our absence, we believe that life, existence, and breath will come to a general pause. Alas! The gap we leave is scarcely perceptible, so quickly is it filled again.

When some intervening cloud has darkened the pleasing scenes of life, or disappointments opened our eyes, vice loses her allurements, the world appears empty, then Jesus and the Gospel beam forth with inimitable luster. Christian virtue gains loveliness and treads the shades with more mortal charms. If tribulations tend to refine the soul and prepare it for glory, welcome distress. These are not judgements or marks of displeasure to God's children. They are necessary and salutary chastisements, as well as tokens of his concern for our spiritual and eternal welfare.

God will prune his people, but will not hew them down. The right hand of His mercy knows what the left hand of His severity is doing. Sickness and disease in the weak minds, the sources of depression. But that which is painful to the body, may be profitable to the soul. Sickness, the mother of modesty, puts us in mind of our mortality. Sickness will, sometimes, kindly pull us up by the ear and bring us to a proper sense of our duty.

Whom the Lord loves He chasteneth, and if we endure chastening, God dealeth with us as with sons and daughters.

There is a sacredness in tears. They are not of weakness, but of power. Tears speak more than ten thousand words. They are the messages of overwhelming grief, of deep regret, of unspeakable love. Despise not woman's tears. They are what makes her an angel. Scoff not, if the stern heart of manhood is sometimes melted to sympathy. They are what elevate him above the brute. We love to see tears of affection. They are painful tokens, but still most holy. There is pleasure in tears. An awful pleasure.

Genuine tears are the involuntary and faithful expressions of the soul. The soul's sorrow or joy. Joy weeps, guilt or innocence. Insulted virtue has its tears. Tears relieve the soul. A tear dropped in the silence of a sick chamber, often rings in heaven with a sound which belongs not to earthly trumpets or bells.

Repress not the tears of a child. They are a purifying vent to the young heart. Repress them not mother, for God has given them to be a comforter in the lone and bitter hour. In manhood, quench not for they are the manifestation of spiritual life. Tears, be ever with every reader and with us all. Our token when we sigh for the absent or for the lost. A sacred witness that our regrets and sorrows are sincere.

It is a striking fact that the dying never weep. It must be because the dying have reached a point too deep for earthly sorrows, too transcendent for weeping. They are face to face with higher and holier things, with the Father in Heaven and His Angels. There is no weeping in that blessed abode to which the dying man is hastening.

He who tastes only the bitter cup of life, is an ingrate to God and a torment to himself. The record of human life is far more depressing than its course. The hours of quiet enjoyment are not noted. The thousand graces and happiness of social life, the loveliness of nature meeting us at every step, the buoyancy of spirit resulting from health and pure air, the bright sun, the starry firmament. All that cheers man on the road, warms the heart and makes life pleasant is omitted in the narrative.

Sorrows are only tempest clouds, when far off they look black. But when above us, scarcely gray. Sorrow is the night of the mind. Sorrow is the firmament of thought and the school of intelligence. Those who are wise extract something that is convenient and useful, even from the most bitter afflictions.

Sweetest of all songs are the Psalms in the night. David sang with the most tenderness when in the gloom of deepest affliction. The saddest song is better than none, because it is a song. The simplest and most obvious use of sorrow is to remind us of God. It would seem that a certain shock is needed to bring us in contact with reality. We are not conscious of breathing till obstruction makes it felt. We are not aware of the possession of a heart till some disease, some sudden joy or sorrow, rouses it into extraordinary action. We are not aware of the God within us, till some chasm yawns which must be filled, or our affections force us to become fearfully conscious of a need.

To mourn without measure is folly. Not to mourn at all is insensibility. There are those who think that to be grim is to be good. That a thought, to be really wholesome, must be shaped like a coffin. They seem to think that black is the color of heaven and the more they make their faces look like midnight, the holier they are. The days of darkness come, and they are many. But our eye, takes in only the first. Patience attains her perfect work while trials unfold. The loftiest of our race are those who have had the most profound grief, because they have had the most profound sympathies.

When a gloom falls upon us, it may be we have entered into the cloud that will give its showers to refresh and strengthen us. There are sorrows too sacred to be babbled to the world. Real sorrow is not clamorous. It seeks to shun every eye, and breathes in solitude and silence the sighs that come from the heart. Every sorrow has its secret sorrow, which the world knows not. Often we call a man cold, when he is only sad. Give not the mind to heaviness. The gladness of the heart is the life of man, and joyfulness of a man prolongs his days. Remove sorrow far from you, for sorrow has killed many. There is no profit in it. Cares bring age before the time. Grief is but a selfish feeling. Most selfish is the man who yields himself to the indulgence of any passion, which brings no joy to his fellow man.

They are the true kings and queens who go with courage to grapple the future, strengthen the weak, to comfort the weary, to hang pictures of faith and trust in the galleries of sunless lives, and to point the desolate to the golden heights of the hereafter.

Causeless depression is not to be reasoned with. You may as well fight with the mist as with this shapeless, undefinable, yet all beclouding hopelessness. If those who laugh at such deep depression did feel the grief of it for an hour, their laughter would be sobered into compassion. Resolution might shake it off, but where are we to find the resolution, when the whole man is unstrung? Christ is a refuge and "a very present help in trouble."

When we lose our friends and loved ones, heaven gains them. When we mourn, they rejoice. If we hang our harps on the willows, they tune theirs in the eternal orchestra above, rejoicing that we will soon be with them. They are ours as ever, and we are theirs. The ties that bind us are not broken. They are too strong for death's stroke. They are made for the joys of eternal friendship. Friendships on earth will not disturb these bonds that link with loved ones on high, nor will our duties here disturb them. They do not see in sorrow.

Debt/Failure/Despair

WELCOME adversity! The voice is stern and harsh, but it is the voice of a friend! There is something sublime in the resolute, fixed, suffering without complaining which makes disappointment often better than success. Adversity deserves to be considered. That affliction moves pity and reconciles our enemies. But prosperity provokes envy, and loses our friends.

He that has never known adversity is but half acquainted with others or himself. Constant success shows us but one side of the world.

Adversity exasperates fools, dejects cowards, draws out the faculties of the wise and industrious and puts the modest to the necessity of trying their skills. It is good for the man that he bear the yoke in his youth. Oaks are made hard by strong discipline. We must take the rough and thorny roads as well as the pleasant, and a portion of our daily duty must be hard and disagreeable. The most dangerous of all states of mind is that of constant pleasure, ease, and prosperity.

The one who stands boldly for the defense of the truth, in the midst of the flood of errors that surround them, are not the lily fingers who have been rocked in the cradle of luxury. But they are those whom necessity has called from the shade of retirement, to contend under the rays of the sun, with the stern realities of life.

Adversity is the trial of principal. Without it, a person hardly knows if he is honest or not. When you feel inclined to cry, just change your mind and laugh. Nothing drys sooner than tears. It has been truly remarked, that many a man in losing his fortune, has found himself. In prosperity, be humble. In adversity, be cheerful. If you have the blues, go and see the poorest and sickest families you know. He is happy whose circumstances suit his temper. But he is happier who can suit his temper to his circumstances. He is foolish who grumbles at every little mischance.

While you are generous, see to it that you are also just. Do not give away what does not belong to you. Let us warn you on account of its moral bearing, against debt. Nothing more effectually robs one of his best energies, takes the bloom from his cheek and peace from his pillow, than debt. Debt is a foe to a person's honesty. Avoid all meanness. Shun as a pestilence, the habit of running thoughtlessly into debt. Let your expenses be always short of your income. Debt is the father of invasions, of self-respect, cares, and double dealing. It will in due season, carve the face into wrinkles. Be sure of it, he who dines out of debt though his meal be a biscuit and an onion, dines in a banquet hall. The person out of debt is the person of liberty. Free as the singing lark above. But the debtor, although clothed in the utmost bravery, is but a serf out on holiday.

Somebody truly says, that one debt begets another. If a man owes you a dollar, he is sure to owe you a grudge too, and he is generally more ready to pay interest on the latter than on the former.

The present indiscriminate credit system is a labyrinth. The entrance is easy, but how to get out, that's the question. Each purchaser who is ultimately able to pay, contribute large sums to indulge those who cannot, and what is worse, those who never intend to pay, thus encouraging fraud. On

every hand we see people living on credit, putting off pay-
day to the last. Make a push at the beginning, instead of the
end and save all this misery. The great secret of being solvent and comfortable is to get ahead of your expenses. Eat
and drink this month what you earned last month. Not what
you are going to earn next month. No man can to a certainty, guard against ill health. No man can insure himself a well
conducted, helpful family, or a permanent income.

Friendships are broken over debts. Forgeries and murders are committed on their account. However considered,
debt is a source of cost and annoyance continually. In no
respect that we can fathom, does debt advance the general
well-being.

In every community there are men who are determined
not to work, if work can be shirked. They begin life with a
resolution to enjoy all the good things that are accumulated
by the labor of man, without contributing their own share of
labor to the common stock. Hence the endless schemes for
getting rich in a day, instead of by slow and plodding steps.
The principal is in all cases the same, to obtain something
for nothing. Everybody knows the history of such men.

Businesses are always changing. Splendid mansions
change hands suddenly. The next season, the house will be
dismantled and a family. A man who makes fifty thousand
dollars, instead of setting half of it on his wife and children,
throws the whole into a speculation with the idea to make it
a hundred thousand. Men who have a good season launch
out into extravagances and luxuries, and these with a gambling mania invariably carry people under.

Americans are always in a hurry when they have an
object to accomplish. But if there is any vocation or pursuit

in which gradual, slow-coach processes are scouted with detestation, it is that of acquiring riches. Especially is this true at the present day, when fortunes are continually changing hands and people are so often, by the lucky turn of the wheel, lifted from the lowest depths of poverty to the loftiest pinnacle of wealth and affluence. Exceptional persons there are, who are content with slow gains. Willing to accumulate riches by adding penny to penny, dollar to dollar. But a mass in business, are too apt to despise such a tedious, laborious, ascent of the steep of fortune. To rush headlong into schemes, for the sudden acquisition of wealth. Hence, honorable labor is too often despised. A man of parts is expected to be above hard work.

There is with a great majority of people, a want of constancy in whatever plan they undertake. They toil as though they doubted that life had earnest and decided pathways. They toil as though there were no compass but the shifting winds, with each of which they must change their course. They beat about on the ocean of time, but never cross it, to rest on delightful islands or mainlands.

No calamity can produce such paralysis of the mind as despair. It is the capstone of the climax of human anguish. The mental powers are frozen with indifference. The heart turns to bone with depression. The soul is shrouded in a cloud of gloom. No words of consolation, no cheerful repartee, can break the death-like calm. No love can warm the pent-up heart. No sunbeams dispel the dark clouds. Time may effect a change. We can extend our kindness, but cannot relieve the victim. We can trace the causes of this awful disease. God only can effect a cure. We can speculate upon its nature, but cannot feel its force until its iron hand is laid upon us. We may call it weakness, but cannot prove or demonstrate the proposition. We may call it folly, but can point to no frivolity to sustain our position. We may call it madness, but can discover no maniac actions. We may call it stubbornness, but can see no exhibitions of reasoning. We may call it lunacy, but cannot perceive the incoherences of that unfortunate condition. We can call it properly nothing but dark, gloomy, despair. An undefined and undefinable paralysis of all the sensibilities that render a person happy and capable of imparting happiness to those around him. It is a state of numb dormancy, rather than a mental disorder of the cerebral organs.

> Me miserable! which way shall I fly
> Infinite wrath, and infinite despair?
> Which way I fly is hell; myself am hell?
> And in the lowest deep a lower deep
> Still threat'ning to devour me opens wide,
> To which the hell I suffer seems a heaven.
> –Milton

It is induced by a false estimate of things, and of the dispensations and government of the God of mercy.

Disappointments, losses, severe and continued afflictions, sudden transition from wealth to poverty, or the death of dear ones may be its origin. These things may cast a gloom over the mind that does not correctly comprehend the great first cause. They may not see the hand of God in every thing. This produces a state of despair, because these things are viewed in a FALSE manner. Fanaticism in religious meetings has produced the most obstinate and melancholy cases of despair that have come under our own observation. Intelligence, chastened by religion are the surest safeguards against this state of misery. Lack of knowledge of this subject and vice are its greatest promoters. Despair is the destruction of all hope, the deathless sting that refines the torment of the repentant and lost. It is that undying worm, that unquenchable fire, so graphically described in the Holy Writ.

Remember this, that God always helps those who help themselves. That He never forsakes those who are good and true, and that he hears even the young ravens when they cry. Remember too, that we must never give up in life's battles. Press onward to the end, always keeping in mind the words—NEVER DESPAIR.

Stepping Stones

STEPPING STONES are advantages, auxiliaries, power, etc., and these are attained in no other way than through personal experiences. Our trials of life strengthen us. Each successive victory raises us higher in strength and power. It is through trials that stout hearts are made. It is through adversities, that our patience and courage are increased.

He who bears adversity well, gives the best evidence that he will not be spoiled by prosperity. Many a promising reputation has been destroyed by early success. Every failure is a step to success. Every detection of what is false, directs us toward what is true. Every trial exhausts some tempting form of error. But scarcely any theory, the result of steady thought, is altogether false. No tempting form of error is without some latent charm derived from truth.

Doubtless a deeper feeling of individual responsibility,

and a better adaptation of talent to the fields of labor are necessary for a better society. But with the adaptation of talent
and means, no man can succeed who has not a fixed and resolute purpose in his mind. An unwavering faith is needed,
that he can carry that purpose out.

Despair not, for disappointment will be realized. Failure may attend this effort and that one. Only be honest and
struggle on, and it will all work well. Yield not to the influence of sadness which sinks us to degrading inaction, that
drives us to seek relief in some fatal vice, or to drown recollection in the poisoning bowl. Arouse, and shake the
oppressive burden from overpowering you. With firm bearing and a stout heart, push on the attainment of a higher
goal. The open field for energetic action is large, and the
call for vigorous laborers immensely exceed the supply.
Much precious time is squandered, valuable labor lost, mental activity deadened by vain regrets, useless repinings, and
unavailing idleness. Let no cloud again darken your spirit,
or weight of sadness oppress your heart. Arouse ambition's
smoldering fires. Burst the shackles that impede your
progress, and cling to hope. The world frowned darkly
upon all who have ever won fame's wreath, but on they
toiled. Place high your standard and with a firm tread and
fearless eye, press steadily onward. Persevere, and you will
surely reach it. None should despair. God can help them.
None should presume. God can cross them.

Prayer is the action of the Holy Ghost, the spirit of simplicity. An imitation of the Holy Jesus whose spirit is meek
and conformed to God. His anger is just, often hindered, but
never hasty and full of mercy. Prayer is the peace of our spirit, the stillness of our hearts, thoughts, and recollections. It

is the seat of meditation, the rest of our cares, and the calm of the tempest. Prayer is the issue of a quiet mind of untroubled thoughts. It is the daughter of charity and the sister of meekness. Anger is the perfect alienation of the mind from prayer. It is contrary to that attention which presents our prayers in a right line to God. Our prayers made with a contrite heart, ascends to heaven upon the wings of the Holy Dove, and dwells with God. Till its return, like the useful bee, laden with a blessing and the dew of heaven.

God respects not the arithmetic of our prayers, how many they are, nor the rhetoric of our prayers, how neat they are. The geometry of our prayers, how long they are. The music of our prayers, how methodical they are. But the divinity of our prayers, how heart-sprung they are. Not gifts, but graces prevail in prayer. Perfect prayers, though not one word may be spoken aloud, always pluck the heart out of the earth and move it like a censer beneath the face of heaven.

Prayer is a constant source of invigoration to self-discipline. Prayer that is sincere, intense, and watchful. To present a petition is one thing, to prosecute a suit is another. Most of our prayers answer to the former, but successful prayer corresponds to the latter. The whole of prayer does not consist in taking hold of God. The main matter is holding on. Though prayer should be the key of the day and the lock of the night, yet we hold it more needful in the morning.

Not a few, owe their escape from skepticism and infidelity to prayers sacred influence. Said the noted John Randolph, "I once took the French side in politics. I should have been a French atheist, if it had not been for one recollection. The memory of the time when my departed mother used to

take my small hands and cause me on my knees to say, "Our
Father, who art in heaven."

> "The parent pair their secret homage pay,
> And offer up to heaven the warm request,
> That He who stills the raven's clamorous nest,
> And decks the lily fair in flowery pride,
> Would, in the way His wisdom sees the best,
> For them and for their little ones provide."

God/The Bible/Religion

THERE is no God! Unite in thought at the same instant
the most beautiful object in nature. If not God, then who?
Who unrolled the blue scroll and threw upon high the legible
gleaming of immortality? Who fashioned this green earth,
with its perpetual rolling waters, and its wide expanse of
islands and mains? Who settled the foundations of the
mountains? Who paved the heavens with clouds and
attuned, amid the clamor of storms, the voice of thunders,
and unchained the lightnings that flash in their gloom?

Who gave to the eagle a safe high nest where the tempests dwell and beat the strongest, and to the dove a tranquil
abode amid the forests that echo to the music of her moan?
Who made thee, O man! With your perfected elegance of
intellect and form? Who made the light pleasant to you and
the darkness a covering, and a herald to the first gorgeous
flashes of the morning?

There is a God! All nature declares it in a language too
plain to be misapprehended. The great truth is too legibly
written over the face of the whole creation to be mistaken. It

is heard in the whispering breeze and in the howling storm. Heard in the deep toned thunder, and in the earthquake's shock. Its declared to us when the tempest lowers, and when the hurricane sweeps over the land. Its declared when the winds moan around our dwellings and die in sullen murmurs on the plain. We know it when the heavens overcast with blackness, ever and always illuminated by the lightning's glare. Is the truth less solemnly impressed on our minds in the universal hush and calm repose of nature? When all is STILL, as the soft breathing of an infant's slumber.

And man, the proud lord of all creation, so fearfully and wonderfully made. Each joint in its corresponding socket. And surpassing all, possessed of a soul capable of enjoying the most exquisite pleasure or of enduring the most excruciating pain. Endowed with immortal capacities, and destined to live onward through the endless ages of eternity. These all unite in one general proclamation of the eternal truth. There is a God, infinite in wisdom who reigns over all, undivided and supreme. God is the fountain of all life, the source of all light from whom all blessings flow. All happiness centers in Him.

The Bible is not only the revealer of the unknown God to man, but His grand interpreter as the God of nature. In revealing God, it has given us the key that unlocks the mysteries of creation. The glass through which to look "from nature up to nature's God.

Who can stand amid the scenic majesty and not feel that there is a moral sublimity to be found on earth? It is in the Book of God and it is the thought of God. What are all these outward visible forms of grandeur, but the expression and voice of Deity the Bible has created in our minds.

The Bible is adapted to every possible variety of taste, temperament, culture, and condition. It has strong reasoning for the intellectual. It takes the calm and contemplative to the well-balanced James, and the affectionate to the loving and beloved John. Not only is this book precious to the poor and unlearned. Not only is it the counselor and confidence of the great middle class of society, both spiritually and mentally speaking. But the scholar and the sage, the intellectual monarchies of the race, bow to its authority.

When the good mother parts with her dear boy, other volumes may be placed in his hands, but we are sure that she will fold among his apparel a Bible. On the seas it goes with the mariner, as his spiritual chart and compass. On the land it is to untold millions, their pillar-cloud by day, their fire-column by night. In the closet and in the street, amid temptations and trials, this is man's most faithful attendant and his strongest shield. It is our lamp through the dark valley. The radiator of our best light from the solemn and unseen future. Stand before it as a mirror, and you will see there not only good traits, but errors, follies, and sins, which you did not imagine until now. You desire to make constant improvement. Go then to the Bible. It not only shows the way of all progress, but it incites you to go forward. It opens before you a path leading upward, along which good angels will cheer you and God himself will lend you a helping hand.

> "We've drank every cup of joy, heard every trump
> Of fame; drank early, deeply drank, drank draughts
> That common millions might have quenched; then died
> Of thirst, because there was no more to drink."

But never a human being went to the Bible, who did not find His words true: "But whosoever drinks of the water I will give him, shall never thirst; for it shall be in him a well of water springing up into everlasting life."

The Bible is a book for the mind, the heart, the conscience, the will and the life. It suits the palace and the cottage, the afflicted and the prosperous, the living and the dying. It is simple, yet grand. Mysterious, yet plain. Though from God, it is within the comprehension of a little child. In the divine book, they study the science of the eternal world.

Take this book from the family, and it will degenerate into mere conventionalism, marriage into a "social contract." The spirit of mother will depart. Natural affection will sink to mere brute fondness, and what we now call home would become a den of sullen selfishness and barbaric lust!

Religion is the daughter of heaven, parent of our virtues, and source of all true happiness. She alone gives peace and contentment, divest the heart of anxious cares, bursts on the mind a flood of joy, and spreads sunshine in the pious soul. By the spirit of religion, are the spirits of darkness banished from the earth. Angelic ministers of grace thicken unseen regions of mortality. She promotes love and good will among men, lifts up the head that hangs down, heals the wounded spirit, dissipates the gloom of sorrow, sweetens the cup of affliction, blunts the sting of death, and breathes around her an everlasting spring. The external life of man is the creature of time and circumstance, but the internal abides and continues to exist. Spirit triumphs over form. We have narrowed the sources of internal comfort, and internal enjoyment. If we have debased the powers, or corrupted the purity of mind. If we have blunted the sympathy or contracted the affections of the heart, we have lost some of that treasure which was absolutely our own.

Above all, if we have allowed the prudence or the interests of this world to shut out from our souls the view or the hopes of something better, we have quenched that light which would have cheered the darkness of affliction. But, if we let God care for our inward and eternal life. If by all the experiences of this life, He is reducing it and preparing for its disclosure, nothing can befall us but prosperity. Though your spirit may be destined to live isolated, you cannot be alone, for God is there.

Old Age and Death

AGE is inexorable. It's wheels must move onward. They know no retrograde movement. The old man may gaze backward with an eye of longing upon the rosy scenes of early years, as one who gazes on his home from the deck of a departing ship. Every moment carries him farther and farther away. Poor old man! He has little more to do than die.

The young who all wish to live, but who at the same time have a dread of growing old, may not be disposed to allow the justice of the representation we now make. They regard old age as a dreary season that admits of nothing which can be called pleasure. Old age, frightful as it may be to the young has no terror to those who see it near. Experience proves, it abounds with consolations and delights.

Among other circumstances which contribute to the satisfaction of this period of life, is the respect with which old age is treated. There are it must be acknowledged, some

Engraved & Printed by Illman Brothers

OLD AGE.

FOR THE ROYAL PATH OF LIFE.

foolish and uneducated persons who do not pay that venera-
tion which is due the aged, but these are not numerous.

The world in general bows down to age, gives it precedence and listens with deference to its opinions. Old age
wants accommodations. It must in justice to man be
allowed, that they are afforded with cheerfulness. Who can
deny that such reverence is soothing to the human mind? It
compensates us for the loss of many pleasures which belong
to youth.

The respect of the world in general is gratifying. But the
respect of a man's own offspring, must yield heartfelt
delight. Can there be a more pleasing sight than an old man
surrounded by his children and grandchildren? All of whom
are emulous of each other in testifying their homage and
affection. Whoever takes a little child into his love may have
a very roomy heart, but that child will fill it. The children in
the world keep us from growing old and cold. A little
thoughtful attention. How happy it makes the old! How
lonely their hours! Often their partners in life have long
filled silent graves. Often their children they have followed
to the tomb. They stand solitary. Why should not the young
cling around and comfort them, cheering their gloom with
happy smiles?

Ought we ever to miss an opportunity of showing attention to the aged, or lighting up a smile by a courteous act or
a friendly deed?

If any must weep let it be the young, at the long succession of cares that are before them. Welcome the snow, for it
is the emblem of peace and of rest.

With death, no sex is spared and no age exempt. All
roads lead to the same place. All terminate, however varied

the routes. "It is appointed unto men once to die." No matter what station of honor we hold, we are all subject to death. It makes us all equal when it comes.

Look at that hero. Their relation with the living world is now ended. It is not! Their familiar voice, appearance, expressions, and influences will be eternally ours to remember and hold to our hearts. They will continue to live, as their abiding spirit awaits us to join them.

This is life. Only a few years do we journey here and we come to that bridge, death. Go where you will and it will find you. Many dread it and try to flee from it as the king of terrors. Is he an enemy, when God sends him to deliver us from pains, follies, disappointments, misery, and woe? Is it fair to death to call him our foe, a king of terrors, an enemy?

Man comes into the world crying, cries on through life, and is always seeking after some desired thing which he imagines is labeled HAPPINESS. He mourns over some loss which makes him miserable. A restless mortal body with an immortal soul that requires something more than earth can give to satisfy its lofty desires. The soul that hails death as the welcome messenger, to deliver it from its ever changing, ever decaying house of clay, called man.

Death is but life to a true believer. It is not his last day, nor his worst day. But in the highest sense his best day, and the beginning of his better life. At death, we leave one place to go to another. We depart from our friends and family on earth to go to our friends and family in heaven. We depart from the valley of tears and go to the mount of joy. We depart from a howling wilderness and go to a heavenly paradise.

Thanks be to that gospel which opens the vision of an

endless life! Thanks be to that Savior friend, who has promised to conduct all the faithful through the sacred trance of death, into the scenes of paradise and everlasting delight!

> "Life! we've been long together,
> Through pleasant and cloudy weather;
> Tis hard to part when friends are dear;
> Perhaps will cost a sigh, a tear;
> Then steal away, give little warning,
> Choose thine own time; Say not, Good night,
> But in some brighter clime Bid us good morning."

THE END.

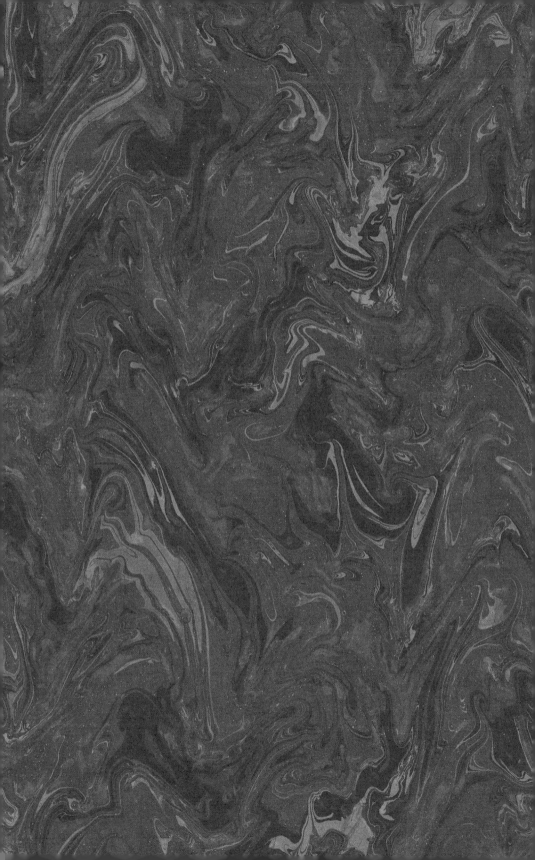